WEALTH
WITHOUT STOCKS OR MUTUAL FUNDS

Testimonials

Praise from the business community

"John is truly a financial wizard when it comes to showing people from all income and wealth levels how to create more income and wealth without having to depend on Wall Street."

—Jack Canfield, Coauthor of the Success Principles™ and *Chicken Soup for the Soul*

"John Jamieson has opened my eyes to many proven methods for building wealth that I never knew existed. Before you listen to all the other so-called financial gurus, learn from his fresh approach."

—Steve Harrison, President and Creator of Quantum Leap Training Systems

"In order to grow most businesses you will need capital. The traditional approach with bank loans is an expensive approach (if you even qualify). In John's new book, *Wealth Without Stocks or Mutual Funds*, he outlines how to turn the tables on the banks and use your own money to scale and grow. If you are looking to scale your already successful business and capital is required (without giving up ownership to investors) this book is a must to study as a financial option. This book is also loaded with dozens of real world wealth and income creation strategies that only an experienced investor and business man like John could put in one cohesive place."

—Scott Letourneau, The Business Formation Expert

"John Jamieson is the epitome of one of my favorite sayings, he is a "Do-ru," not just a guru! John walks the walk; he really does profitable deals and shows others how to do the same. I have had the distinct pleasure of knowing and working with John for 7 years now, I can tell you there is nobody I know that is more passionate about helping people, not only create more wealth for themselves, but preserve it as well; helping people have a

legacy that they can pass down. John's first book has changed thousands of lives for the better and this one is an absolute masterpiece, a MUST have!"
—Chris Lombardo, Real Estate Investor, Educator and Mentor

"John Jamieson has been a friend and an inspiration to me now for many years. He has dedicated himself to providing quality service and education together with wealth building techniques that have proven to be innovative and life changing. I have been fortunate enough to collaborate on a few projects with John and always learn something new in the process. I look forward to seeing what new information John has to share moving forward as he has proven himself to be someone to watch and learn from."
—"Big Daddy," Mike Biglane, Biglane Mentoring Services, Inc.

"I love this book! Jamieson strips away the veneer and hits us between the eyes with the naked truth about succeeding in the world of wealth creation. Impossibly, he delivers more in his second book than in his record-shattering first."
—Tracie Taylor, Lifestyle Entrepreneur, Wealth and Wellness Coach

"John Jamieson deeply understands the non-traditional secrets of how create true wealth. His newest book, *Wealth Without Stocks or Mutual Funds,* provides the reader with the inside secrets of the Key 11 Pillars of Wealth. This is a Must read book!"
—Howard Edward Haller, Ph.D., Real Estate Investor, Speaker, and Best Selling Author

". . . I have the unique pleasure of having Mr. John Jamieson at my church on several occasions. He has been the keynote speaker on Sunday mornings working with us on a better business model for automatically and systematically creating tax free generational wealth. As a result of his unique blend of faith and wealth strategies, he has been labeled the "Pastor of Finances" by New Breed Church.

"I am confident that Mr. Jamieson has the expertise to help civic, ecclesiastical, business; private and non-profit groups reach their financial goals. He is intelligent and has great economic cognizant skills to reverse the deep thresholds of traditional stagnated poverty. In my opinion, Mr. Jamieson is a financial guru with a revolutionary cutting edge approach to wealth building. I stand in full support and highly recommend Mr. John Jamieson to all."

—Dr. Ken Howard, M.S., M.Div., D.Min., President and Senior Pastor, New Breed Church

"Hey John, I just read *Wealth Without Stocks or Mutual Funds*. WOW! In a confusing world, you really know how to break down seemingly complicated programs and explain them in an easy to understand manor. You're the best I've met at laying out adverse risks (wealth drains) to be aware of and how the average investor can combat those drains. *Wealth Without Stocks or Mutual Funds* is a huge wealth of cutting edge information and is a must read for everyone!"

—Brady Black, Vice President of Marketing, Gradient Annuity Brokerage

"*Wealth Without Stocks or Mutual Funds* is loaded with more real life income and wealth strategies than I have ever seen in one book. Every chapter is loaded with strategies that everyone can use in their real lives and businesses. John does an awesome job of simply explaining seemingly complex strategies so that anyone at any level can use the information. I also loved the fact that I can get help with actually implementing almost every strategy in the book. This book is for anyone, at any level, who wants to get ahead financially. I can't wait to get the finished copy in my hands and start referring people to buy their own copy!"

—Christy Harris, CTM Investment Group

What Real Estate Professionals had to say about John and his trainings

"John, I wanted to take a moment to thank you for presenting your wealth building seminar at our RE/MAX of Southeastern Michigan Special Event.

"I was truly impressed, as were our agents, with the wealth strategies that you presented for the real estate industry. It was exciting to learn how the concepts from your Perpetual Wealth Systems and Real Estate Agents Build Wealth programs can dramatically improve an agent's income and net worth.

"Your presentation style was both professional and entertaining. We have had a very positive response from our agents that attended this event. I am pleased to hear that a number of our associates have contacted you to work with them on their personal wealth strategies. Great job on the entire event!

"I look forward to partnering with you in the near future on other events that will help and enhance our membership's financial opportunities."

—Joe Sabatini, Vice President and Regional Manager, RE/MAX of Southeastern Michigan

"John Jamieson presented his wealth building seminar at our annual Master Sales Society Event earlier this year and he was universally appreciated and we intend to have him back next year.

"John's skills as a platform presenter and salesperson are matched by his subject knowledge and enthusiasm for it."

—Mike Pallin, Floyd Wickman Team President

"*Wealth Without Stocks or Mutual Funds* is a MUST READ!! Whether you are a savvy investor or just getting your feet wet, this book is full of simple strategies to build wealth without risking the ups and downs of the stock market. Even though I have been a Realtor® for 25 years this book has opened my eyes and showed me why I should be investing in the area I know & understand. John, you knocked it out of the park with this book I can't wait till it hits the shelves, I will be referring it to everyone I know."

—Brian Thomas, RE/MAX First

"I wanted to take a moment to let you know that I truly appreciated your sharing of your time and talent at the Lunch and Learn Seminar at RE/MAX Suburban.

"I must say that I was initially skeptical of your claims prior to your visit to meet with our team. To claim to have new information to build wealth which is radically different and contrary to what we have all been taught was indeed, quite a claim!

"I was blown away with what you shared—you delivered exactly what you promised, and more. Your ideas and concepts are indeed totally different that I had ever heard before, and made a lot of sense.

"Your professional presentation and adept speaking style was informative, energetic and kept the attention of the group. Since your seminar, I have had a number of our team come to me to let me know that they had felt similarly, and that they would be contacting you to obtain more information and to move forward with what you proposed.

"Great job on educating our team with what seems to be a great way to build wealth, with a twist! Bravo."

—Dave Tuscany, Broker/Owner, RE/MAX Suburban, Inc.

"Best wealth building presentation I have ever heard; wish I could have started using this 30 years ago."

—David M., Realtor®, Adrian, Michigan

"The content that John Jamieson presented was more valuable than I would have ever expected."

—Jane D., Clarkston, Michigan

"Very cutting edge information."

—Rick Rosen, Realtor®, Shelby Township, Michigan

"I learned idea's from John that I have never heard before."

—Ray N., Realtor®, Sterling Heights, Michigan

"My eyes have been opened. I learned so much. Very well worth my time. Everyone should hear this."
 —Kathy Z., Associate Broker, Adrian, Michigan

"Great info and several new and innovative ideas about creating and accumulating wealth.
 —Sharon O., Broker, Shell Knob, Montana

What Clients and Students had to say about John and his trainings

"In the last two years I have sat down with several financial advisers and listened to them explain what products that they thought would suit my needs best. I am not a risk taker; I am a widow, a single mom and a business woman who was looking for a product that would build wealth for my retirement as well as for my children without having the risk of possibly losing it all. The first time I met John I knew he was going to be the guy to understand what I wanted and to help me achieve that goal! John has taken all of my fears out of how to invest my monies. With John's guidance I know I have set up a fantastic retirement for myself as well as a great nest egg for my family generations to come!"
 —Kim Z., Michigan

"I first met John during a real estate training seminar back in November 2010. I was very impressed with John's knowledge of all aspects of real estate, but the concept of Perpetual Financing piqued my interest. I've been investing in stocks, all types of options, commodities and currencies for more than fifteen years and I had never heard of the concept of Perpetual Financing. My wife and I are currently using the funds in our whole life insurance policies to purchase four homes in Detroit this year at a discount from the peak market of 80% and renting them with a positive cash flow per month of $550.00. By pulling the funds from the policies we continue to get the dividend on the total policy balance, plus the rental cash flow, plus the interest for the using the funds goes directly back to our policies. Finally, all the earnings within the policy grow tax-free.

"John and his team simplified and automated the entire transaction process. From setting up the whole life insurance policy, finding high quality properties in Detroit at great discounts, closing, taxes, insurance, renting to high quality tenants and property management.

"Finally, we plan to hold onto the properties for three to five years with the monthly positive cash flow and eventually sell the properties at an estimated 100% return, or more on our funds. John and his team will also handle the selling of the properties once the time is right. A complete end-to-end solution."

—Jay H., Washington

"I just spent three remarkable days with John Jamieson who was the main lecturer for a seminar in Los Angeles. He is a natural teacher, experienced investor and for me the whole package . . . John has hit the top of my Guru Chart . . . I recommend to all those investors who have been looking like geniuses because of a strong local economy it's time to listen and get some real methods and ideas from John Jamieson who knows how to make money in a challenged market."

—Candice J., California

"Mr. Jamieson was recently facilitating a training class in real estate. His knowledge, experience, and communication skills really helped open my eyes and perception into new ideas, concepts and strategies into the Real Estate Market. Mr. Jamieson's methods and strategies are tested proven and allotted economic gains for himself and his business. I highly commend his support, expertise, and facilitating techniques in the area of investing settings."

—Semi P. S., Washington

"As a national professional speaker, I always thought I was an outside the box thinker when it came to marketing my business dealings. What a treat and literal paradigm shift when John and I had the chance to work together. I was coached by the master himself!"

—Dennis Dinoia, National Trainer, Florida

"We first thank you for all your help with our first home. Besides being a great instructor in which you taught us a lot. You were great at answering our questions about this whole process . . . We followed your advice and got a toll free number and put the house on our website (that was so easy). We had our first open house on a Sunday. We had an offer four days later and closed on the property in two weeks. Our profit was $25,000."
  —Jacqui and Chris H., Michigan

"Excellent Training! So much information that is not available anywhere else. John and the instructors he invited know their subject matter inside and out. They are honest trustworthy folks with a sense of humor!"
  —Reggie W., Louisiana

"This seminar was amazing. I wish you had been doing this 20 years ago and I had found you then. Thanks, I can't wait to get started with you."
  —Colin M., Connecticut

"I've been to a lot of real estate/money making seminars and I found this one to have the most value of them all. It's a complete package using your own bank to real estate acquisition. The team was very knowledgeable and interested in our success."
  —Margaret Tom, Hawaii

"This is one of the best seminars I have ever attended. Content was excellent and the presentations were very well done. This is definitely a game changer."
  —Tom M., Michigan

What Medical Professionals are saying

"I would highly recommend *The Perpetual Wealth System* to anyone. My father has always been a huge proponent of whole life insurance. After reading John Jamieson's book, I realized how powerful owning a "properly designed" whole life policy can be. *The Perpetual Wealth System* explains the benefits of owning a whole life policy such as tax deferred growth, death benefits, long term care benefits if necessary, etc. The book then explains how to utilize the policy to essentially create your own bank from which you can take loans against. Mr. Jamieson also goes into various strategies to use that bank to grow your wealth. The book was a very easy read and a huge eye opener for me. I have had the opportunity to speak with John twice since reading his book and will say that his communication skills and candor are impeccable. I hope to be working with John for many years to come. There is absolutely no excuse to not read this book."

—Dr. William Soscia, Florida

"John is a knowledgeable, trustworthy, and helpful financial wizard. His depth of knowledge on the financial products and how they coexist with the current financial markets is a true asset. After discovering John, speaking and working with him, I now have a much more predictable and promising future. As a small business owner, I wish I found John sooner in order to become my own bank to self-finance business capital that I need. Because of John, I know have the financial plan to sustain my needs now, my retirement years and beyond. I highly recommend anyone to work with John if they are serious about a secure future."

—Dr. Taj Haynes, North Carolina

"I happened upon John at an ideal time in my career. My private practice was growing and my investments had increased markedly since the stock market crash of 2008. I was searching for a strategy to deleverage my market exposure without decreasing my return on investment. I took a chance and contacted John after viewing some of his on-line tutorials and reading his book *The Perpetual Wealth System*. His knack for simplifying complex investment strategies and his willingness to openly discuss not only his greatest achievements as an investor, but also his failures and how he learned and improved as a result of them, immediately earned my respect. There are plenty of financial "experts" who can pitch an investment strategy without ever having walked the walk. John is a true and tried investor which makes for an ideal advisor and mentor. He listened to my concerns and suggested an approach involving real estate and whole life insurance. I now own four investment properties and an insurance policy that are both sources of guaranteed income regardless of how the stock market performs. The cash on cash return on my investment has already exceeded what I imagined, and the whole process from concept to implementation was seamless. I would recommend John and his team to anyone and look forward to doing business with him for years to come."

—Dr. Robert Berls, New York

WEALTH WITHOUT STOCKS OR MUTUAL FUNDS

The Ultimate Blueprint of Little Known Powerful Strategies for Building Diversified Wealth and Income

JOHN JAMIESON

PERPETUAL WEALTH SYSTEMS
DETROIT

 Published by JC Press
www.wealthwithoutstocksormutualfunds.com

Cartoons © Randy Glasbergen, glasbergen.com
Cover design by Tracey J. Henterly, Freelance Graphic Designer, Cleveland, OH
Interior design by Dorie McClelland, springbookdesign.com

ISBN: 978-0-9851976-0-5 paperback
ISBN: 978-0-9851976-1-2 ebook

Printed in the United States of America

This book is dedicated

to John and Dorothy Jamieson as well as all my other family members who have passed away. Combined you made my life a true gift with too many good memories to fit into a book.

I also want to thank my wife, Marybeth, who handles so much for our family that gives me the time to write books, work with clients, and help change people's lives. To my sons, John and Luke, I hope this book will always be a constant reminder to you of being the best you can be in your own lives and chosen professions. If you end up half as blessed as your old man, you're in for great lives indeed.

Thank you to my assistant, Colleen Zalewski, who has been a huge help with this book as well as our day-to-day business operations. I also would like to thank all the friends and business associates who have participated in this project that will help many thousands of people grow their incomes, wealth, and financial options.

Lastly, this book is dedicated to all of you who have been told that you can't achieve great things in your life because you lack the proper pedigree, college credentials, or background. The fact is, you can start from wherever you are today and make dramatic improvements in every area of your life over a very short time frame. You must have a desire and a belief in yourself that you can accomplish anything you set your mind to achieving. Today, you can start a trajectory for your life totally different than the one you are on right now. This trajectory can make your life almost unrecognizable from where you started in just a few short years. Some people want it faster than a few short years but the fact is the time is going to pass regardless of what you desire. Set up a plan to transform or improve your life in every major area. Never let anyone else's opinions of what you should be dictate what you will accomplish with your life.

Read and listen to positive information every day and your life will never be the same.

Your life is meant to be designed by you and you alone. You have in this book a great launching pad to help you in your money and business life. Use its platform to start to network with other like-minded people and begin to mastermind with people who have not just lofty goals, but also the fortitude to work and make them a reality. Your past does not have to equal your future and don't let someone's opinion of your talent get you down. I was a high school failure and college dropout who was told to find some trade I liked because that was what I was best suited to do with my life.

I am glad I was too damn dumb to know I couldn't do what I do today! Sometimes being "dumb" is an asset.

Thanks for ordering *Wealth Without Stocks or Mutual Funds*. I would like to give you a free gift of further education as a small token of my gratitude for investing your money and your time to get ahead financially.

I have a special DVD entitled "The Flow of the Money Stupid" and "Not Your Father's Life Insurance Policy" which has world class information taken from a $995.00 home study course. This DVD will be a perfect fit for the self-banking and one account chapters.

After you send us your completed request form we will get you out this DVD along with other wealth building material that will help you in your journey.

Truly,
John Jamieson
President of Perpetual Wealth Systems
Author of *Wealth Without Stocks or Mutual Funds* and *The Perpetual Wealth System*

Yes, please rush me out my free DVD and other wealth building material!

Name

Address _____

City _____

State_____ Zip Code_____

Phone number _____

Email address_____

Email or fax the fully completed form to info@wealthwithoutstocks. com or 586.273.1507 and we will rush your Free DVD and additional wealth building information to you. There is no cost or obligation. Thank you again for ordering this book.

CONTENTS

Preface   *xxi*

Introduction   *1*

Chapter One   Beat the Bank by Becoming the Bank   *13*

Chapter Two   Your "One" Account   *27*

Chapter Three   Reduce Income Taxes by 50% or More   *41*

Chapter Four   Fast Turning Houses for Big Paychecks   *51*

Chapter Five   Fast Turn "No Equity" Homes   *79*

Chapter Six   The Secret IRA Your Financial Advisor
                               Doesn't Even Know Exists   *93*

Chapter Seven   Private Lending—No Banks Required   *103*

Chapter Eight   Nationwide Turn-key Income Properties   *117*

Chapter Nine   Million Dollar Marketing   *131*

Chapter Ten   Million Dollar Internet Marketing   *147*

Chapter Eleven   Million Dollar Media Strategies   *175*

Chapter Twelve   Create Your Own Private Pension   *193*

Chapter Thirteen   Mobile Home Park Investing   *209*

Chapter Fourteen   Mortgage and Debt Payoff in Record Time   *221*

Chapter Fifteen   Double Digit Returns Paying Other People's
                               Taxes   *231*

Chapter Sixteen   Network Marketing in the 21st Century   *241*

Chapter Seventeen Wealth Without Stocks or Mutual Funds
                               Game Plan   *253*

About the Author John Jamieson   *265*

Become a Wealth Without Stocks or Mutual Funds Team Member   *267*

More Education from Perpetual Wealth Systems   *268*

Preface

The 21st century is in full swing and starting to establish its place in history. In the world of finance, business, and investing the 21st century world can be a scary place. The complexity of financial markets combined with technology advances, have scared many Americans into a state of shock when it comes to building their own wealth. There are literally tens of thousands of financial advisors and experts all spouting off about how to grow wealth. With all the different products and programs available to us as consumers, deciphering what makes the most sense and gives our families the best chance at success can be a massive undertaking!

What I noticed in all my research and studying over many years is that almost every one of those financial experts focus on pie charts and predictions based on the stock market. I just Googled® "stock market investing" and pulled up just under 82,000,000 hits of people discussing all their strategies to "beat the street" with this play or that play. Walk into any traditional financial advisor's office and you will be offered any number of strategies, stocks, mutual funds, and money managers. There is almost always a place for the stock market in any well rounded wealth building plan but certainly there are more options to grow wealth and increase income.

A diversified portfolio of stocks and funds is a myth. The 21st century's instant information age and 24 hour news cycle has made the stock market a massive worldwide interconnected beast. The whole beast often moves in sympathy (be it up or down) with certain segments of the beast depending on what the beast is focusing on that particular day. The "modern portfolio theory" that is sold to most investors is in fact not modern at all but actually based on a theory that has been around for about 60 years. There is nothing new or innovative about this age old strategy. This strategy is designed to lull you into a false sense of security because your money is "diversified."

However when the market tanks again, as it always does, almost all of your stocks and funds will tank in sympathy. Why utilize financial strategies that were designed to accommodate a totally different kind of world than we have now? If you had to go in for heart surgery would you want the best technology and strategy the 1950s had to offer? Wouldn't it make more sense to bring the most up to date, current strategies and technology to the table during your operation? It's time for you to rethink those old financial strategies and come into the 21st century with your income and wealth creation efforts.

A truly diversified yet powerful wealth strategy must include investments and strategies outside of the stock market completely. Needless to say this will not be welcome news to many in the stock market community so be prepared for blow back. If you really want diversified holdings with the chance at serious wealth creation you will need to own and understand different asset classes. You will need to diversify your income both now and in the future to provide rock solid stable income month after month for your entire life. This is actually not as difficult as you may have been lead to believe.

You will have to work what I call the 11 pillars of riches and they are laid out step by step in *Wealth Without Stocks or Mutual Funds*®. You have the ability to take control of your financial future and this book will be a huge step in the right direction. Don't ever believe you are not smart enough to handle some of your own money and make it grow quickly. What you need is the desire and blueprint for making sound financial decisions in your life. Financial success boils down to these simple truths:

1) Don't spend all that you make

2) Lose as little money as possible when you make an investment

3) Stop or slow down your 4 main wealth drains as described in the book

4) Put the power of true compound interest to work for you as much as possible

5) Minimize your taxes with simple strategies as much as possible

6) Always be learning and improving

7) Spend some and save some

These 7 truths are not difficult and you have taken a huge step in the right direction by investing in this book. Pay attention to the suggestions toward the end of the book on what steps to take first after you have read the content of the book. There are literally dozens of real world strategies between these covers and your job is to determine which ones to implement first and which ones to employ as you move forward. The conclusion of the book will help you determine what might be the best steps based on your current income, age, and wealth levels. You will also have the ability to reach out to us for help after you have finished reading this book.

Sit back and enjoy the *Wealth Without Stocks or Mutual Funds*® ride!

"If at first you don't succeed, press 1. If life gave you lemons, press 2. If you're a squeaky wheel that needs to be greased, press 3. If your actions don't speak louder than words, press 4. If you have all of your eggs in one basket, press 5."

Introduction

As I sit down to write my second book, I'm feeling very fortunate.

Until two weeks ago, I had no intention of writing another book—at least not for a few years. Writing a book, I've found, is a tremendous undertaking that requires hundreds of hours to put out a quality product.

I'm still having flashbacks of terror when I think about finalizing my first book, *The Perpetual Wealth System*—and that was three years ago! Now I stand at the beginning of an exciting new adventure far sooner than expected. The reason I'm doing this now is that a few weeks ago I was struck by a lightning bolt. You might call it providence.

When the idea came to me, it was a direct hit. It made me sit up and take notice.

I was in Manhattan at an event where I was pitching the media on why they should do stories about me and my business. When you're at an event like that, you've got about 120 seconds to make an impression and cut to the heart of the matter. Journalists quickly try to discount you and find out why you're not a match for their audience. It's up to you to prove to them that you, in fact, might be a great fit for their audience.

If you can pull that off in the two minutes allotted to you, then you have a great chance of getting media coverage in the form of newspapers, magazines, websites, radio shows, and TV shows.

I was about to pitch a man from *Investor's Business Daily* on why I should be included in one of his upcoming stories. Your first couple of sentences are critical because you have to hook the producer and make him want more information. I'd used many "hooks" in pitching the media during prior times. Some that went over well and some that were dogs. I usually have the hook and first few sentences ready to go, but this time I didn't—and thank God for that.

By Divine providence, I blurted out, "I show people how to create wealth without stocks or mutual funds."

He was fascinated.

I decided to keep using the same pitch, and everyone I spoke to wanted to know how it was possible. Surely I couldn't have been the first person to pitch this concept to the media, I thought. There must be books or writings with this same angle. After the third person I spoke with loved my pitch, I sat down at a table in the hotel lobby and called my assistant and asked her to check domain name availability for www.wealthwithoutstocks.com, even though I was sure it was already taken. I asked her to get me something as close as possible.

Ten minutes later, she texted me that the domain was available.

I was floored.

Then she told me that I now controlled that domain. I quickly secured several other versions and extended it to also include www.wealthwithoutstocksormutualfunds.com.

It was at that moment that I knew I'd given myself a brand-new project, and I needed to get it to market as soon as possible. When I got home, I contacted my attorney about trademarks and copyrights and before I knew it, I was off to the races.

But how is it possible that this is such a unique concept that no one had thought of before? How could the media not have been pitched this idea before I showed up on the scene?

Well, it turns out it has been pitched—by many people—but nobody that I'm aware of ever tied it all together in such a strong, all-inclusive package before today. In fact, I personally pitched the same media with variations of this title. I tried many other pitches, but none were as perfect or summed up my brand nearly as well as this title.

Many of my financial articles have been targeted at wealth seekers, showing people how to create tax-free generational wealth, how 401ks are for suckers, how to be your own bank, and how to create a real estate cash flow machine.

All of those took me to a certain point, but I knew my new idea was going to be even better—not only for me, but for my readers, students, and clients.

Looking back, it's little wonder why the man from *Investor's Business Daily* and the other financial media people were fascinated by my "hook." After all, people want to know: How is it possible that you can create and protect wealth without owning stocks or mutual funds?

Conventional wisdom tells us that to create wealth; you have to invest in solid public companies by purchasing individual stocks or mutual funds. These people had never really been shown any other way to create wealth without stocks or funds.

The ever-present stock market

Turn on your TV, your phone, your computer, or any other device, and you'll almost certainly be greeted by the day's stock averages: the Dow Jones, the NASDAQ, the S&P 500. You'll be instantly updated as to the direction of the market. There are entire television channels that are on 24 hours a day, seven days a week, which do nothing but report on the stock market.

How boring do you have to be to follow those for hours every day?

The media has been bombarding us like this for generations now, so it's no wonder people don't realize they can, in fact, create wealth without stocks or mutual funds.

This book is not anti-stock market. There's certainly a place in every wealth plan for stocks or funds somewhere along the way. The problem is that the vast majority of people have no idea about some of the many other ways we can grow and protect our wealth.

When my team and I work with clients from all over the country, people are always fascinated when we discuss the subjects of this book. The topics I cover here are virtually unknown to most of the world, but when used properly they can be extremely powerful.

As I write this, I'm so excited to put all of these wealth vehicles in one place that I can't wait to finish this project and get it into as many people's hands as possible. By writing this book, I want to help you learn more about each topic and give you the chance to set these programs up in your lives.

Most books like this convey information, but you're usually left to your own devices to actually implement anything you've learned. Instead, I want to put a turnkey solution in your hands for as many of the strategies discussed in this book as possible.

If you're serious about wealth creation, further education is a must. I know some of you might feel a bit leery once you see the training programs available to you after you read this game-changing book. But there's just so much more I can teach you outside the pages of a traditional book. That's why my company and I produce so many recordings and live events for you to take advantage of above and beyond this book. Every year, I spend thousands of dollars on my education—and I know if I didn't make that investment, I would fall far behind in the marketplace. In this rapidly changing world with instant information if you don't learn anything new very often you quickly become antiquated and not as valuable in the marketplace. In short, you get left behind scratching your head.

You're holding in your hands a virtual bonanza of ways to create wealth without stocks and mutual funds. I can honestly say I know of no other book like it, and I feel like I was meant to write this book. This is the culmination of almost 25 years of business, investing, and hard-earned education put into one place. The knowledge I'm sharing with you will give you options you never knew existed. If you've heard of some of these strategies, then maybe this will be the push that gets you over the top to start using them in your own life.

We all know the stock market is a major force in almost every investor's life, but you don't need any real expertise to put your money in the market. Most Americans simply choose what kind of investor they are (aggressive, moderate, or conservative) when they sign up for their 401(k); which will be their main retirement savings and investing plan for the rest of their lives. More than 80 percent admit to having little clue what they signed up for and no knowledge of how their money is actually being invested. They just get their investment amount taken out of every check and let it ride!

The good news with that philosophy is that you don't need any market expertise; the bad news is that you're making one of the biggest financial decisions of your life blind. You're investing (not saving, in most cases) money, which is far better than not doing anything at all and just blowing all of your income. It's fast, easy, and painless to get started funding your future. So you don't have to be a financial expert to begin to accumulate wealth. That system is hands-off from you and will allow you to focus on other things that are also important in your life. The money is given to Wall Street (most of the time) and invested through mutual funds into many different kinds of stocks. However, that system also comes with enormous costs in the form of market losses and huge opportunity costs that we'll explore later in this book.

The wealth without stocks system is not that simple (it's pretty easy, but not that simple) and will require you to learn how to take advantage of the markets available to you—but only with some additional study on your part. If you're reading this book, then I'm going to assume you're the kind of person who's willing to shut off the TV—even for just an hour a night; that you're willing to sacrifice time on Facebook® and Twitter® every other social media time suck.

If that's true, then you have the opportunity to grow and protect wealth at an accelerated rate that should far outpace your colleagues who've bought into the old 401(k) plan. I want to congratulate you for being one of the few who'll actually take the time to design your finances and secure an abundant future.

You're about to enter a secret world (unlike the stock market and mutual fund world) that will actually make sense to you. This book isn't meant for you to use every strategy in every chapter. That would be a tall task, and it isn't necessary. There are a few chapters, however, that I think are a must for every family to read in order to grow their wealth simply and securely. There are other chapters that are very powerful but might not directly pertain to you at this point in your life. There are also chapters with separate strategies that could work great together under the right set of circumstances.

Think of this book as your own personal wealth buffet—you're free to choose whatever you like and leave the other strategies on the table. However, what will happen for many of you is that you'll implement one or two of the strategies and then come back to the book to see what else might be a fit for your goals. Just because it's not a fit for you today doesn't mean it won't be a fit for you tomorrow.

I recommend that you browse the table of contents and see what jumps out at you. Then read the chapters on being your own bank, creating tax-free wealth with life insurance, and reducing your income taxes. Those three chapters are a must for everyone because they'll be the cornerstones of your wealth. You might be skeptical of this now, but once you understand how they all work together to turbo-charge your financial future, I promise you'll see the light.

I also want to point out that creating wealth inside the stock market is very possible, and many people attribute their fortunes to it. My philosophy is not an "anti-stock" philosophy, but rather an alternative one. One of the biggest mistakes investors make is not allocating their money to correspond with their stage of life. I'll discuss this more in depth later in the book, but, for instance, does it make sense to have all your retirement invested in equities (stocks and funds) when you're getting close to retirement age?

Ask someone who did that in 2007 or 2008. Far too many of our fellow Americans could not retire on time, or—worse—had to come out of retirement and try to find a job to bring in a paycheck.

Wealth Without Stocks or Mutual Funds® is filled with money making, money saving, wealth creating, and wealth protecting information. We are dedicated to give you many options to grow your income and wealth so you won't suffer the fate of never having the option to not only retire, but retire in style! We need to talk about an important overall structure and content so the information will have structure and meaning. Everything I teach will be encompassed in 11 major financial structures or pillars of wealth. The first are the 4 wealth drains of taxes, interest and fees paid to banks, money lost in the markets, (all markets not just the stock market) and depreciation lost on major purchases. I discuss these 4 drains in depth in an upcoming chapter so pay close attention.

The other structures are called the 7 gears of riches. Those gears are:

1) Income gear—income stream from your job and/or business
2) Investments gear—which is considered anyplace you put money where it can grow or lose value
3) Cash gear—cash on hand for liquidity and emergencies
4) Guaranteed income gear—income sources from investments or passive residual income
5) Long-term care gear—structure to make sure all your other 6 gears don't get eaten alive
6) Debt gear—to handle, reduce, and eventually eliminate all personal debt
7) Legacy gear—to provide resources and options to people and organizations after we're gone

The 7 Gears of Riches

Our goal is to always reduce or eliminate the 4 wealth drains while filling in the appropriate seven gears with money so those gears operate together like a well-oiled Perpetual Wealth machine. Consider this your rough blue print for both short and long-term financial abundance. This is your 10,000 foot view of a wealthy and balanced financial life. Some will address just one area but most will address several of the gears and/or drains. You get to decide for yourself which drains and gears are most critical in your life right now and focus on the chapters that support your most urgent need.

If you're lacking enough income and are truly struggling just to get by on that income, it does you no good to focus on long-term care or longer term passive income. You need to take steps immediately to get your gross and your net income higher to give you some breathing space.

You might be doing great with gross and net income and that is not a huge need for you right now but you're giving too much of that income away to several of the 4 wealth drains. This takes away from your ability to grow wealth at a rapid rate and in such a manner that you know the wealth is yours to stay. Your other 6 gears could be very much out of balance and not spinning together. When gears don't operate in tandem and together it creates a rough running engine and eventually leads to the engine seizing up and stopping. We want your gears to work in harmony for the rest of your life starting today!

1) Income from job and/or business is your life blood to live your life and pay all your bills. I don't feel we were put on this earth just to live, pay bills, and die so this cash flow must be large enough to pay your bills and live a certain lifestyle with options such as vacations, nice home, automobiles, charity support, etc. When your cash flow is weak you cannot plug up your wealth drains nor can you grease the other 6 gears. You should be working toward a results driven income so you are not limited by other people's opinions of what income you should make. One of my mentors told me years ago that profits are better than wages. He was so right and for many reasons.

   This book will give you several ways to immediately increase your income. Some of those ways would involve you working with my company and some won't. I wanted to give you several options to make extra money and for some of you that might lead to an entirely new career in the future. There are millions of families whose lives would be greatly influenced for the better if they just brought in an extra $1,000 to $2,000 of monthly income. That is here for you in this book and much more if you will put in some time and effort.

2) Investments are the second critical gear and there is a seemingly endless supply of places you can invest money that could make you wealthy and another seemingly endless supply of places that could also take all your money and leave you poor. The secret is to find a few core investments that you understand very well and work those investments. Become an expert at even one or two (this book will help you get started to expert status) solid investments and focus your efforts in those areas. One of the biggest mistakes people make is to put all or most of their efforts to just their investment gear and little effort into the other main gears or drains of their financial life. We will give you an easy plan to lead a much more balanced financial life and keep these gears working together with as little resistance as possible.

3) Cash on hand is seemingly self-explanatory and is not a difficult concept. However, even though it is a simple concept many people focus on putting so much into investments that if a short-term cash need arises they might not be able to satisfy that need. They also might be able to satisfy the need but at a cost of selling investments at losses or incurring penalties and fees to get their cash needs met. Cash set aside is usually thought to be low interest bearing but that does not have to be the case. There are great financial vehicles out there that will allow you quick access to cash while still giving you a decent return on your cash as it sits in the account

4) Guaranteed income is the income we can count on after our job or business income either goes away completely or drops significantly. Do you know how much income you need every month to live your current lifestyle? Would you like to live even better? Most retirement accounts such as IRAs and 401ks make no guarantees on how much monthly income they will provide in your retirement years. Do you have a pension? How much will you receive from Social Security? Will Social Security be there in the future for your retirement years? The Social Security Administration's own web page says that if you

retire after a certain year you will only qualify for 77% of the current amount given to you as your projected retirement account. A successful and abundant retirement will require safe and stable income. Most of your retirement accounts are not built to provide these guarantees but this book will show you how to reallocate those accounts to provide you with safe stable income for life

5) Debt elimination or reduction will be critical to a worry free life and retirement. If you have a $2,500 house payment and $2,000 of that amount goes toward principal and interest you will have $2,000 a more net monthly positive cash flow if you can pay that home off in full. You will learn how to do that faster and easier than you ever thought possible in this book.

6) Long-term care or home health care in your older years. Most people's plan for dealing with long-term care boils down to one word . . . Hope! Hope is not a strategy but there are strategies that are little known that can aid you should you ever need extra money for long-term care or home health care. If this one gear falters it can systematically destroy all the other gears you have been working so hard to build. Many times, by simply reallocating existing assets you can control the potential huge expense of long-term care or home health care without expensive long-term care insurance policies.

7) Estate or legacy is what you would like to leave behind in this world after you move on to the next one. Would you like to give family more options in their lives as far as education or opportunity? Do you have a special cause or foundation you would like to help long after you're gone from this life? Would you like to make sure that all your hard work doesn't go to Uncle Sam after you pass away or to a greedy court system? A proper estate plan is critical to closing out your financial life and leaving a positive influence behind generations after you're gone from this world. If you want to determine who is entitled to what than a simple estate plan is a must.

We are going to show you how to build out all your 7 gears of riches while at the same time plugging up your 4 main wealth drains. This book is dedicated to changing your financial future for the better. You hold in your hands a completely new way to look at money and wealth. We can't wait to get started helping you down your path to financial independence and abundance!

"You need more time to prepare for retirement.
Sign this to legally change your age to 25."

Chapter 1

Beat the Bank by Becoming the Bank

When I train people how to be the bank they're almost always fascinated by this concept, but they struggle to understand how it could benefit them. So before you read another word of this book, get out a pen, paper, and calculator and do this simple exercise:

Add up all the payments you've ever made in your life to a bank or finance company on every debt you've ever had. This includes cars, real estate, boats; any motorized anything, business loans, business equipment, student loans, etc. Now whatever that figure is (it will largely be a figure of age and income), double it. For instance, if you've shelled out $1 million in total payments, your number would be $2 million.

Why do we double that figure? Simple: By giving up control of all your money in the form of monthly payments for all those years, you turned over the growing power to the bank.

Depending on your age, even if you'd kept that money and earned a modest interest rate of 4 percent to 6 percent, your money would've easily doubled once—and, for many of you—doubled twice.

Now that we have your money lost score, let's add up your money kept and invested score.

Simply add up all the money you've saved in your IRAs, 401ks, and other retirement accounts. Grab your most recent statements and add them up. This entire exercise can be done in 10 minutes, and I challenge you to do it before you read another word.

How much have you saved and invested for retirement?

Which of those two totals is bigger, the money you paid to the bank—or the money you set aside for yourself?

Now ask yourself who's getting rich with that personal finance model.

The answer, of course, is obvious: the banks and Wall Street. This business model works like a charm for them. Wall Street is flat-out drunk with money and has been for decades.

When I do this exercise in front of a room, it always draws a laugh from the crowd because they realize that those monthly payments have deprived them of most of the wealth in their lives.

You borrow money your whole life and don't care, as long as the interest rate is low. The problem is this keeps you in financial bondage to the banks. Whatever money you're able to put away goes into a "qualified plan" and is then handed over to Wall Street.

The average participant in my workshops might tell me he's shelled out $2 million in payments and lost growth over the years, and has only $70,000 saved for retirement. Which figure would you rather have for yourself? This is math that any fifth grader can do, and it makes sense to anyone with an open mind.

Now to be fair, very few people can afford to self-finance their first car or house, so the numbers get skewed because you probably didn't have the option of self-financing those things. But your ultimate goal should be to self-finance your life. Think of it as one giant income wheel. Income comes into the wheel, but most of it gets spit right back out the other side.

Your goal is to keep as much of that money coming in on the wheel as possible. It's important to understand that I'm not advocating just paying cash for items the way many financial gurus incessantly preach. I'm talking about using your capital just like a major bank.

If you took out a loan from the bank, do you think they'd mind if you didn't pay it back? Or if they'd mind that you paid them no interest? (Don't be fooled by those "0 percent loans" because there's always a cost; sometimes it's hidden in the actual price instead of in the finance charges.)

The answer to both of those questions is of course they would.

So if you're acting as your own bank, why would it be acceptable to not pay yourself back, especially without interest? It's never acceptable just to pay cash (especially for anything over $10,000) and not pay the bank back—even if you own the bank.

I'm going to show you how to make money on every car you ever own from this moment forward. When I teach this concept in my workshops, I always get someone who wants to show me how smart he is who says, "I don't pay any interest on cars because I pay in cash." These people want to prove that they don't get robbed by banks, that they're more sophisticated than most of us.

But the truth is that paying cash for a car does very little to stop the wealth drain of the car. The biggest expense you have when you own a car (not including operating expenses like gas, oil, and maintenance) isn't the interest you pay on a loan, although that can substantial. The biggest expense is actually the depreciation.

Let's look at a typical American car-buying experience:

Bob buys himself a new car (that's his first mistake; he'd be far better off buying a used car that's two to three years old, after the lion's share of the depreciation has already occurred) or even a used car for $25,000. He takes out a loan for $25,000 for five years at 5.25 percent interest, giving him a monthly payment of $475.

So what will this transaction look like in five years?

At that point, Bob owns the car free and clear, but he's shelled out a total of $28,500 (the original $25,000, plus $3,500 in interest). All he has to show for it is a $5,000 asset.

His loss on his "investment" is $23,500 over five years—and getting worse with every month.

So where did his biggest loss occur?

It wasn't in the $3,500 interest paid, but in the car's steady depreciation.

Interest lost to the bank: $3,500.

Money lost to depreciation: $20,000 (and climbing every month).

Anyone who thinks paying cash for a car is a good idea is living in a fool's paradise. The cash left sitting inside the car disappears like magic.

That money must be volumized and velocitized to recapture the massive depreciation and create interest in your favor instead of working against you.

Some gurus will tell you to pay cash for everything and drive around in a $2,000 jalopy. But what self-respecting adult wants to drive around in a "beater"? This is a great way to create a sense of scarcity in your life and actually repel wealth from your family. Driving a beater can have a huge negative effect on your personal wealth thermostat, causing you to subconsciously believe that you're only worth what your "beater" car says your worth.

Instead, you can drive a nice car that's in your budget and finance all or part of it yourself. That way you get the nice car and don't lose your shirt in the process.

I would like to show you why you might be better off buying your car than funding your 401k. I know that sounds like financial heresy but I can prove it with fifth grade math. I'm going to ask you to do another exercise right now. I have a video that will show you in just a few short minutes what I am talking about and why any fifth grader could figure this out for themselves in about 10 minutes.

Visit us at www.MultipleWealthStreams.com to watch why buying a car might be better than funding your 401k. Search for the video entitled "car vs. 401k" and give it a watch and a share on your social network if you like what you hear. Many other training videos are available there so take the time and join our YouTube® community.

Plug up your 4 biggest wealth drains

The four wealth drains in most Americans' lives are income taxes, interest and fees, market losses, and depreciation. In order to grow your wealth, regardless of what happens to any market, these drains must be stopped. I'll elaborate on them throughout this book, especially on the biggest wealth drain of all: taxes.

The traditional financial model that we've all been brainwashed with says to put 10 percent of our income into our retirement accounts, such as a 401(k) or an IRA. But that money is almost always put into mutual funds and the stock market.

If you're one of the few people who puts away 10 percent or more of your income for retirement, congratulations! You're in better shape than most Americans. The bad news is that even you are getting bamboozled by the biggest magic show on earth.

The best magicians and illusionists are masters at having you focus on one area of the show, while at the same time using their other hand to actually achieve the "magic."

This is a perfect analogy for our four wealth drains. The "magic" occurs when you focus on your investments and whether they're going up or down. You ask yourself, "When should I get in the market? When should I get out? Should I buy stock or sell it?"

But while you're focusing on the investment portion of your life, you can become oblivious to how you're transferring your wealth almost every month to everyone but your family.

While you're busy looking at your investments, here are the wealth drains you're ignoring:

- Income taxes
- Interest and fees paid to banks and others
- Market losses from your investments, which steal the compounding curve
- Massive depreciation on assets (such as cars)

If we could stop or seriously slow down all of these wealth drains, wouldn't we automatically create more wealth for our families? And wouldn't that wealth accumulate regardless of what happens in any investment market? Could we set our watches by that wealth as opposed to just our investments?

Of course, the answer to all of these questions is a resounding YES!

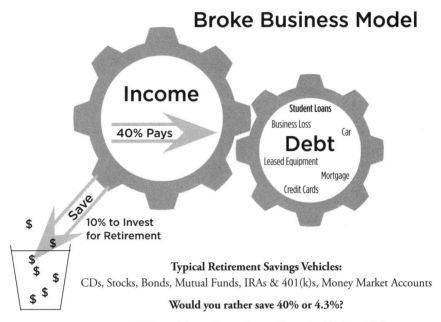

Broke Business Model

Typical Retirement Savings Vehicles:

CDs, Stocks, Bonds, Mutual Funds, IRAs & 401(k)s, Money Market Accounts

Would you rather save 40% or 4.3%?

(US National Average Savings Rate as of December 2014 was 4.3%)

Ben Franklin was right and wrong

As we know, Benjamin Franklin was one of the wisest men this country has ever known and helped lay the foundation for America, along with some other very talented men. His most famous saying is "A penny saved is a penny earned."

When I'm talking to live crowds, I often ask this question:

"If a penny saved is a penny earned, then would $250,000 saved be $250,000 earned?" The crowd almost always says yes, and for the longest time I thought that was right.

But then I wised up.

To actually save $250,000 from your income for yourself, you probably have to make around $450,000. Why? Because you have to pay taxes on that new income.

So $250,000 saved is not $250,000 earned, but rather $250,000 saved is $450,000 earned!

This is one of the reasons I have dedicated an entire chapter to income taxes and how to legally and ethically reduce your income tax exposure every year. Since income taxes are one of the biggest expenses we have in life don't you think it makes sense to know how the system works so you can arrange your affairs in such a way to pay the least amount of taxes allowed by law?

You might consider going to the chapter on taxes now or simply arrive there in the natural course of reading. Either way the information is not to be missed and once learned, please make sure you act upon the new strategies you'll learn.

Interest and fees paid to banks

This massive number has already been made crystal clear in the exercise of adding up your payments and doubling that amount we discussed earlier. How would you like to recapture even 50 percent of your figure from the previous exercise and keep it for yourself and your family? To do so, we will take a close look at how banks really make money and how you can employ the same strategies. This is covered in an upcoming chapter in depth. Once this information is understood you will want to take steps to use these banking strategies for your own wealth creation efforts.

Market losses steal your compounding curve

Albert Einstein supposedly said that "compound interest is the eighth wonder of the world." Compounding is a seemingly magic elixir that has the power to create wealth for anyone who grasps it. But for those who choose to ignore its power, it can be a real wealth-stealer.

Compound interest can be killed in two ways:

1) By withdrawing money from a financial account in which it was earning compound interest. When investors break the compounding curve like this, it can be a serious setback, so you should only withdraw these funds in an emergency.

2) When your investment loses value, it erases the compounding curve and puts it years behind the pace it would have been on if the money had not been lost. True compounding of money is interest on profits with no backward movement of the original principal or the interest already earned.

A different kind of interest

It's important to understand that not all interest is the same. There's **simple interest,** which is annual interest on a specific amount, calculated daily. Then there's **amortized interest**, where the amount of interest is preset and added on to the loan amount and then divided up in equal installments over a certain period of time. Almost all normal loans (real estate, auto, boats, etc.) that are for a specific period of time are amortized. Then there's **average rate of return interest**, where the investment gains in some years and loses in other years. You add up the gains, subtract the losses, and divide by the number of years to obtain your average rate of return. It is actually very possible to have a positive average rate of return over time and still lose actual money. This is because the losses occur early in the cycle and the gains later on in the cycle are based on much less money.

Last but not least, there's **compound interest**, where money earns interest on profits and grows every year, with no losses. (Preferably, this also happens with no income taxes, but more on this later.)

In a perfect world, you would borrow money with simple interest (lines of credit are usually simple interest) and get compound interest paid to you. But it almost always works the other way, where you borrow on an amortized basis. This, of course, works in the lender's favor.

You might have heard that if you make just one extra payment a year on your 30-year mortgage, you can pay that loan off in more like 20 years, saving you loads in interest. This is true, but when you do that, your monthly payment doesn't change. Instead, your same payment is credited differently on an amortization schedule, where a greater portion of the payment goes toward the principal every month.

TIMING OF PROFITS AND LOSSES

This illustrates two hypothetical investments and is for informational purposes only.

Starting Principal: $500,000
Income: 5% of first year principal
Inflation: 3%

If you averaged 8.43% return over 20 years, will the sequence of your profits and losses matter?

In this example the average remains the same; just the order has been reversed.

Age	Annual Return	Investment A Ending Balance	Annual Return	Investment B Ending Balance
66	32%	$ 633,450	-37%	$ 290,000
67	-3%	$ 588,000	5%	$ 280,171
68	30%	$ 740,641	16%	$ 298,028
69	8%	$ 769,759	5%	$ 285,343
70	10%	$ 819,213	11%	$ 288,250
71	1%	$ 801,045	29%	$ 341,938
72	38%	$ 1,072,227	-22%	$ 236,519
73	23%	$ 1,287,663	-12%	$ 177,673
74	33%	$ 1,685,558	-9%	$ 129,818
75	29%	$ 2,134,671	21%	$ 124,513
76	21%	$ 2,550,208	29%	$ 126,500
77	-9%	$ 2,283,278	33%	$ 134,095
78	-12%	$ 1,976,381	23%	$ 129,239
79	-22%	$ 1,502,887	38%	$ 141,094
80	29%	$ 1,896,101	1%	$ 105,142
81	11%	$ 2,063,447	10%	$ 76,791
82	5%	$ 2,124,645	8%	$ 42,524
83	16%	$ 2,419,867	30%	$ 14,160
84	5%	$ 2,510,157	-3%	$0
85	-37%	$ 1,537,562	32%	$0

This is basically compound interest going backward. Very few people ever actually do this, and the main reason is that they have a hard time seeing 20 or 30 years into their financial future. They also know that if they pay more on the balance of their loans, their present-day cash flow isn't any better because their payment remains the same.

Ask yourself this: "Would I have much more money today if I never lost a dime of my capital over all these years and my money always went forward?"

The answer is absolutely!

It's not pre-ordained that you have to lose your money in the stock market and hope that it comes back. The stock market is a pure creature of average rate of return. So be wary when you hear that a particular fund "averaged 8 percent over the last 30 years." The reason is that averages are not compounding of money!

People will quote you an average based on any time frame that suits their point. If their five-year average rate of return stinks, they'll map out a 10 to 100-year average. Every average rate of return can be skewed based on when the average is calculated.

Depreciation

The biggest wealth stealer that almost nobody talks about or writes about is depreciation. Almost everything we ever buy in our lifetime experiences massive depreciation. Let's say that two years ago, you bought yourself a couple of beautiful business suits and spent $800 for them. What would they be worth today, assuming you wore them even a little? Even if you could find someone your size, would they give you anything for them? Would you even try to sell?

What about the pair of shoes you bought to match? Or the shirts, ties, scarves, and bags that were the perfect accessory at the time? Let's say you spent $1,500 for all of these things. Today they'd be worth about $300.

Most of us won't sell them, of course. We'll wear them into the ground or let them sit and die inside our closets until we give them away, hoping for some kind of tax deduction.

That original $1,500 is now gone, and you might still owe interest if you bought those things on credit. Of course, we all need clothes, food, and other essentials, but this is the nature of how we spend our money on consumer items. I have clients tell me sometimes they don't know where their money goes. That's usually because they've never really thought about the depreciation on all the things they buy. Of course, we can't totally stop depreciation in our lives, but we can certainly slow it down, especially on big-ticket items such as cars, boats, equipment, office machines, and jewelry.

The truth is that most of our wealth gets spent on consumer items and is then lost through depreciation. The more we can reverse that trend, the more money we have for our families. The only way to stem the tide of depreciation is to make a commitment to be the bank and "loan" yourself money on any consumer item over $10,000 or whatever figure is appropriate in your own life.

When you accept the loan as a consumer from your own bank, you make a rock solid commitment that any loan you accept yourself will be repaid to your own bank—with interest. Pick a reasonable payback time and set up your own amortization schedule (there are loads of free schedules available online) for payments. If you borrowed the $10,000, you must use interest volume and velocity to recapture the depreciation you'll inevitably experience on the item. In my first book, *The Perpetual Wealth System*, I discuss these principles at length.

So what is interest volume?

Very simply, interest volume measures how much of every payment is going toward interest (normally to an outside bank) and how much of that payment is going toward debt pay down. The pay down part helps your net worth; the interest part helps the bank's net worth.

Let's say you just closed on a new home with *principal* and interest payments of $1,000 a month. If your interest rate on the loan is 6 percent, that doesn't mean your interest volume is 6 percent. Your interest volume in the early years of a loan is close to 80 percent and shrinks over time as you start to pay *down* the original loan balance. So you and I could have the same payment and interest rate, but very different interest volumes, depending on the age of our loans.

This is why you shouldn't be in a big hurry to refinance everything all the time.

Interest velocity is nothing more than the speed of *money*. Velocity is not unique to money and is critical in any business. If you've ever waited tables, you know velocity all too well. If you had a section of eight tables during the night and you could turn those tables over three times instead of twice, would you make more money in tips that night? Of course you would because you'd get paid on eight more bills.

Interest velocity is nothing more than how many times can we lend out the money to ourselves or others and collect new fees and another income stream back to the bank. We'll discuss private lending in an upcoming chapter, but for now remember this: If you could loan out money and get paid two origination points up front every time, would you want to loan that money three or four times during the year?

The answer is obviously four times because that way you'll earn thousands more in fees.

A centuries-old business model

Banking has been around in some form or fashion for thousands of years. If you could bring your oxen to the temple in biblical times, you could get a loan out on it for a fee. Any business model that's been around that long is obviously a killer business model and has created untold fortunes for bank owners. Our problem as a society is that we've only been trained to be borrowers—not lenders. Owners of banks understand volume and velocity, but few Americans truly understand how banks have been making money off us for centuries.

Now is the time to understand that there's a fortune to be had by using a pool of money—just as a bank would—to put volume and velocity on your side in your wealth-creation efforts. This is the powerful, time-tested strategy you need to stop the four wealth drains and grow and protect your wealth for you and your family.

There are many fantastic real-life strategies packed into these chapters, but this chapter's strategy of being your own bank can be combined with all the other chapters. Very few people will use the information in every chapter, but I hope that everyone will combine this chapter with the next chapter to achieve financial *independence*.

In this chapter, we covered banking and how banks have historically controlled us. But it's critical to realize that you can take control of your own money and your own cash flow.

We've all been told we should put our money in the stock market and just let the "financial experts" handle it for us. I agree that almost everyone can participate in the stock market at some level. And I also agree that a good investment representative can be a major asset to you in your wealth-creation efforts. But it's important to remember that there are many ways for you to control your own wealth. Many of these will have nothing to do with the stock market.

Being your own bank and putting a stop to the four wealth drains is critical to your financial success, and I hope you'll start to pool your own money immediately, either all at once or by gradually building your bank.

Start now and don't delay.

Now let's talk about the best place to pool that money.

"We've done everything we can do, Mr. Johnson.
Unfortunately, there is no cure for bad insurance."

Chapter 2

Your "One" Account

What I am about to tell you might fly in the face of some of the financial advice you may have been given over your lifetime. I know that was certainly the case when I was first exposed to some of the concepts in this chapter. You owe it to yourself to be open minded and really explore all the points that are made here before you dismiss the powerful information contained in this chapter.

A truly wise person is never closed down to the possibility that there are better ways to accomplish goals. This is how progress is made in all areas of life and human endeavor. I know I am very knowledgeable in many areas of investing, real estate, personal finance, and business. However, I would be an absolute fool to believe I "know it all" in any area. Put this to the test—but only with an open mind. I did this by spending the first 3 weeks after I was shown some of these concepts trying to poke holes in them. I soon realized that the information I was given before about this topic was very one sided and closed-minded. There is an old saying: "if you can't beat 'em, join 'em," and that's what I did when it comes to the information you are about to learn.

Most of you by now have seen the light and are starting to understand that you should have your own pool of funds and use them the way banks have used funds for centuries. The next question on your mind should be where you can pool these funds before you loan them to yourself or other people.

Where is the most optimal place to operate this bank from and use volume and velocity? Should you just use a checking or savings account?

Maybe you should use a money market account? After all, the account must be very liquid and easy to obtain funds. The truth is there is only one account that will be your optimal place to fund your own bank. That account is a PROPERLY DESIGNED WHOLE LIFE INSURANCE CONTRACT. This fact flew in the face of what I was taught by financial gurus when I first started getting my financial education years ago. I was told that you should never put money inside a whole life insurance contract because it was a lousy investment. Many of the famous gurus of today still teach their students the same idea that whole life insurance is a lousy place to put money.

I believed that financial myth for over 20 years and so I never did own a whole life policy. I believed the untruth, "buy term and invest the difference" that's still being told to the masses. So why is there such a difference of opinion between me and those gurus? To be fair to those that still teach that whole life is a terrible place to grow money, according to what they understand about how most policies work, they're correct. The problem (as with many things in life) is you don't know what you don't know.

You see, most whole life insurance policies are written just for the death benefit and very little thought given to the cash value. Why? Because most whole life policies start off with very little—if any—cash value in the first few years and are only starting to grow cash many years into the future of the policy. However, what almost nobody understands (even people who sell life insurance) is that there are some insurance carriers that will write a policy that will allow very high cash values from day one and design the policies to grow nicely over time. You can basically exchange a lower death benefit or coverage amount in return for more access to your cash and greater growth.

A traditional whole life policy in which you contribute $10,000 a year into the policy might get you a $1,000,000 death benefit but with zero cash value year one and maybe only $500 after two years of premiums. This would NOT be the type of policy we could set up to use those funds as a bank. If we were working with the right insurance carrier, maybe we could contribute the same $10,000 into the policy and only take out a $500,000 death benefit. In return for the lower exposure for the insurance carrier, they agree to give us $7,000 starting cash value from the first day the policy is open. After the second premium payment of $10,000 we might have $16,000 of cash value. These are funds that we would have access to in our wealth creation efforts and not have them locked away inside a traditional whole life plan. You will give up access to some of your money in the early years, but in mid to later years, your premium deposits will grow very nicely. Your cash value will start to compound on a tax-free basis, and as you add more funds, the compounding dollars will increase exponentially!

Big Myths Exposed About Whole Life Insurance

Myth #1: Buy term and invest the difference

The thinking behind this strategy initially appears very sound. Because the cost of whole life is more expensive than term in the early years of a policy, you should buy the same coverage for much less premium using a term policy and invest the amount saved between the two premiums into mutual funds. This difference over time will create more wealth for you and your family, while at the same time giving you plenty of coverage should you die prematurely. When you get older and the term policy gets far more expensive due to your advancing age, drop all coverage because you will have accumulated enough wealth to self-insure and leave money behind for your estate.

When I was 22 and wet behind the ears, I thought the above paragraph was gospel and preached it to anyone who would listen. As with most myths, there are some truths in the myth and this is no different. The costs of whole life premiums are more expensive in the early years for the same amount of death benefit when compared to term rates for the same coverage.

Now here is the other side of the coin. Nobody (or very close) actually invests the difference in their premiums into an investment vehicle. So if their whole life annual premium is $2,400 and their annual term coverage is $400.00, the theory is you are saving $2,000 annually or $167.00 per month—so put that amount every month inside a mutual fund and in 30 years you will have loads of money. The biggest hurdle is putting away that $167.00 every month. If you are still a buy term and invest the difference kind of person, have you done what is described above? If you have, congratulations—you are part of the ½% crowd of people. Almost nobody is actually employing this strategy but plenty are talking about the theory. Also, even when this concept is applied, it fails to take into account many variables that will greatly impact the results.

Financial success is not about theory but about actual results. If almost nobody is using the strategy, then it's great for sound bites, but lousy for results. Let's also examine if you will need life insurance toward the end of your life. You need to look no further than the ads on television to see the huge market for life insurance at the end of life. Big companies with celebrity spokespeople have been on the air every day for over a decade paying for advertising, selling small end of life burial insurance. The advertising budget alone is staggering, which begs the question: how many policies do they have to be selling to pay for that advertising and their other expenses, and make their profits? Truck loads according to the Life Insurers Council and CSG Actuarial Report. In 2013, over $400,000,000 of these policies was divided between over 613,000 individual policies just in that calendar year!

What does the information tell you about this nation's financial model? Why would you buy one of those expensive policies in your later years? (Yes, they are expensive in relation to the amount of coverage you receive for your premium.) The only reason is because you are not sure if you have enough liquid money saved to bury you and cover your final expenses! This is a great barometer of how buy term and invest the difference has done in servicing the American public.

In my own life, my mother passed away just after the huge economic collapse of 2007 and 2008, before any real rebound in any of the financial or real estate markets occurred. My mom had done well for herself and worked hard starting at the age of seventeen. She certainly had acquired enough to cover her final expenses and leave behind a nest egg for her three children. However, she happened to die at a very inopportune time in financial history. Her home had decreased in value by 35%, as did most of her investments (my Mom was very independent and did not ask for my help until the damage was done). I found out she had lost a good portion of her money inside market vehicles that had gotten pounded during the previous few years.

So when she passed away, she left considerably less of an estate behind than she believed she was going to just a few years earlier. She was not unique and that same scenario happened to millions during those years. This will again happen to many millions more when the markets nose dive again if they don't set up a simple plan to avoid this fate. I am very grateful for the money she did leave to me and my family and we are fortunate that we did not "need" her money to survive. Had someone shown these life insurance and self-banking strategies to her 30 years before, she would have left behind millions of tax-free dollars for her estate. This is true of millions of people who passed away during those terrible down cycle years for the economy.

As you will learn in a future chapter, my mom should not have been in market accounts at that stage of her life. There were far better options for her that would have preserved and made her estate quite a bit larger even without using life insurance.

Myth #2: Life insurance is a lousy place to put money

What I described before about designing policies is very true but there are also some other facts that blow this myth away. Simply ask yourself this question: if life insurance contracts are such a lousy place to put money, why do the biggest and most wealthy institutions put loads of their own money into life insurance products? Major banks, large corporations, and family dynasties have been putting boat-loads of money into these kinds of policies for generations. Are they that stupid about money? Hardly. They are very savvy with money, which is why they use life insurance contracts and other products to grow and protect their wealth.

Major Banks' High Cash Value Life Insurance
As of 12/31/2014, Federal Financial Institutions Examinations Council Call Reports

JPMORGAN CHASE	10.6 BILLION DOLLARS
WELLS FARGO BANK	17.995 BILLION DOLLARS
BANK OF AMERICA	20.794 BILLION DOLLARS
PNC BANK	7.699 BILLION DOLLARS

Myth #3: Whole life insurance is too expensive

When someone tells me that, I simply respond, "in relationship to what?" If you are just comparing it to premiums for a term policy on the same coverage amount, you could be correct. However, because of the tax-free, guaranteed compounding of a proper life policy, many of my clients will overcome the actual cost of the insurance in the first few years of the policy. These policies will get to the point that they self-complete, which means the insurance company owes you more than you owe it in minimum premiums. If you decided to, you could have the basic premium paid out of cash value and your cash value would still grow and move forward. So in twenty years, if you still want coverage and attempt to extend your old term insurance policy or buy another one, get ready for the shock of the new premium based on your attained age. If you had strongly funded a life policy twenty years before that policy's death benefit, it would have been growing for those twenty years (all part of the proper design of the policy with a proper carrier) and no additional funds would be required to maintain the policy due to the huge cash values you have accumulated. You would also have had access to large cash values to use for other wealth strategies as described in this entire book.

Myth #4: Universal life or Indexed Universal life does the same thing as whole life

This is such a myth that I need more than the space required in this book to let you know how these policies really work over time and why the cost of insurance will skyrocket over the life of the policy. Please download my free report at my website at www.wealthwithoutstocks.com and click on the

Resources page, where you will find the indexed universal life report. You can also go to www.theperpetualwealthsystem.com and click on the Video of the Week. Then scroll down and download the entire free report I wrote about these types of policies. Don't you dare buy one of these policies until you read this free report. If you already have one of these policies, get the report and be thankful there is probably something we can do to help you. Ask us about a 1035 exchange of that kind of a policy for one that is better suited for long-term and being your own bank.

Myth #5: I am too old or in too bad of health to obtain a life insurance policy

I have clients all over the country who once believed this to be true, but now own life insurance policies. If you like the concepts of self-banking and insurance policies, don't assume you can't qualify for one of these policies. You may be able to qualify, and the numbers will still make sense. If you indeed cannot qualify, there are other options.

Many of my clients take out policies on their children or grandchildren, which means the younger, healthier person qualifies for the insurance, but my client owns the policy with all the benefits. I have clients in their seventies who took out new policies but the policy was on their adult children. They then went on to use the funds in the policy as their own bank. Contact us to see if this might be an option for your situation as well.

When I am speaking to a crowd on this topic I often call a properly designed whole life policy the "one account" because it is so truly unique and powerful. It is the only account that I am aware of that can function with many different uses that all work together. It is the only account that can be all of the following:

Savings Account:

When you're not using your money, it's sitting inside of the life insurance contract collecting much more in interest than it would if it were sitting in a bank. As of the time of this writing, most savings accounts are paying 0.5% or less and some life carriers' dividend scale is almost 6.5% on life policies. Even after you take out the cost of insurance in the early years

33

of the policy, your money still does far better than dying a slow death in a traditional bank. You have easy access to your funds just like a savings account, so why keep most of your money in the bank doing nothing for you or your family?

Your Personal Bank:

Just as described in the last chapter, you can put these funds to use to plug up your four massive wealth drains and help you grow wealth as the bank. Because you are doing this inside of your life insurance contract, your earnings are tax-deferred inside the policy, and when done properly, can be accessed tax-free. Also, with some policies and carriers, the money you lend out will still be credited with growth and dividends. This is not common, but there are carriers that allow this and we can help you determine which carrier is best for your needs.

Retirement Account:

There will come a time when you desire to pull an income stream out of your policy. You will be able to either withdraw the money as you see fit (which is not optimal most of the time) or take policy loans that you will not pay back. In most cases, policy loans are optimal because you don't have to pay taxes on them. If you choose, you don't have to pay the policy loans back during your lifetime. The loans can be paid back out of the death benefit after you pass away. For instance, say you have a $1,000,000 death benefit but have lent out $250,000 in policy loans and deferred interest and you pass away; your family will receive the $1,000,000 death benefit less any outstanding policy loans—which, in this case, are $250,000. This will produce $750,000 tax-free to your family after you pass away.

Rainy Day Fund:

You should never borrow all the cash value out of your policy but rather keep a chunk of money in the policy in case of emergency. This is a rainy day fund that produces solid interest rates and return.

Estate Creator:

Let's not forget you are creating all this wealth inside of a life insurance contract which will automatically leave behind money for your family and/ or anyone else you choose after you pass away. My mom, as she aged, started to worry more about leaving money behind for her family instead of living as abundant a life as she should have lead. This is the only kind of program in which you can spend every nickel during your lifetime and still leave behind extra for your family. Wherever you have your money saved or invested currently, ask yourself if that account has all of the benefits listed below. These are all benefits of a properly designed life insurance contract that we can help you set up.

Do your current investment or retirement accounts accomplish all of this?

1. **Give you principal protection against any downside market risk. Initial cash value and all subsequent premiums are principal protected.**
2. **Your money will grow every year, contractually guaranteed by very old, solid companies.**
3. **Non-taxable growth and dividends paid to the account.**
4. **Allow you to access your funds at any age, for any reason, with no penalty or taxes, without fees: a significant difference from 401ks and IRAs that have very strict guidelines and timetables for withdrawing or borrowing money from the account.**
5. **Total control of what you use your funds for, including for investment, personal, business, and emergencies.**
6. **Ability to put large sums of money into the account while maintaining the account's tax-free growth and access. The maximum most qualified accounts (IRAs and alike) will allow to be contributed annually is around $50,000. There is no such limitation on whole life insurance contracts.**

   (NOTE: While #6 is true please don't think you have to be a high income earner to make this program work. We have

clients putting in as little as $300.00 per month into their program. We also have clients putting in multiple six figures into their plans every year. This is truly a strategy for most income levels.)

7. Tax-free withdrawals, when done properly. These structures have a similar tax structure to a Roth IRA but without all the rules and red tape for accessing the funds.

8. Easy in and out of the policy means you can use this account as your personal bank and recapture lost depreciation and interest you might otherwise normally experience.

9. Very difficult for creditors to attach judgments and liens and be able to collect the funds. (Always consult with a good asset protection attorney.)

10. Money creates a large death benefit that will also pass tax-free to your estate. (Certain maximums apply; check with your attorney.)

11. Very easy to borrow money from the insurance company for the rest of your life. Not having to "qualify" for a loan as with traditional sources for funds. Truly taking control of your finances for generations to come.

12. Guaranteed insurability for life once you're approved. Once you have this policy in place, you and your family are covered for life, assuming at least the base premium is paid as agreed. It is important to understand that the base premium might be able to be paid out of existing cash value in years you don't want to fund it with any more outside money. Unlike term policies that only insure you for a specific time frame. Many people are shocked to find out they cannot get new coverage because they have been diagnosed with an affliction that makes them uninsurable. You will also be able to stop funding the policy in the future and have it in force for the rest of your life without new premiums

13. The freedom and flexibility to combine these policies with almost every other strategy outlined in this book. Your life insurance

policy or private bank will be your centerpiece and cornerstone wealth creator. Many other wealth streams will flow around this rock solid base. Would you like to invest in real estate, make private loans, buy tax liens, buy gold, and buy discounted notes and discounted debts? You can use this policy to do all of the above and more.

When you properly design a life policy with a proper carrier who embraces these types of policies you receive all these benefits. I always get the question, "How do I get one of these set up?" If you go to your normal insurance agent please don't be surprised if they look at you like a deer in headlights when you start describing this type of policy. There are only a handful of agencies who understand these concepts (to their fullest degree, not just, "yes, I have heard of it") and I am sure you will not be surprised to learn **that my company writes these policies all over the country and has done so for years.**

We are experts at these policies which is why people seek us out from all over the country. I am a big believer of supporting friends and families in their business ventures whenever possible. However, this is an account that you will be using for the rest of your life and will affect your family for years to come. This is the time to use experts to get this done correctly. So, yes, this is a shameless plug and a huge asset to you at the same time. When I envisioned this book I didn't see just the book—I knew I wanted to create ways for readers to get more cutting edge information and when possible, to give them the people and companies that could take years off of their learning curves in all of the wealth strategies covered in this book.

I also work with other wealth strategists all over the country who have embraced the wealth without stocks program. Many of these people are fully trained, licensed, and have access to great insurance policies with top carriers. If one of those people supplied you with this book, please go to them to get your policy up and running. I really appreciate my joint venture partners and have no desire to take any hard earned clients from their businesses. If they are offering these types of programs, you are ready to get started. If you currently do not have a person as just described, reach out to our office today.

After all, what good is a book loaded with world class information if most readers don't take action on its content? I wanted this project to be different and if I have experts in all of these areas that can help you, why wouldn't I make these connections for you? Well in this case, and in this chapter, the experts you need happen to be my staff and me. Feel free to go to our website or email us directly at info@perpetualwealthsystems.com.

What I love about this concept is it does not require you to learn much new information. You just have to combine the last chapter with this chapter to begin creating automatic and systematic wealth for generations to come in your family. Do you know how to make payments? There is not a reader out there that doesn't know how to make payments. The problem is who you have been making payments to for your entire life. Reverse your outgoing cash flow to incoming cash flow and house that captured cash flow inside a guaranteed tax-free environment. Then watch how quickly and safely your wealth accumulates.

"The bad news is, they want to raise taxes on the wealthy.
The good news is, if you buy me everything I want,
you'll never be wealthy!"

Chapter 3

Reduce Income Taxes by 50% or More

This chapter will show you the US tax code as you probably have never seen it before. The tax code is over 70,000 pages of boredom and confusion and is designed so badly that even the authors of the tax code really don't have an idea of how the system actually works. You can be sure that the code is designed to be difficult and keep you as the taxpayer intimidated and paying the most money possible to your old Uncle Sam.

Income taxes are the single biggest expense most Americans will ever have and yet very few people have a real clue how the system works. It is my belief that since you are going to pay taxes for your entire working life-time—and probably even some taxes after you have died—that you should have a handle on how they actually work and how to legally pay the absolute lowest amount of taxes allowable. Determining how to pay the lowest amount of taxes possible is your responsibility and not your tax preparer's or CPA's. Nobody will ever care more about your money than you do, so think of this chapter as your spring-board to saving a fortune in income taxes over the course of your lifetime. You will be amazed by how relatively simple it is to legally and dramatically reduce the amount of taxes you pay each year.

Let me say upfront that I am not a CPA or a tax attorney. I am just a taxpayer like you that wanted to understand how I could get the tax system to work in my favor as much as possible. I have read countless books and listened to live presentations by many experts on the subject of taxes. Here, I have brought a tax expert to you who has been teaching taxes all over the country to thousands of people for twenty years. He blew my mind when I saw him speak, with all his rich information. We have become friends and had many business dealings together over many years. His name is Patrick and he is a major contributor to this chapter. Take it away Pat!

Thanks, John. Hi there and thanks for reading this. As John already told you my name is Patrick and I am going to try to simplify some of the 70,000 pages of the tax code and supporting documents to help you capture more deductions and ultimately save you thousands of dollars on your taxes every year. I wrote a book and would like to give it to you for FREE. Just go to www.wealthwithoutstocks.com/taxes and you can get your FREE eBook. The following is a sampling of what I cover in the book:

- Why People Over-Pay Their Taxes
- Two Tax Systems in America
- #1 Tax Strategy in America
- Profit Motive
- Business Trips VS Vacations
- Travel Rule Basics
- Ski Trips
- Cruises
- Meals & Entertainment
- Golf & Other Activities
- Dutch Treat
- Automobiles—Your KEY to a HUGE Deduction
- Motor Homes & Yachts
- Medical Expenses
- Tax Deductible Gifts
- Insurance Premiums
- Depreciation
- Deducting Your Spouse & Kids
- Work Clothes
- New Business Start-Up Deductions
- Deductions for Employees W-2 Wage Earners

Obviously I can't cover all of these topics in this one chapter so I will just pick a few (five to be exact) to give you an idea of what's possible.

First we need to understand why people over-pay their taxes . . .

Most people over-pay their taxes for 3 reasons:

1) Fear of the IRS and being audited.

As long as you are following the laws in the Internal Revenue Code there is no need to fear an audit. The IRS just wants to make sure you are doing things right and following the laws.

2) Not keeping good records therefore missing out on deductions.

Would you be willing to spend just a few minutes a day, (about an hour a month) to put $6,000 of your hard earned money back into your pocket? That would be a great use of your time. You have the ability to make that a reality but you will need the "know how" along with the desire.

3) Not knowing the rules — What's deductible and what's not.

This chapter and free book will open your eyes to available tax deductions most people don't even know about. Remember to consult with your tax professional to make sure you qualify and are documenting your deductions correctly.

TAXES — COMPLEXITY:

The U.S. Tax Code is very complex and confusing. No one, including any of the 100,000 or so IRS employees, really understands it in its entirety. With this book, we have attempted to break down and simplify some of the over 70,000 pages of confusing tax code so you can begin the process of reducing your overall tax burden.

TAXES — THE LARGEST SINGLE EXPENSE:

The average American pays about 30% of their gross income in taxes (Federal, State, and Local), representing their single largest family expense. Taxes cost the average family more than housing and medical care combined.

Yet few families ever realize the great expense that taxes cost them. While many people budget for food, clothing, and other necessary expenses, they typically do nothing when it comes to planning to legally reduce their biggest expense: taxes!

We have all heard that middle class Americans pay the bulk of the taxes—there could be some truth to that. Let me explain. You see, for the average American wage-earner, a W2 employee, there are about a dozen tax deductions they are entitled to; however, if you are doing something in your life with the intent to make a profit on a regular and consistent basis, you can be entitled to hundreds of tax deductions.

The #1 Tax Strategy in America:

Do something with the INTENT to make a profit from your home!

The "Business" tax breaks were passed by Congress for 2 reasons:
1) To stimulate the economy by creating more businesses and more jobs.
2) To encourage people to have additional sources of income to pay off their debt and contribute to their retirement.

An activity with the INTENT to make a PROFIT, can be considered a "Business" and qualify for "Business" tax deductions. You can do this as a sole proprietor (in your own name) or as an entity (corporation, LLC, etc.) either way works. In order for a business to be able to deduct all ordinary and necessary business expenses it must be able to show that the business is being run with the reasonable intent of making a profit. You do not need to actually make a profit as long as you intend to make a profit. (I cover this concept more thoroughly in the e-book on page 11.)

Here are the requirements set forth by Congress:
1) Have the intent to make a profit
2) Work your business on a regular and consistent basis
3) Treat it like a business—keep good records

Meet these 3 requirements and you can qualify for thousands of dollars in new tax deductions!

Let me share with you just 5 of the many Tax Deductions that I cover in my book.

TAX DEDUCTION 1 Deducting Travel:

You cannot deduct expenses for attending a convention, seminar, or similar meeting held outside the North American area unless:

1. The meeting is directly related to your trade or business, and
2. It is reasonable to hold the meeting outside the North American area.
3. It is considered "REASONABLE" to have a business meeting in any of these countries!

See chapter 1 of IRS Publication 463.

The following countries to not have this requirement because they are considered to be in the North American area:

American Samoa	Baker Island	Barbados
Bermuda	Canada	Costa Rica
Dominica	Dominican Republic	Grenada
Guam	Guyana	Honduras
Howard Island	Jamaica	Jarvis Island
Johnston Island	Kingman Reef	Marshal Islands
Mexico	Micronesia	Midway Islands
Northern Marina Islands	Palau	Palmyra
	Puerto Rico	Saint Lucia
Trinidad & Tobago	USA	U.S. Virgin Islands

TAX DEDUCTION 2 Travel Rule Basics:

Basic Rule: For each business day of travel, you can deduct 100% of your lodging and 50% of your meals and entertainment.

Workdays: You can count a business day as any day during which your principal activity during normal business hours is the pursuit of business. You must work more than half of the workday.

Tried-to-work days: You count a business day as any day you intended to work but circumstances beyond your control prevented you from actively pursuing your business objective.

Weekends, holidays: If a weekend or holiday falls between two business days, the weekend or holiday is considered to be a business day and is tax deductible. This applies only when it is not practical to return home for the weekend because of time required or expense involved.

Saturday night travel: Airlines sometimes charge less if you stay over a Saturday night. If you can save money by staying over Saturday night, you can count the stay-over as a business days.

Travel days: Travel days are business days.

TAX DEDUCTION 3 Meals and Entertainment

The IRS considers "entertainment" to be any activity that provides "entertainment, amusement, or recreation, and includes meals provided to a customer or client." You are permitted to deduct 50% of all of your ordinary and necessary meals and entertainment costs for your business. The 50% limitation applies to all meals (whether local or in travel status) and entertainment expenses.

In order to qualify for the deduction, you must discuss business during the entertainment (directly related entertainment) or immediately before or after the entertaining—within 24 hours (associated test for entertainment expenses). You must be able to document Who, Where, When, What & Why. Most receipts have the Where & When printed on them—you just have to document the Who, What, & Why.

- The Tax Code does not provide any guidance as to what constitutes a "substantial and bona fide" business discussion for purposes of meals and/or entertainment.
- There are no rules that specify how long the discussion must be before it constitutes a business discussion for deducting your meal or entertainment expenses.
- Your business discussion does not need to take a greater amount of

time than your non-business discussions for the meal or entertainment expenses to become deductible.

- As long as a business discussion is the primary purpose of the entertaining, the expenses will qualify for a deduction.

TAX DEDUCTION 4 Dutch Treat

How to deduct "Dutch Treat" business entertainment: many business expenses do not involve paying the expenses of clients or prospects. They are Dutch Treat, meaning everyone pays for himself or herself. But how do you handle Dutch Treat expenses? How do you know if they are deductible?

General Dutch Treat Rule: IRS regulations state that the taxpayer may deduct entertainment "even though the expenditure relates to the taxpayer alone." The IRS says its objective test precludes arguments that "entertainment" means only the entertainment of others. Further, the IRS acknowledges that business entertainment may include an activity that satisfies a personal, family, or living expense. The IRS notes that an individual in business may deduct the entertainment cost, including his personal benefit, as a business expense.

Translation: Business entertainment deductions aren't limited to the costs of treating others; you're also allowed to deduct your own costs if you "go Dutch."

TAX DEDUCTION 5 $25,000 Vehicle Deduction

Per Section 179, you may be able to expense some or all of the business use of your vehicle. Basically, if your vehicle weighs more than 6,000 pounds, you can expense up to $25,000 the first year the vehicle is used in your business. You also must use the vehicle at least 50% for business in order to qualify. The $25,000 deduction assumes 100% business use. If you use your vehicle 75% for business, you would get 75% of the $25,000 or $18,750.

($25,000 x .75 = $18,750).

EXAMPLE: You bought an SUV that weighs 6,220 pounds. You use it 75% for business and 25% for personal use. You may be able to claim a maximum Section 179 deduction of $18,750.

Car Used Less Than 50% for Business

If the business use of your car drops to 50% or less, certain rules apply. These include:

1. You cannot take a Section 179 deduction for your heavy vehicle.
2. You must use the straight-line method of depreciating your vehicle. While the five-year period still applies, this will result in a lower depreciation deduction in the earlier years.

These five strategies are just the tip of the iceberg, but you will receive loads more information by downloading our free book mentioned above. I am very excited to have been asked by John to participate in Wealth Without Stocks or Mutual Funds.® I hope to meet you in person at a live event and hopefully I can help you even further with your income tax reduction efforts.

Thanks Patrick!

Something extra for you successful business owners

If you are already a successful business owner and are paying $150,000 or more in annual income taxes there is also a little known company structure that may help you save 50% or more on your income taxes every year. We call this our income efficiency strategy and work in conjunction with a very high level attorney to structure these programs. It is very unlikely your current tax professional will be aware of this business structure but this attorney has been utilizing them for clients since 1998. However, the attorney who sets these up will be happy to have conference calls with your tax professionals to explain the program in depth. This attorney is not trying to replace your current professional but rather to work with them to implement this plan for your business.

I don't want to bore you with details here, but if you are in that small group who are paying those kinds of taxes we have a real solution that has been looked at by the IRS several times since 1998 and every time there were no changes required for the client. In other words, this is not some kind of a scam or loophole, but rather a very specific company structure that will fit into your existing business model to dramatically reduce your income taxes. Send us an email at info@perpetualwealthsystems.com with the subject line "income efficiency strategy" and we will have one of our professional teammates reach back out to you to see if we can help.

"Paralysis by analysis — nobody knows exactly what
it means, but it rhymes, so it must be profound!"

Chapter 4

Fast Turning Houses for Big Paychecks

My first love is real estate investment because it took me to levels that I could not have achieved without getting to be an expert in that arena. Before I bought my first property, I was in college for two years, and before that I was a juvenile delinquent and high school failure.

Your life can change in 30 minutes

My second year in college my grades were respectable. I was not winning any awards but I was doing far better than I had ever done in high school. The main reason was a reality check from my mom who told me in no uncertain terms that if I received the same grades in college as I received in high school that she would be cutting me off from my education funding. I couldn't blame her as who wants to waste big money on someone who is not taking it seriously? Even though my grades were fine I hated every second of my two year college career. Won't bore you with the details here but that is the only two years in my life I can remember not being happy.

Then late one night I watched an infomercial (brand new marketing strategy in the late 80s that has now become common place) and it was talking about buying properties with no money, no job, and no credit. I had all of those so I figured I could make it happen. After some research and investing in that home study program, I decided my second year at college would be my last. I jumped into the real estate investment business full time and eventually would also be a loan originator and real estate agent in addition to an investor.

I found out that you could indeed buy properties starting with nothing if you had some cutting edge knowledge. I spent years and tens of thousands of dollars acquiring that education through books, tapes, and live seminars plus the real life education I learned on the streets. I want to pass that real world information to you as much as possible in this book.

I went on to train people all over the country in multi-day seminars which people spent thousands of dollars to attend. I really love teaching people the power of real estate and how it changed my life. I obviously don't have time or room to put all of those trainings into this chapter but I am going to load it with top notch real world information that you can put to use right away in your own life.

Who knew there were TV shows about flipping houses?

My young son loves to torture me with Real Estate "Reality Shows" because for some reason he is fascinated by the housing business. This will likely change as he gets older but if he wants to go into that field he sure was born into the right house! I have written this chapter as if I were gone and trying to teach my sons the down and dirty of how to make money by fast turning or "flipping" houses. If they do what they learn on those "reality" shows they will certainly go bankrupt quickly.

Reality shows meet true Reality

I rarely watch these shows but when I do it becomes obvious they have little to do with the actual business of real estate investing and much more to do with drama and before and after photos. By the way, there is nothing wrong with this drama because people are tuning in to be entertained and not to be educated. The only problem is when people don't know the difference and believe the television show is actual how-to education. So let's cut out the drama and get down to making real money.

Big paychecks are very possible in this business and are even possible starting with nothing. You see "no money down" does not generally mean there is not money in the deal, it just means that it does not have to be our money. My first property was bought as a rental when I was 21 years old and did not require one dime of my own money. I used two strategies combined that allowed me to use a partner and seller financing to accomplish this first deal. My second deal was also no money down and I received about a $7,000 paycheck on the resale. Now $7,000 isn't all the money in the world but when you are starting from scratch with none of your own money at 21 years old, $7,000 was a windfall! Thankfully the deals and checks got bigger, but those first two deals were critical to my future success in real estate.

I want to take you through the 5 steps of any profitable fast turn on a single family home. The 5 essential steps are:

1) Find a good deal
2) Analyze deal quickly
3) Make offer and close on accepted deal (or follow up on deals that didn't get done but were close)
4) Repair for maximum profit
5) Sell quickly

Seems simple enough doesn't it? Inside each one of those 5 steps are the details that will make you either become successful or struggle in this niche business. Let's examine each one more in depth:

Find a Good Deal

The term good is such a broad term and is in the eye of the beholder. My definition of good and yours might be totally different. From the perspective of a guy who has bought and sold tens of millions of dollars of real estate, let's talk about what constitutes a good deal. This assumes you want to buy a cheap fixer upper and rehab the property for immediate resale. This also assumes you're going to cash out of the transaction by selling to a retail buyer who wants to live in the property. You will see in the next chapter that is not even close to the only way to sell properties—but for this chapter, that will be the focus.

You must buy your property at a big enough discount off its retail or repaired value to allow you to make repairs, pay holding costs, pay sales costs, and make a nice profit. The first thing you need to know is the value of the home once you have put it in nice shape. One of my first mentors, Mr. Nick Koon, told me, "Son, until you know value, you know nothing!"

Next, you need to know what similar homes in the same area are selling for, and at what prices they are being listed by other sellers. You are looking for as close to your style, size, lot size, school district, age, bedrooms and baths as possible. Does the subject property have a basement? Does it have a garage? These are the biggest factors in pulling the comparables—or comps, as they are referred to in the trade.

Some comp sites you can reference are listed here and under Resources on www.wealthwithoutstocks.com: Zillow, Real Estate ABC, and Trulia

The sites above all have free versions and paid versions and of course if you pay you get more bells and whistles than if you use the free version. There is also a new player on the scene that is called the Investors MLS and is a one stop shop for many attractive features on properties all over the country in one place. The demonstration I was shown was awesome but as of this writing it's still in "beta" phase. Please visit www.wealthwithout-stocks.com and view under resources for the most up to date version of this great new tool for real estate investors.

There are many sites on the internet that will allow you to gather comparables but none will be as good as the local multiple listing service (MLS for short) that Realtors® have at their disposal to conduct their business. Working with a real estate agent will be a huge asset to your business but make sure you don't waste their time. I would use these other sites to get a ball park estimate and then ask my agent for their comps. By the way, real estate agents and brokers pay big money every month to have the best information in the marketplace, so they should have the best and most up to date information.

If my prospective investment home is a 3 bedroom, 2 bath, 1,500 sq ft ranch, then that is the kind of home I am looking for to compare against my home. On the same street or in the same subdivision would be great, but at least as close as you can get. You are looking for a range of value because no two homes, however similar, are ever exactly the same. If I see similar homes in nice shape selling for $240,000 to $260,000 then my value will be about $250,000. You would like sold comparables to be within 45 days, or more recently when possible, for the most accurate snapshot of current market value.

A simple formula that will keep you profitable

Determine the "After Repaired Value" and multiply that amount by 70% to 75% maximum. Then subtract your estimated repairs. This figure will give you your maximum offer on a fixer upper. It would be optimal to buy it for less than this figure—this figure represents the maximum you can pay. Deviate from this formula at your own risk. This will allow you to make a nice profit on the deal. By paying more you put your profitability at risk. The "After Repaired Value" is what your property would sell for, assuming it was fixed up nicely to compare with or even be better than the other properties that have sold in the last 60 days.

Thus, you need to buy this $250,000 home (depending on repairs) in the $170,000 to $190,000 range. We will discuss this strategy further in the analyze section. We will first focus on bringing good prospects and leads to us so we can find a good deal as described above, and particularly a few key ways to find good deals in this chapter—but we can only scratch the surface. I would like to give you 100 best sources to consistently find good investment prospects. Please visit www.wealthwithoutstocks.com and chapter 4 "Fast Turning Houses for a Big Paycheck" for a free download of the 100 ways to find great deals.

1) The local Multiple Listing Service: This is usually only a good strategy when the overall market is very slow and there are large numbers of unsold inventory on the market. During those markets there is usually enough inventory in any good sized market to keep you busy. Most local MLS's download to www.realtor.com where you can access

millions of listings from all over the country. When your market is hot you can expect to find very few deals on the MLS and the rare times there is a great deal listed it will most likely have multiple offers.

2) Getting the word out that you are a serious investor and are looking for good deals in any condition:

a) Get business cards made stating that you buy houses, in any condition, any area, and close quickly. Buy 1,000 and leave them all over and pass them out as often as possible.

b) Print oversized flyers stating the above as well as domain name for a website. Consider passing these out (services do it for cheap) or mailing to a certain geographic location if you really want to own properties in that area.

c) Good old-fashioned bandit signs still work. These are usually yellow signs with permanent marker hand written on them and placed all over town. Get a service to put them up for you but check with local zoning ordinances so you don't get fined. Add a 21st century technique to the sign and put something like text to "webuyhouses123" for a quicker response. This will get you cell phone numbers from prospects instead of just bad email addresses.

d) Pay an ant farm to bring you deals. After you download your 100 ways to find deals find all the people on there that are around houses all day every day and make connections with as many as possible. Tell them if they bring you a lead that ends up as a successful investment you will play them $300.00 or some figure that makes sense to both of you. If I was in a higher priced market like on the east or west coasts I would expect to pay more per deal because my profit on a $500,000 will almost always be more than on a $200,000 property. You also might just pay them $10.00 per each lead sheet they bring you back filled out with the information you need to make a decision. Think of having 20 or 50 "ants" in the field bringing you solid leads. This is leverage at its finest!

e) Put up a website and get a decent domain. Many sites do this but the one I prefer is GoDaddy®, www.godaddy.com. The site does not need to be fancy or expensive but prioritize making it solid and clean and keeping it current. So many sites get put up and are immediately forgotten about, which blows their credibility. I suggest a 4 minute video every month to post to the site. Keep the site relevant and use the domain in all your marketing. Study the chapter on internet marketing for more tips on a great website.

f) Make up your wedding list. Imagine you are getting married and going to have a huge wedding. Who would you invite? Get that list together and get all their contact information and let them know periodically (at least every quarter) that you are looking for real estate investments.

g) Find out who in your area handles bank foreclosures (otherwise known as REO's or real estate owned by a bank) and send those agents a letter introducing yourself. Follow up these letters with calls and ask for a one on one appointment and buy these agents and brokers lunch. If there is a good sized foreclosure market in your area this one strategy can be a gold mine for your business.

h) The internet is loaded with properties but depending on the site the information can be very old so nothing will replace building relationships with real human beings who are in the world of real estate.

i) Estate properties sometimes can offer a great opportunity at a bargain. I have bought dozens of properties from my local probate court lists. When people pass away many times they leave a will that will have to go through probate court. These probates are public information and usually posted in a county legal news and/or website. These notices will include the person who passed away and the person who is the personal representative for the estate. These are the people in charge of the opening and closing of probate and the estate. A well placed letter and follow up phone call have provided me with some great deals and large profits. I always get more excited when the personal representative is located out of town because they are sometimes more motivated to get the estate closed as quickly as possible. I would never send letters to spouses who just lost their mate; they have enough on their minds without me seeing if they want to sell. Most of the time you can tell by the address of the decedent and the address of the personal representative. If Ken Jones passed away and Lisa Jones is the personal representative and both live at 1234 Maple Street it means that Lisa is probably Ken's wife. If the representative lives at a different address, they are more than likely a child and that property will more than likely be sold in the next 30 to 90 days. I also got better deals when there were several siblings, which meant the money was being split by several people. A $40,000 price reduction might only be $10,000 per person and easier to accept.

When you receive leads from the above and some of the other 100 ways on the downloadable list, they will come in 3 basic categories of properties:

1) Ugly
1) Semi-ugly
1) Pretty

When you are looking to buy and sell for a profit most (but certainly not all) of those deals will be ugly (they need a lot of TLC and money to bring them up to snuff), or semi-ugly (needs work for sure but more simple cosmetics than real contractor television stuff).

Before you even go to the next step of analyzing the actual property from the lead, first pay attention to why the seller is selling the property. What is their true motivation for selling? All sellers sell for only two reasons: the need for cash or the need for debt relief. Yes, there are dozens of sub-reasons such as divorce, pending foreclosure, settle estate, relocation, getting a non-performing loan off the books (REOs, aka bank foreclosures) and many others. All of those sub-reasons go back to the two main reasons above.

Is the seller's reason for selling strong enough that might allow you to buy this property under its current market value? The stronger the reason the bigger the discount on the price you could expect to receive. If a seller wants to sell because they are upgrading their home and need more space, will that usually allow you a chance for a deal? No it will not! On the other hand, if the seller has inherited the property, lives out of state, and has just been informed the property is a beat up old mess, does that sound like you might have a better chance at the kind of property we are trying to secure? Much higher chance of success based on that need to sell.

At any given time across America there are really two real estate markets. The first is the regular or retail marketplace. This is usually about 95% of the market and this world is inhabited mainly by Realtors®, builders, banks, mortgage brokers, home owners, home inspectors, mortgage originators, and any other group of people that focuses on helping "normal buyers and sellers" buy and sell properties. You will be selling many of your properties for top dollar in this world so you must get to know how it works.

There is also a secret sub culture of the real estate market. This second market is usually around 5% to 10% of the total marketplace. This world is inhabited by investors, REO brokers, and agents (bank foreclosure brokers and agents), private money lenders, hard money lenders, foreclosures, probate properties, highly motivated sellers, contractors, subprime buyers, and anyone else that's geared toward the investor buyer/seller and subprime buyer.

The profit for the savvy investor is dealing only with the 5 to 10% of the marketplace that will allow you to make the profits you require for your business. So many beginning investors will waste the bulk of their time dealing in the 95% world and wonder why they don't buy any properties or the properties that they buy are subpar deals.

Make a decision right now to only deal in the 5 to 10% world and your life and business will be far more enjoyable and profitable. You need to become an expert in dealing with the 5% world and all its players. There are great deals all around you but you must be the prospector and focus only on the gold and not the dust.

In my over two decades in real estate I have been through every kind of market imaginable from red hot multiple offers in hours kind of market to a free falling value market where it seemed you could not give properties away. I have found that unsuccessful investors will always find reasons why they are not doing well or finding good deals. See if any of these sound familiar:

"The market is too hot here to find any good deals."

"This market is so bad that nobody is buying."

"You can't do those kinds of deals in this market."

None of these are true and I don't care what cycle your target real estate market is currently experiencing. During red hot markets I bought properties and got great deals. During dead dog slow collapsing markets both my clients and I have bought killer properties at rock bottom pricing. During a red hot market you really need to stay tuned to the 5 to 10% of the market. When you buy in these markets most of the houses are never "officially on the market" but rather the properties were found by you or your ant farm using the marketing strategies above. They also might have been on the open market and did not sell. They had some kind of problem that the agent and owner did not know how to solve. If the property hits the MLS and is a super bargain, it will always be hard not to overpay for the property. The rule of thumb is the more people that know the property is for sale, the more money you can expect to pay to acquire the property.

That's the bad news; the good news is because that kind of market is so hot you don't always need as big a discount to make the deal work. The hotter the market is when you go to resell, the quicker sell you will have and less holding costs you will need to pay. When you are dealing with very slow markets, many times you can pick and choose the deals you want to buy right off the MLS and find solid deals that make sense. You must customize your buying and selling machine based on the market conditions.

The third type of property is pretty homes and those are homes that require a whole different approach than the ugly and semi-ugly homes. These are covered at length in chapter 5.

Analyze Deals Quickly

The next step once you have found what you think might be a good deal is to run your fast turn numbers. Here is a simple formula to use every time.

1) After Repaired Value (what you believe it will sell for after repairs are made based on comps)

    Repairs to be made (more on figuring these later)

    Holding costs (utilities, taxes, insurance, lawn, snow; budget 5 months minimum)

    Interest on funds (interest paid to outside lenders or your own bank (remember being the bank?)

    Buying closing costs such as points on money, insurance, title company fees, etc (check with local investors and title companies to get an idea)

    Selling costs such as real estate commissions, transfer taxes, title insurance (check with local investors and title companies to get an idea)

    Cost over runs and oops factor

    Your minimum acceptable profit

    Maximum offer allowed by you

	$200,000	After Repair Value
Example		
	$15,000	Repairs
	$2,000	Holding costs
	$4,200	Interest on money
	$1,000	Closing costs (buying)
	$11,000	Closing costs (selling including commissions)
	$3,000	Cost over runs
	$36,200	
$200,000		
($36,200)		
$163,800		
($25,000)	Minimum Profit	
$138,800	Maximum Offer	

NOTE: DON'T WASTE YOUR TIME PULLING COMPARABLES UNTIL YOU KNOW YOU ARE DEALING WITH A PROPERLY MOTIVATED SELLER. OTHERWISE YOU WILL SPEND ALL YOUR TIME DROWNING IN PAPERWORK ON DEALS YOU HAVE NO CHANCE OF BUYING. ONCE YOU KNOW THE MOTIVATION IS RIGHT AND YOU THINK IT COULD BE A GREAT DEAL, PULL YOUR NUMBERS AND COMPARABLES.

Down and Dirty Rehabbing

There are full 3 day courses you could take on nothing but rehabbing houses. I like to keep it simple and tell you that in most areas of the country and for most types of homes from 1,000 to 1,500 square feet your rehab budget will be between $0 to $30,000 to renovate the subject home. This seems like a huge range but let's break it down to $5,000 increments.

- $0 to $5,000= painting, carpeting, small handyman repairs, outside sprucing up, and general clean up
- $5,000 to $10,000= all of the above and popping in a kitchen and a bathroom (builder grade)
- $10,000 to $15,000= all of the above plus a new furnace and ac unit
- $15,000 to $20,000= all of the above plus a new roof or maybe some concrete work
- $20,000 to $25,000= all of the above and new electrical and some plumbing
- $25,000 to $30,000= all of the above and everything in the house has to be redone new

It is rare that any rehab for the above described bread and butter home would ever be more than $30,000 barring some ridiculous foundation problems. If you're in an area where labor and materials will be more expensive, plan accordingly for the higher numbers. Most of your rehabs on the bread and butter properties described above will fall between the $10,000 and $15,000 range. If you will be dealing in bigger homes in nicer areas make sure what you can expect to pay because you will generally have to put in higher quality materials. Once you have done a few you will get the ranges down better. When you have done hundreds of them as I have it gets as easy as buying a sport coat or outfit at your local store.

Rehab to fast turn or to lease?

The amount of rehab work you do on a particular home will also be dependent on what your intention is with the home. What is your exit strategy? In this chapter we are assuming that our exit strategy is to sell to an end user buyer who is qualified and can obtain outside financing from a bank or mortgage company. In these instances, buyers have access to any home on the market in their price range, so you are very much in competition with other nice homes. I will spend more money to repair a home in this scenario than I will if I am selling to a tenant buyer or a land contract buyer. The retail buyer is pickier and will walk away from your home quickly if they don't like what they're shown. They can afford to be picky because they have access to the entire marketplace.

The tenant buyer or land contract buyer (discussed more in depth in the next chapter) have far fewer homes to choose from so they are more willing to overlook a few perceived deficiencies the retail buyer would not accept. This is also true of tenants who are just going to rent your properties. We are not going to rent out junk houses by any stretch of the imagination. However, they will probably not be in the same top-notch condition as the homes we are selling on the retail market.

If I am going to spend $15,000 to repair and resell to a retail buyer, I might only spend $10,000 on the same home if my exit strategy is different. It is critical to always know your exit in the transaction before you decide on your entrance into that same property.

In the beginning, work with contractors to verify your estimates but don't call a contractor out every time you want to make an offer because you will quickly burn that bridge from wasting a lot of their time. After you make an offer and get it accepted, that is the time to bring out your contractor to make sure you are in the right range.

Making offers 101

1) Use the offer to purchase form that is most common with Realtors® in your area. Many times you can get a blank offer template from a local agent or title company you build a relationship with to use for your offers. If it is a listed property, and you have an agent who will be collecting a commission, have them prepare the offer (sounds fancy, but really just means filling in some blanks and adding a couple of custom clauses).

2) Make your offer subject to home inspection or contractor inspection within 3 to 5 days of offer acceptance. If the contractor verifies what you believed is true, you are in the go zone. If his numbers are way off you will be able to either back out of the deal with no financial loss or renegotiate the price or terms based on new information.

3) Make the offer as attractive as possible with a decent Earnest Money Deposit (EMD) of 3 to 5% of purchase price. EMD's are not required to make a contract legal (contrary to popular opinion) but they do show good faith and put a seller and broker at ease. This is especially important if there are competing offers. I have had offers that were less money than competing offers get accepted because of a strong earnest money deposit. The money is not at risk if you put in your escape clause as described above so why fight or lose a good deal over a small matter? (Every time you make an earnest money deposit, don't give it directly to the seller but rather have a title company or the broker who might be handling the sale hold the deposit. A deposit is used to show good faith by the buyer, but remember you don't even know who owns the property yet or if the title is clean. Until you can verify all of that by using a title insurance company, the seller does not get your deposit. If you ever violate this rule, don't be surprised if you never get back your deposit money if the deal does not close.)

4) Try to close as soon as possible. 10 days for cash sales or 30 days or less for deals requiring outside financing. This is especially true when buying bank owned homes. Many asset managers who handle these properties are given bonuses based on when properties close. I have seen many deals that were not as strong in the price department get accepted because they could close quickly and the other offer couldn't.

Do you even want to repair the home or would you like to fast turn the home to another investor for a profit? Many times during my career I have been able to obtain a good enough deal on the property that there was room for me to mark it up $5,000 to $20,000 and sell the contract or property in as is condition. This is called wholesaling and can be a business within the business. This would become too long of a discussion for this book, but understand that the strategy exists. If you would like more information on wholesaling, consider investing in the program at the end of this chapter and obtaining a real estate coach.

1001 Creative offers sellers can't resist

This was the title of one of the first books I ever read about real estate when I started many years ago. This title sounded good—I mean, who wouldn't want 1001 offers that sellers can't resist as a real estate investor? It made a thick, impressive book but I still didn't understand why you needed so many offers in your tool chest. The fact is there are loads of creative offers one can dream up on a piece of property but dreaming up creative offers doesn't get the deal done or you paid.

Easily structure a creative deal with a just a few tools in your tool chest

When you are constructing offers on properties, it boils down to just a few things to have a solid chance at picking up a nice deal.

1) What are the seller's true wants: cash or debt relief? Sometimes it is both of these, but always one motivation is much stronger than the other.

2) How motivated and creative is the seller, and can you structure something simple that they would understand? The 1,001 creative offers will confuse the snot out of them and a confused mind always says NO!

3) What resources do you have either personally or access to that will help get this deal done? Do you have cash? Self-directed IRA? Cash Value Life Insurance? Or access to private funds? We have a national private lender that will loan you money on good deals that meet their criteria. Visit www.wealthwithoutstocks.com and click on the US Private Lending tab to apply.

4) How much does the seller owe on the property? This will tell you their main reason for selling. If they have little to no equity, they are trying to get out from underneath their payment or debt relief. If they have a high equity position, they are more than likely selling to gain some of that equity in cash. Is their mortgage current with payments, and if not, how many months are they behind and how far along in the foreclosure process have they progressed? Every state has different foreclosure time tables and some even have redemption periods after the foreclosure sale. Spend some time studying your home state's foreclosure time tables.

The best way I know to teach you to how structure financing on a home with the limited space available to us is to give you a few real life examples. These examples range from the silly simple to the awfully creative but all have worked for me many times in my business over the years.

Example: You find a home worth $250,000 after repairs are made that needs $20,000 in repairs to bring it into nice shape. The seller has inherited the home, lives out of state, wants a fast painless deal, and is willing to sacrifice top price for that convenience. You are able to buy this home for $160,000 but you must pay cash and close in 20 days. If this deal was presented to you today could you do the deal?

Offer strategies

Offer all cash and use your own funds or borrow money from a private lender (See chapter 7 about using private lending to create wealth from the borrowing and lending side of the fence) at 2 points and 8% interest. This is a private loan, not a hard money loan, and they are really two different animals, even though most investors think they are the same product. Check out our site www.wealthwithoutstocks.com to see if we have some national lenders that could help you do these deals until you build your own private pool of investors. I can tell you now that lenders who do this nationally as a business will be more expensive than 2 points up front and 8% interest. However, if the numbers make sense even with paying more, and that is the only way you can do the deal . . . get the money and get your deal closed!

You put $20,000 down and borrow $140,000 from the private lender plus $20,000 in repairs, bringing private loan to $160,000. You quickly bring the home into shape and sell for $250,000; after holding costs and sales expenses, you make a net profit of $40,000. This is a fantastic return on your $20,000 investment in just four months. The rate of return on this deal was 200% but remember that was over the course of four months and rates of return are figured annually, so the annualized return should be multiplied by 3 = 600% return on your $20,000 investment.

Will you treat this as a business or an investment?

The rate of return above seems too good to be true but this was not just a rate of return on an investment of money. It is also a rate of return on your time, efforts, and education. Rather than just blindly throwing $20,000 into the stock market with little to no knowledge, you have taken the time and spent the money to get trained. In short, you have earned the right to collect these kinds of paychecks. You also spent time and some money finding the deal. You most likely analyzed dozens of deals and made a dozen offers before you found this gem. So you should make far greater returns because this is an investment and a business at the same time.

Now let's look at a couple alternatives to getting this financed and closed on the buying side. We offer the seller the $20,000 down and ask them to finance the rest with a first position land contract or contract for deed (what it is called will vary depending on what part of the country you transact business) for just 6 months. We might start off offering them no interest for such a short-term loan but would agree to pay them a reasonable rate of return if needed. I would always try to get a lower rate than I could get from a private or hard money lender. Don't assume the seller needs all cash on the day of closing. Many times they will need all cash, and sometimes they will be happy to take a short-term pay off. I would simply tell them that you need some time and are going to spend your money to get this house in tip-top shape so the more they can help you with this endeavor, the better deal it will be for both parties.

You could also combine the two strategies above if the seller needs more down payment than you have but is still willing to take back (carry) a seller-held mortgage. Let's assume everything above is still the case but the seller needs $50,000 down minimum and you still need $20,000 in repairs. You simply ask the seller to subordinate their lien to a new first loan on the property. This is a fancy way of saying you will borrow $70,000 first loan from a private lender (very safe loan for the private lender) and ask the seller to carry back a $110,000 purchase money second mortgage for a 6 month term when the loan becomes all due and payable. I would offer no interest and no payments to the seller but might expect to make payments on the $70,000 to the private lender during the time I hold the property. So you would have a $70,000 loan recorded as the first lien and $110,000 recorded in second position for a total of $180,000. You then would sell as above to a retail buyer and expect to pay some selling costs and holding costs. Because I will have fewer holding and closing costs with this kind of arrangement or with straight seller financing, that creates more value in this deal from my perspective. This means that I might be willing to pay a little more for this deal. If I can save $10,000 of holding and closing costs I will make more money. This gives me room to be able to sweeten the offer price if needed to get this deal done. This still should be a nice, profitable deal.

Private loans are critical to make this side of the business (ugly and semi-ugly houses) work. Why no banks? There are places for banks in real estate investing but usually not in single family homes that you plan on fast turning. Remember these homes will need work and sometimes enough work that they will scare the bank appraiser and the bank and cause them to deny you the loan. Also there are many parts of the country in which the bank can sue for deficiency judgments if you default and the selling of the property does not satisfy your entire debt obligation. So in the interest of safety for you, speed, and easy access to cash, private lending will become a huge part of your rehab investing business.

Another strategy is to partner with someone who is strong in an area in which you are weak. I would advise only a joint venture per property and no long-term commitments and entanglements with a partner. If you are weak with money, then maybe you need to find someone who has money that you could borrow to do your deals. This could just be a private loan as we talk about in more depth or it could be on a partnership basis with profits getting split. I bought my first two dozen homes this way but that was before I found out about the power of private lending.

A more creative example

I bought a home in 2011 that was a huge rehab job that was even a little more than the $30,000 talked about in this chapter. The situation and the numbers looked like this (remember this is in metro Detroit at the height of the real estate collapse so the numbers will look very low to most people reading this book, so forget about the numbers and pay attention to the concept):

One person in my ant farm told me about a house that was in a great area but was in need of a total renovation. It was a solid brick home in really nice suburb of Detroit. The home, repaired, was worth $90,000 (at one time this home would have sold for $160,000) and I could buy it for $25,000, but it needed about $30,000 in repairs. This was a bank owned property (REO or foreclosure) and they wanted quick cash. Banks are rarely a candidate for the split funding described above so you always need access to cash. I borrowed the money to buy the property and to repair it from my own life insurance policy (I actually do this stuff—I just don't talk about it) and structured a 9% loan back to myself. I had enough in the policy to buy the property and do the repairs. I had the property repaired at a cost of about $35,000 (major rehabs will almost always be a little more than you think) so now this home showed like a new construction. Now I went to sell the home and a buyer presented himself right away. There was a problem in that he could not qualify at the time for a new mortgage. He had lost his previous home in foreclosure just a year before and was unable to obtain financing through traditional channels. Prior to his foreclosure he had never missed a payment on anything for 25 years so this was a solid man who went through some short-term financial troubles. Just because someone lost a house doesn't automatically make them a bad credit risk. Look at their total history and not just a credit score number.

I agreed to sell the home to him for $93,000 with him putting $20,000 of his own money down (which he had) and I would finance the $73,000 balance. I really did not want to finance that much and leave my money tied up in that one deal (remember velocity of money in the previous chapter?) so I came up with a little more advanced strategy. I split the land contract I carried back into two different liens. One was a first lien for $63,000 and the other was $10,000 recorded in second position and both loans were at 8% interest.

I then went out and got a private lender I had a good relationship with to buy the first land contract from me at a small discount off of its face value. She agreed to pay $59,000 to me in cash for the right to collect on that $63,000 8% first lien. I carried back the $10,000, which was some of my profit and not my original capital for 3 years at 8%. This satisfied everyone's needs and I just recently received full pay off (as did the private lender who had the first lien) for my $10,000 lien. The buyer worked on his credit and was then able to pull a conventional mortgage and now has that standard loan on his almost new property.

This deal had a little bit of everything between the buy and the sell. I borrowed funds from my established life policy, which was paid back at

9% to mostly my benefit, and very little to the insurance company's benefit. This means I made a nice profit on my real estate investment and my private bank made a nice safe loan and a nice return on the money. I also had easy, quick access to the funds to tie up and close this deal. I also used private money, subordination, and seller carry back to get the property sold fast and for top dollar.

When you are dealing in the ugly and semi-ugly house business, raising cash will be critical. Please pay special attention to the private lending chapter and the self-directed IRA chapter, as these will be critical to your success.

Building Your Power Team

When you are entering the real estate investment world it will be important to build a power team as you move forward. It is not necessary to have all of these people in place before you start. This will cause analysis paralysis and stop you from ever getting started. These people can be put in place over time and mixed and matched as needed for a particular deal. Also, you will wonder, where do I find all these people that deal with real estate investors and understand what you are trying to accomplish.

Start to get involved and attend meetings at your local Real Estate Investor Associations. They are usually called REA groups for short. Go to www.nationalreia.com and find a group or two you could be involved with and attend some meetings and mixers. Almost all of these groups will have a newsletter and you will see professionals, like the ones mentioned above, advertising their services. You can also ask experienced investors who they use for certain tasks and if they are happy with that company's performance. These groups are also a great place to find private and hard money loans as well as cash investors who might want to buy your contract or property in as is condition. (Remember wholesaling above?) Another option to find real estate investors is through Meetup™, www.meetup.com.

Some of the professionals you will want to be putting in place are:

1) Cash investors
2) Private lenders

3) Real estate attorneys (for real estate law and landlord-tenant issues, including evictions)

4) Investment real estate agents (not just real estate licensees but investors who also have a license)

5) Home inspectors

6) Handymen

7) Contractors including Plumbers, Electricians, Carpenters, Floor layers, Tile Professionals etc.

Just get out into the marketplace with cards and start attending some meetings and these people will fall into place as time moves forward. From the beginning, the most important person on the list is a good all-purpose handyman who is licensed and insured. These people will be the backbone of your real estate investment business.

There are many resources online that provide some initial due diligence for you as well as former customer reviews such as www.angieslist.com or www.homeadvisor.com. Make sure any contractor understands that you are looking for a long-term team member for their particular trade. Most will give you a far better deal if they really believe you will use them many times in the upcoming years.

I found my very first handyman from a referral from another investor. I met Joe and he was one of those guys that could do just about anything and hated to spend money even if the money wasn't coming from his own pocket. He was honest, trustworthy, and reliable. Joe ended up becoming a great friend and a member of my team for 20 years until his passing. Look for similar qualities in your contractors and handymen. A license will be required for your bigger trades but many handyman tasks will not need a license. Make sure they have some insurance to protect you against any injuries that might be suffered on the job.

Selling for Cash to Retail Buyers

You have found a property, analyzed it, made the offer, gotten it closed, repaired the home and now you must exit out of the deal by selling to a retail home buyer. As discussed above, these will be the pickiest buyers but a few headaches will be worth a great investment and big paycheck.

Start building a buyers list by pre-marketing your home. When you get the home cleaned out or things ripped out and it is starting to look like something, that is the time to put your sign out and get your online ads going. You might be able to pre-sell the property and even let the new buyers pick out a few things like their colors for paint, counters, cabinets, etc. You will start to draw activity to the property and the easiest way to handle that activity is with a website. Have all signage go to a website and maybe even a toll free 800 number with a pre-recorded message. You can pay a small monthly service fee to many companies that will give you a toll free number plus dozens of mailbox extensions in which you can record messages that are available 24 hours a day. Many people still like to use the phone, and if you can give them a phone number and a website, it makes it easy to give them information. If you would prefer, you can route calls directly to your business or cell phone. Please check out our site for our resource page to get a few suggestions on services that could help you with this step.

If you are only looking to do one rehab a year or even less, building a buyers list will be less important. If your goals are a little loftier, then you need to get contact information for as many buyers as possible. If you sell this one but have one or two others coming up, wouldn't it be nice to have buyers before you even start the rehab process? This is the power of a buyers list. At least capture their email addresses and put them on your email contact board with their own group. There are also services that will host your list for a fee every month and you can also market to your list using that same service if you wish. (See chapter 10 for more on this and we will have the list under the Resource Tab on www.wealthwithoutstocks.com). The fee is usually based on how many emails addresses you have or how many emails you send out every month. Most are quite reasonable and you could get started for around $15.00 per month for a small list of names and emails. At the beginning, you could also use your normal email provider if you just want to send out group messages to a handful of people.

When you receive an offer on your property, insist on seeing a pre-approval letter from a lender and call the mortgage professional to see how far along in the mortgage process. Make sure they have been to an actual underwriter for their approval and not just the word of the mortgage originator who thinks it all looks good. Collect an earnest money deposit of at least 2% of the purchase price and the more the better. Check in with the mortgage representative every week and see what you can do to help the process and try to get it closed in 3 to 4 weeks maximum. One of the biggest expenses you have with fast turning houses is the holding cost of taxes, interest, utilities, and upkeep. This is why it is critical to get your properties turned and closed as quickly as possible.

Have a backup plan

Every once in a while, the best laid plans go astray and the property might not sell either as quickly as you anticipated, or for as much money. This is why it is important at the beginning of the transaction to be comfortable with your numbers and have a backup plan or two if things don't go quite as anticipated.

You may want to consider listing your property with a top notch local agent who can give it maximum exposure right away, which will cut down on your closing costs. Yes, you will have to pay a commission but if you're going to give the agent multiple deals over the years then a discount off of the listing portion of the commission could be negotiated. Be careful about discounting the amount offered on the MLS to any cooperating agents. If the "local norm commission" is 3% paid to the buyer's agent and your listing agent is only offering 2%, you are many times slitting your own throat. If you were the Realtor® and could earn 3% on 9 listings or 2% on your home which might you not show? If you are going to list it, make sure the Realtors® are working with you and not against you. You should always budget to pay a commission in your original numbers when you're analyzing this investment. If you sell it on your own maybe you will get to keep the commission. If you don't you want to sell it on your own, have it already in your budget to pay a reasonable commission to sell the investment.

Another backup plan might be to keep the property and simply rent it out to cover payments and expenses. This could be a straight rental or maybe a rent to own agreement described further in the next chapter. You might want to refinance the property to pay off any higher interest mortgages or private lenders with lower interest long-term financing. Find out what are the terms of refinancing loans before you make the investment.

Yet another back up strategy (you might even make this your main exit strategy) is to hold what is known as a 10 day sale. This is basically a strategy to give an auction mentality to your sales and get the most money possible in the shortest periods of time. This is an entire strategy in and of itself, which I don't have room to discuss here. Please check out our website to see the trainings we have on this topic that you can use to sell homes quickly. I have used this strategy successfully several times in the past.

You also might approach the private lender (another huge benefit of using private money) and ask them if they would like to keep the loan in place for another couple of years. Some will be happy to do so and leave things just as they are and some might agree if they adjust the rate or maybe collect a point or two extra from you for the privilege. This allows you to sell the home to a new buyer without them having to qualify for a new loan today. You could collect a down payment and payments over a period of time and maintain the payments on the underlying private loan you originally took out when you purchased the property.

You could also consider selling on terms which we will discuss in further depth in the next chapter or simply cutting the price to get it sold and gone. Don't fall in love with any property and understand it is just a business. Sometimes you make what you think or even more and sometimes you don't. Learn a lesson on every deal and move on down the road.

You have just read about the side of the real estate investment business that is most commonly discussed and taught. Basically buy low, fix up, and sell high for cash. This is a great business but it is only one side of the real estate world. There are also some downsides that should be considered when using this type of strategy:

1) Usually cash intensive (not necessarily your cash but cash will have to be raised) as many of these homes will be bank owned and banks want to be cashed out up front.

2) Higher holding costs due to using private money and having vacant homes during rehab and selling period and all utilities being paid with no income to offset.

3) If not using an IRA to buy and sell, all profits will be taxed as ordinary income assuming you cash all the way out and do it in less than 12 months.

4) More competition because this is the most well-known strategy by many people.

There is always more to know and if you have read this far you have proven to be a lifelong student of wealth and improvement. In my former life I was an REO agent and also bought many millions of dollars of bank owned properties. I condensed all that knowledge in a complete home training system that covers the material in this chapter and much more.

I have made it available for a fraction of its value to readers of this book. If you find the information in this chapter and the next valuable, you owe it to yourself to get more information on both sections, which can be easily accessed in the audios and manuals at: www.wealthwithoutstocks.com and chapter 4 "Fast Turning Houses for a Big Paycheck"

"This home practically pays for itself. It's located
on a very windy street, next to an ATM machine!"

Chapter 5

Fast Turn "No Equity" Homes

The previous chapter is what most people think of when they hear the term "flipping houses" for profits. The buy low-sell high method is as old as time and usually requires very little creativity. You must find a good deal, fund it, fix it, and flip it to a new retail buyer for cash. This is a very profitable end of the real estate business but by no means the only or even the best way to successfully fast turn houses.

There is a whole other world of profits available to you in the real estate world that very few investors will ever understand or try to implement. This end of the business is buying at higher prices but with attractive terms. When you buy with attractive terms you can also sell using creative terms, creating chunks of cash up front, monthly cash flow, and another chunk of cash a couple years down the road. This end of the business will require you to understand financing real estate at a higher level than just the buy low - sell high business. Most of the properties in this side of the business are in nice shape, requiring little to no repairs.

My goal with this book is to help you down the road of becoming a real estate transaction engineer. This would mean that any motivated seller that comes your way you will have the tools to make them an offer (or several different offers) that would make sense to both of you to get a successful deal closed. I want you to be able to make an offer on any deal that comes down your lead pipeline that is owned by a motivated seller. If you only know the ugly or semi ugly house business you are limiting yourself and your income potential.

Think of this chapter of a continuation of the last chapter but starting after the "finding" section. The finding part is almost identical. You are looking for flat out motivated sellers that have problems that you can solve with your offer. This will open up possible deals you could have never done with just the buy low and sell high method. When a motivated seller is talking with you and you quickly realize that they owe $195,000 on a $200,000 house, will you be able to buy this at a huge discount? Almost never—except for the occasional short sale (I will not be discussing short sales in this book because they are not nearly as profitable or common as they once were) or if the seller is willing to bring $50,000 to the closing to sell to you at this time. That will happen about never. This seller has to relocate and is motivated but cannot sell this house at a cash price that will make sense to us and our criteria. For most investors that is the end of the conversation because they are one bullet hunters. They are the "Barney Fifes" of the real estate investment world.

I do want to add one extra strategy for finding the kinds of homes we are going to talk about in this chapter. A great pool to fish in will be expired listings from your local MLS system. You will either need to be an agent with access to this system or work closely with one that is willing to share information with you in exchange for your loyalty when you or someone you know needs a good real estate agent. A great lead source (for the kinds of houses described in this chapter) are expired listings that occur every day in your own backyard. Listings expire for many reasons but one of the most common is that the list price is too high. Why is it too high? Again, there are many reasons including a thick-headed owner that does not understand the free market telling them that their house is listed too high in relation to other similar properties. The condition of the home is secondary. After all, you can always adjust the price to accommodate almost any problem with the condition.

Many times the price is too high because the seller owes too much on the property and is trying to sell the home for enough to pay off the house and pay a real estate commission. If they are unsuccessful with this route they will need other solutions. Some in this position will just stay and wait it out but others will still need to solve a pressing problem and you have a solid solution for those that want to play ball.

If you are not licensed as a real estate agent, reach out to a good Realtor®, develop a solid working relationship, and explain that you are looking for these low or negative equity houses. They can set you up on an automatic email program through which you will be sent new expired listings that come up every day. Then get a letter out to the owner right away (or have an assistant, either real or virtual, handle this every day for you) and see what happens over a period of time. You will start to get calls and find these niche properties that very few of your competition know how to handle. Visit our site for an example of the letter you might send out to these expired listing prospects.

Once I realize I can't steal this house with a great price I switch to terms mode. What kind of loan is the $195,000? Is it a nice solid 30 year fixed with no balloons, a low interest rate, and affordable payments? Why is the seller selling? We said he is relocating but what is the real core reason he is selling? Is he selling to gain cash? No! There is no cash to get because there is no real equity in the home. He is selling for debt relief. In a perfect world for the seller, a nice normal homebuyer would come along and buy this home for at least the amount owed and pay this loan off in 30 days. This is not a perfect world and that buyer has eluded the seller, which is why he wants to know if you can help. So how about if I offer to take over his $1,400 total payment with payments starting in 60 days? If he agrees to this or something similar (30 days for a payment) we will enter into a lease option or rent to own agreement on this property with the right to sublease.

You explain to this motivated seller who is looking for a solution that you will find a quality rent to own tenant/buyer to occupy the home and pay all (or most) of the maintenance expenses. You further explain that you are going to make their house your personal project and will do everything in your power to prescreen a tenant who actually wants to own this lovely, well-maintained home. This is the only way you can be of service to them, given their no equity circumstances. If they are still balking, then I simply say, "Mr. Smith, is me installing a solid tenant and future buyer in your home a deal breaker here for you today?" This language lets them know that you're just about done trying to convince them and are ready to move on to another prospect. Most sellers will respond by saying, "No, it isn't a deal breaker," in which case you proceed with the deal. If it is a deal breaker, better to find out quickly so you don't waste any more time. Most of the time I will have this discussion on the phone before I even see the place. I want my cards on the table before I jump in my car and waste an hour or two looking at a home I have no chance of buying.

Now what do I do with this home once I have gotten the seller to agree to the offer?

There is a huge group of people who would like to own a home but cannot qualify for a normal loan at this time. This does not mean they cannot afford a home or don't have any money, it just means they don't qualify under the bank's current, stringent guidelines. They in fact might have a down payment and be able to comfortably afford the monthly payment. You just have to find them and that will be easy when you know where to look. In the old days you would run an ad in the rental section of the newspaper saying something like, "Don't waste your money on rent, lease with an option to buy with a small down payment and $1,600 per month." This is still a great strategy, but now of course you would also run ads online using sites such as Craigslist® and other sites where tenants and home-buyers might be looking. You would also put the word out on Facebook® that you have this property and will be having a steady supply of similar homes.

You are building a buyers list of people who are interested in properties that they can put some money down, and have the potential to actually own the property in a couple years. These buyers have a much longer shelf life than the normal retail buyers who might buy your rehabs. Therefore, it is important to build a strong list of potential terms buyers. Many times it is possible to get a property sold before you even close on it with your seller. Now let's assume you have a buyer who likes your home and wants to lease with an option to buy from you.

Your buying transaction is you are agreeing to lease the property with the option to buy at the mortgage payoff amount within 5 years from today.

You agree to pay the $1,400 payment and all expenses on the property up to $500.00 with the seller agreeing to pay for any repairs over that $500.00 threshold. You both agree that your making the payment will start 60 days from today. You have put nothing down on this agreement but your signature and promise to pay. I also have done deals like this but asked the seller to still pay a portion of the payment during the lease option period (5 years in this case). This made payments that were too high work because I was not promising to pay the entire payment. The seller might pay $200.00 per month toward the total payment just to get the much bigger payment off of their books and their move completed.

You agree to lease option this same property to a new tenant who wishes to enter into a lease option agreement with you to buy the home outright within 3 years for $215,000 and for a monthly payment of $1,600. The tenant is willing to give you $8,000 as non-refundable option consideration money to secure the deal. This $8,000 will be credited toward the purchase price (not mandatory but customary in most areas of the country) meaning you are still owed $207,000 upon you being bought out within 3 years down the road.

Assuming the buyer can qualify for a loan in two years he will buy you out for the $207,000. You will at the same time payoff the underlying loan that is now down to $191,000. This means you will walk away with another $16,000 plus the $8,000 you received up front for a total profit of $24,000. Also you received $4,800 of positive cash flow payments during that two year period for a total profit of just under $29,000. All of this from a deal that all the Barney Fife investors passed on because they could not steal the property and knew of no other way to get it done to everyone's liking. In other words, most investors only have one bullet in their gun. That one bullet is to buy it cheap or not at all. You're a real estate assassin with many bullets in your automatic weapon!

You have zero money in the deal and no risk. You did not personally guarantee any long-term debt. You minimized any downside on the lease by taking out a one year lease option with the right to renew for four times for another one year period. You also should be using a company name to transact business to really mitigate any risk in this deal. You must act in good faith and attempt to fulfill any promise made to the seller. I strongly advise you to set up a legitimate company and structure for your business use both now and in the future. The most common kind of company for small business has become the Limited Liability Company or (LLC). I have an associate that specializes in setting these up for customers as well as other business structures all over the country and also shows you how to make sure they are compliant every year to maximize their protection and tax deductions. If you would like to have your own company or companies set up, please go to our site and find my associate under our resource tab. You will find a link to a great company that specializes in setting up simple entities quickly for their clients. They also are a great resource of information in entity structuring.

A very important point here that made you thousands of dollars more was when you were negotiating the deal to lease option with the original seller you said you would have the right to buy the property (option means the right but not the obligation) for the mortgage balance whenever you exercised the option. In other words, during the 5 year period you were getting the benefit of the mortgage pay down making you more profits in the deal. Most investors would actually give the option purchase price of $195,000 which is the starting mortgage balance. By doing it that way the original owner will get the benefit of the mortgage pay down and not you over the same 5 year period. The seller will not care one bit when you are negotiating this and will never kill a deal for this minor point. Always put yourself in that seller's shoes. Do you think they really care about a few thousand dollars 5 years down the road? They have much bigger pressing issues today and need those resolved immediately.

Case Study: Free and Clear House

You locate a property that is in good shape where the seller is motivated to sell and willing to be a little creative. Let's assume it is worth $200,000 and has no mortgages on the property. The seller has inherited the property and does not need all the cash right now and would rather have some income.

They won't let you in for a zero down payment as with the highly leveraged property described above but is willing to take 10% down and finance the rest at 6% for 4 years. The 6% interest is far more they can get in the bank so they are content with that rate on your new loan.

You offer $180,000 but end up agreeing to $185,000 as the purchase price. You agree to the 10% down and the 6% interest on the seller-held mortgage. The seller will carry a $166,500 mortgage or land contract with Principle (P) and Interest payments (I) of $998.00 per month. The property needs no work and is nicely updated. You go to your buyers list or advertise again for the right buyer to sell. You sell the property for $210,000 (top dollar because of the attractive terms you are willing to offer unlike all the all cash only sellers) with $20,000 down from the new buyer. You agree to carry back a wraparound mortgage for $190,000 at 8% with P and I payments of $1,394.00 every month for a period of 3 years. Then the buyer will agree to cash you out at that time.

You only make $1,500 in cash when you sell but you have structured almost $400.00 per month of positive cash flow with none of your cash still in the deal. If you could negotiate a smaller down payment when you would buy you could pocket more cash on the front end of the deal. You also might find a buyer who has more money to put down than $20,000. However even if it played out like this, you were able to obtain a big enough down payment to rotate your down payment back (velocitizing your capital) and create a $400.00 per month income for up to 36 months totaling $14,400 in cash flow. In this example we will assume the new buyer pays us off after 3 years and still owes us $188,000. We still owe the original seller $165,000, meaning we pocket another $23,000 for a grand total of $38,900 profit off of one little terms deal that most investors had no clue could even be done this way.

Here is a huge tip that could make you thousands of dollars more in these kinds of seller-held transactions. Any time you are going to pay off a seller mortgage early, ask them for a discount for cash. The note holder might like to have his cash now instead of waiting another few years. If you owed them $165,000, offer them $155,000 for the early payoff and see what they say. They might tell you to go jump in the lake because they like those steady payments, they also might tell you that sounds good but they won't take any less than $161,000, or they might just say yes give me the $155,000 within 30 days and I will take the $155,000 cash for my $165,000 note. It never hurts to ask, and for this to be effective you probably can't have the home for sale on the open market because the seller will deduce that you're paying them off anyway.

NOTE: DO YOUR OWN RESEARCH ON THE DODD FRANK ACT TO SEE WHAT NEWER RULES ARE IN PLACE IN RELATION TO EXTENDING CREDIT TO BUYERS OF HOMES. IF YOU ARE DEALING FROM INVESTOR TO INVESTOR THERE IS LITTLE TO WORRY ABOUT. HOWEVER, IF YOU ARE DEALING WITH AN ACUTAL OWNER OCCUPANT THERE ARE STEPS THAT MUST BE FOLLOWED. WORK WITH A COMPETENT ATTORNEY WHEN DEALING IN THESE CREATIVE DEALS. Here is a website to get you started: https://www.sec.gov/spotlight/dodd-frank.shtml. You will want to get in the habit of dealing with company structures such as LLC's and Corporations, not individuals, when it comes to buying and selling properties. We will talk more about this in the upcoming chapter on private lending.

There are many things I really like about the kinds of deals above and why you should as well.

1) Very little competition with these creative terms deals because most investors know very little about these strategies
2) Gives a seller several options to be able to do business with you if they can't let the property sell for a big cash discount
3) Takes a seeming no deal and turns it into a good deal for all involved
4) Much easier and faster to sell when you can offer terms instead of just all cash
5) Much of your profits made are usually taxed at long-term capital gains instead of ordinary income which is different than flipping for cash
6) These deals can be done inside of a self-directed IRA that has very

little money in the account. This makes all profits tax-deferred or tax-free depending on what type of IRA

7) Allows you to buy from any truly motivated seller that needs to sell regardless of their situation

8) Allows you to sell to any buyer that has either cash or credit. No need to have both, but they need one of them. Opens up your properties to a huge group of potential buyers

Case Study

A seller calls you with a property they are willing to sell at a good discount for cash but not a big enough discount for you to go out and raise money to buy the deal. The deal looks something like:

Repaired value of home $200,000 and needs little to no repairs.

Seller will sell for a 20% discount ($160,000) but wants to get cashed out. You know that if you pay cash for this and go through all the cost described in the previous chapter, it will be very hard to sell this property for cash and make a decent profit.

You offer the seller a 60 day option to buy his home at $160,000 and cash him out. An option is a one way agreement which means he would have to sell to you if you come up with the $160,000 but you don't have to buy the property at the end of the 60 days. The seller agrees and you execute a simple option agreement.

You now go to your buyers list and tell them you have a great property that you can sell for $15,000 under market, or $185,000. A buyer makes you an offer for $180,000 and goes and gets his mortgage and puts money down. The deal closes in 30 days and you make the difference between $160,000 and $180,000 as profit minus a little expense. You make $20,000 for understanding an option and how to market properties.

What if the seller balks at keeping his property tied up for 60 days? You say, "Mr. Seller, you're telling me that if we didn't tie up your property, you would do this deal?" He says yes. You simply say this to him: "If you find another buyer in 60 days we will step aside and you owe us just $500.00 for our expenses." I might not even require the $500.00 but would ask for it first. If the seller finds a new buyer before you do, you walk away. If he doesn't, he has you working on this deal night and day to get it done and make your profit.

As you can see, there is no money due from you except to market the property, which we are talking about funds in the hundreds not thousands. If that is the case, why be happy in dealing with $200,000 properties? What about $1,000,000 properties with similar percentages? Instead of making $20,000 why not make $50,000 or $100,000?

In a traditional option an option fee or "cash consideration" might be common-place. This would be a non-refundable option fee paid to the seller for you tying up their property with the option. If you don't exercise the option, you are NOT entitled to your option fee being returned.

However, since you have offered the seller the right to sell to some-one else, if he chooses, should you agree to pay an option consideration? I would never agree to an option consideration fee unless I was actually getting the exclusive right to buy and for at least 6 months. In this circum-stance we are not getting an exclusive right to buy and we are asking for far less of commitment than 6 months.

You might want to try the auction strategy mentioned above to get the property sold after you have your option agreement signed. There is a spe-cific way to do these "round robin" sales that we don't have time for in this chapter. I have drawn it out for you step by step and you can get that blue-print for free at www.wealthwithoutstocks.com at the Fast Turning Houses for Big Paychecks page; use code **WWS15** to access this information.

To make these deals work, you need to negotiate a nice sized discount, but not the amount needed to go raise new funds and actually close on the home described in the previous chapter. This allows you to pay more because you are not raising money, making payments, or doing repairs. The seller has nothing to lose because they can still sell the property—most will not even try but you have removed their fear. It is important to remember that for this strategy to be effective the property must be in nice shape and need no repairs. It might need a little sprucing up or cleaning and you can negotiate to have the current seller do some very minor spruce ups before you bring in your buyer leads.

Case Study

There are millions of homes across this country that are still in a zero or negative equity position. As I write this, the national real estate market is off of its lows but not far enough off the bottom to make everyone even again. Many homeowners/sellers have elected not to give the house back to the bank and just walk away if they can avoid it by holding on until equity returns. Even before the last real estate collapse there have always been and will always be homeowners who have little or no equity in their homes. There will be various reasons for this but when you run across these don't be in a hurry to decide there is no deal that can be done. Many times you would be wrong!

Unfortunately for the sellers, many of them will be forced to sell for other reasons such as job transfer or maybe a divorce. If you have a home that is worth $185,000 and you owe $200,000, your prospects are limited when you have to sell. The seller could bring the shortage in with them to closing in the form of cash. This assumes the seller has the cash or will use it for this purpose. Most will not entertain this option. The other option is to let the payments go and give it back to the bank or apply for a short sale. Many sellers don't want to attempt either of these two options for a multitude of reasons. (www.forbes.com/sites/erincarlyle/2014/05/20/9-7-million-americans-still-have-underwater-homes-zillow-says/)

If you're reading this and the market has bounced back more please understand that in any market environment and in all areas of the country you will always run across homes that have little, no, or negative equity for many reasons. Now you will have a strategy to work with all of them and generate profits.

The only thing that will cure this problem for the seller is time. In time, the values may rise to put equity back into the home. Also in time, the mortgage balance will be paid down enough to build equity into the home. Let's assume you receive a call from your marketing and the numbers are described above—what would you do?

FLUP THE HOUSE!

This means you will be flipping an upside down house using terms, a strategy called flupping. The deal goes something like this after you talk to the seller. You offer them a 10 year lease option with the price being the loan balance whenever you pay off the loan. (The 10 years are negotiable on our end but no less than 7 due to the current negative equity) The payment must be reasonable and because of the very low interest rates we have had over the last 10 years and more, most of these loans offer low long-term interest rates with attractive payments. We tell the seller that their mortgage will be paid off in full within that 10 year time frame and the sooner the better.

You explain to the seller that you will find a long-term buyer who will be happy to take over the payment and pay all the expenses on the property. This buyer will also eventually either obtain new financing and pay off the over financed loan or sell the property several years down the road, thus paying off the loan. The seller gets their problem solved (debt relief) and let's face facts, they have very few other options. They can get out from under their payment and give this a chance instead of just walking away and giving the home back to the bank. They are close to doing that anyway but now you have offered them a lifeline and a chance to get out from under this mess.

Now what do we do with this over-financed house?

Now we go to our buyers list and tell them we have a nice home for a long-term lease option. They will agree to pay the payment and all expenses on the property. They can also have the right to buy the home for the loan balance within 10 years. Most lease options want them to perform in 2 to 3 years and a 10 year lease option is almost unheard of in the traditional market place. That long-term lease option has tremendous value. You ask them how much they have for a down payment on a nice home and they say $10,000. Who would give you $10,000 for a lease option on an over financed house? Many people will be happy to give you this money to secure a long-term living arrangement and the right to buy the home for the loan amount. They might even give you more than $10,000 depending on the sales price. If you are in an area of the country that has much more expensive homes then you should be getting $30,000 to $50,000 up front for this long-term strategy. You are simply going to assign your interest in this long-term agreement for cash to the new buyer. This will be done with the full knowledge and approval of the original seller.

Let's look at how the numbers might play out:

In 10 years that mortgage will be 15 years old, assuming it was about 5 years old when we did this deal. This means the loan balance is now $142,000, which means the new buyer can buy it out or resell the property by paying off the $142,000. Assuming a modest 3% appreciation rate during the same 10 years, the value of the home would be around $250,000, creating over a $100,000 equity position for the tenant/buyer. Was that worth their $10,000 investment at the beginning? You bet it was and many buyers will be interested in a nice home with these terms. Many tenants hate having to move every 2 or 3 years so with this strategy they can put down roots and build equity.

If your buyer moves out and the deal still doesn't make sense in regards to paying off the mortgage, sell it again! This is a killer strategy and none of your competition will have a clue how it works. Now you are truly loaded for bear in the real estate investment world. Is there more to know? Without question but there is no way I can teach you almost a quarter century of real estate investment in a couple chapters. Consider investing in our real estate training program and getting one of our coaches to help you launch your real estate investment business. Coaches and advanced trainings have been an invaluable part of my business life and should be part of yours as well.

Just visit us at www.wealthwithoutstocks.com and click on our Coaching tab to get real live help to get rolling in the real estate investment business. It is so much easier to do deals with confidence when you know what you're doing. The only way to do that in your launch phase is to work with a coach or mentor. We have very experienced coaches who are willing to work with you and are worth many times your investment in the coaching program.

In an upcoming chapter, I address how to build a Perpetual Real Estate cash flow machine with income properties and provide you with ready-made teams to help you do this in some of the best markets in the country.

**Investments and
Financial Planning**

"I retire on Friday and I haven't saved a dime.
Here's your chance to become a legend!"

Chapter 6

The Secret IRA Your Financial Advisor Doesn't Even Know Exists

The most popular retirement plan in America is the 401k. There are over 800,000 plans in effect with just below 6 trillion dollars in assets in these accounts. Just because it's the most popular plan doesn't mean it's anywhere near the best vehicle to save or invest for retirement. If you have invested in this book, I am guessing you are not sold on a 401k as your best retirement account.

There are several reasons why the 401, or its little sister the 403b, have become the 800lb gorilla in the retirement world.

1) These plans are touted by the mainstream media and by employers as a huge benefit to the employee and have largely replaced the defined benefit plan (pensions) as the main way workers save for retirement

2) These plans are set up by the employer and the employee simply has to fill out a little paperwork to participate and start funding the plan. This requires very little knowledge or effort on the worker's part to begin a retirement plan

3) Some employers offer some sort of matching of funds for the worker. This means that an employer will also contribute to your retirement plan and it's called a match

4) These and other qualified plans are touted as being tax advantaged (I believe this is huge myth with every account except for the ROTH style account)

5) Wall Street has spent vast sums of money and blocks of time to tout these programs and their benefits but never educate the public on the many downsides

Most people have no idea about the downsides of these accounts because they are rarely discussed and when they are, the average person just isn't paying attention. When I have an initial meeting with a potential client they are quite shocked by what they give up when they use a 401k. Here are a few downsides and reasons to rethink the most common retirement plan:

1) You are giving up control of your money to a plan administrator and will suffer heavy future taxes and penalties if you want to use that money prior to retirement of age 59½ (current age but can change at any time, locking up your money longer)
2) The money will mostly be invested in the stock market and subject to ups and downs without you having much control once the money is put into the account
3) You don't really get a tax deduction for your contributions but rather a tax "deferral" which then shifts the amount of tax to the future at an unknown tax rate and on a bigger pile of money
4) Some of your money will be eaten up with fees and some of these fees will be cleverly hidden

There was an entire show put out by Frontline that examined the many flaws with this overall program that I would highly recommend you watch. I have the link under the Resource tab on my website, www.wealthwithoutstocks.com, and encourage you to watch the full hour-long program, "The Retirement Gamble." The program just confirms what I have been saying for years. The traditional personal finance model we all have been taught is set up for banks, Wall Street, and Uncle Sam to make money and not for most Americans to profit. This is why this book is such a huge tool for anyone who has had enough of the status quo and is looking for an entirely new ball game.

There are far better ways to create wealth than with a 401k but most of them will require a little extra time and knowledge rather than simply blindly putting funds into your 401k. Two of the best ways to replace your 401k saving system is to study the chapters on beating the bank by becoming the bank and setting up a properly designed life insurance policy. These plans, when used together, should be a centerpiece for your wealth creation and preservation efforts. Many clients immediately stop funding their 401k accounts in favor of a properly designed life insurance structure.

What about the money I already have in my 401?

It will depend on your current plan administrator as to what can be done with those funds. You must call the plan administrator and find out your options. Here are some generalities that you must verify for your specific plan:

1) If this is an active 401 (or other type plan) at your current employer, your access to the cash will be very limited

2) If this is an old 401 account from a previous employer, then you should have no trouble rolling those funds over into an Individual Retirement Account (IRA) and by using the strategies in this chapter, getting access to your funds for many investment opportunities

3) If this is an active account at a current job and you are older than 59½, you should be able to roll over a large portion of the account (if not all of it) into an IRA, giving you flexibility and the options described in this chapter

4) If this is a 401 at a company of which you are the owner (or one of the owners), you will most likely be able to access your portion of the 401k for a rollover into a more flexible and powerful account

Make it a priority to call your plan administrator and find out what you may be able to do with your own account. Make an action plan during the time you're reading this book and afterwards as well and make sure a call to your plan administrator is on that list.

How is an IRA different than a 401k or 403b?

The IRA can be in addition to a 401k or used in lieu of access to a 401k. Many people have both types of accounts. Both the traditional IRA and 401 are taxed the same way, allowing for a tax deferral for contributions, profits grow tax-deferred, taxes are owed upon withdrawal. The exception to this would be the ROTH style IRA in which you are not allowed a tax deferral when the money is contributed, but you also can use the money tax-free in later years.

The IRA stands for "Individual Retirement Account" and is set up for the account holder's benefit. Unlike the 401k that has a plan administrator chosen by the employer, the individual account holder with an IRA can choose their plan administrator. This allows for much more flexibility on your part as to who your administrator is and what assets your IRA can own on your behalf.

Would you rather pay tax on the seed or the crop of the money?

I would rather pay a known amount of tax today (of course only what I legally have to pay after all legitimate tax deductions are taken) and get it out of the way on the seed of my crop. If I delay the taxes until later, I don't know what tax rate I might be paying and neither does anyone else regardless of what they claim. The old argument is that when you access your retirement account you will be making less money so your tax rate will be less. Great, so I just have to make poverty level wages to get the low tax rate in the future! I don't believe tax rates will be lower in the future. With the massive amount of debt this country is in I believe strongly that tax rates will be increasing. If you believe they are going to be increasing as well, then why are you agreeing to defer your tax today to pay more in the future? This is just one of many old financial myths this book challenges or destroys. I prefer to get my taxes out of the way today and then put the money to work in solid investments that produce cash flow and future wealth with zero future taxes owed on that wealth whenever legally possible.

What is a Self-Directed IRA?

A self-directed IRA is nothing more than an IRA (either traditional or Roth) that is administered by a company that is approved from the government to allow you to invest your retirement money in nontraditional retirement assets. Nontraditional generally means anything besides stocks, bonds, or mutual funds. Here is an example of some things (but not everything) that your retirement money could be investing in once you have it set up in a proper, approved account.

- Real estate of all types including residential and commercial
- Flips for chunks of cash
- Rentals
- Flips for long-term cash flow
- Lease options
- Straight Options (real estate not stock options)
- A "for profit" business (LLC's or Corporations)
- Private loans
- Gold and other precious metals

When you ask your traditional financial advisor about these options they might tell you that your account is "self-directed" and to an extent they are correct. You probably have the right to choose from multiple mutual funds, stocks, and bonds within your current IRA administrator's plan. This is not true self-direction—it is more like multiple-choice within the same asset class. If you tell them you want to buy a fixer-upper and flip it as described in the fast turn chapter, they will usually look at you cross-eyed or with a haze in their eyes. Most of the time, they will tell you that you can't buy real estate with your IRA. They're very much mistaken!

The traditional financial world is not trained on self-directed IRAs at all because that would defeat their purpose. That purpose is to keep all your money under management in one spot and that spot is obviously with their company. They have no interest in anything that does not further that goal. The best way to illustrate this is with a real life client of mine. His name is obviously changed but the story is total fact as told from him to me during our initial phone conversation.

Jim had read my first book and found it fascinating. He jokingly said he was upset with me because I changed his whole financial paradigm. Jim is a successful young physician who was looking for alternative means to invest for his future. He went to his then-financial advisor and brought up some of the topics discussed in that first book about self-banking and life insurance policies. His advisor was not excited about these ideas and this puzzled Jim. I asked Jim if he was excited when he lost a patient to a new doctor with some new or different forms of treatment. He very quickly understood the comparison and we chatted a little more on this topic. Thankfully for Jim, he knew he was on to something and wanted more information and called our office to schedule a personal wealth strategy consultation with us over the phone.

Jim set up a life insurance policy with our help and intended to use it as his personal bank as we have already discussed. However, during our meetings, he shared with me that he really wanted to buy more income property but didn't think he could because his money was mostly tied up in an IRA. I asked him if anyone had ever told him about a Self-Directed IRA and he very quickly said "no" and asked me to elaborate. Within four weeks of that conversation, Jim had done a tax-free rollover of about half his account to a Self-Directed IRA company which freed up that money to buy properties. Jim (actually Jim's IRA) now owns four solid free and clear homes in suburban Detroit. The income from the properties is flowing tax-deferred into his IRA. When he eventually liquidates these investments, his appreciation profits will be tax-deferred as well. This one simple strategy has altered Jim's financial future. He also has plans to make private loans out of his self-directed IRA.

The story above would never have come to pass if Jim would not have found my book, read it, and then reached out to us to get his questions answered. Unfortunately, I know many more people get exposed to these kinds of concepts and programs and think they seem too good to be true. Many stop their search at that point but many will also go to the step of talking to their traditional financial advisor about what they have learned. Most meet with misinformation that they take as the truth and never actually use these concepts. Don't make that mistake! Learning new information is great but if it is never acted upon the time has been wasted.

No Can Do

Self-directed IRAs are a wonderful way for the active investor to use their retirement accounts to invest in all kinds of real estate and business opportunities. They allow you to invest with more control than just blindly sending money to mutual funds and into the stock market. If you are educated in real estate, business, and private lending, these accounts allow you to invest in what you are an expert (or soon to be expert) in, allowing you to have much more control of your own financial future. If you are drawn to any specific area in this book your IRA can help you do these deals. However, there are some restrictions as to what you may not do with the money:

1) No self-dealing or loaning yourself from your IRA money. Your IRA considers you, your spouse, kids, grandkids, parents, and grandparents as actually being you for all intents and purposes. So, no loaning money to these prohibited groups. Anyone from your direct linear chain, be they older or younger than you, are prohibited transactions and should be avoided.

2) No transferring of existing assets that you own into the IRA. If you own an investment home you may not transfer that home into the IRA. The IRA may purchase new investments only. This is also true of existing businesses. Only new business ventures should be owned by your IRA. However, newly created stock in an existing company could be acceptable (always check with the plan administrator to make sure).

3) No personally guaranteeing borrowed funds. Depending on which state you live in, you may be subject to deficiency judgments on borrowed money if you default on the loan. In other words, if you don't pay and the underlying collateral does not satisfy the loan, you may be personally sued for the difference. Your IRA can borrow money

from outside sources but it cannot personally guarantee the debt. The loan must be on a "non- recourse" basis, meaning the IRA can lose the property but cannot be sued for any shortfalls. When you borrow money in the IRA, that will also change the tax-free status and taxes will be owed on some of the profit due to the leverage. Get more details on this from your future plans administrator.

4) No investing in collectibles such as art, stamps, cars, baseball cards, etc.

Setting up your own private vault

What you are learning in this chapter alone will be a huge game changer for you if you will act on the information. Do you want to invest in properties but think you are too cash poor? How many people do you know that would like to get a nice safe and steady 6% to 8% return on their money? How many of them do you think know about the information contained in this chapter? There are bucket loads of money in retirement accounts that you could lend to your real estate deals and provide solid rates of return for the investors with very little risk on their part. I hope you will pay close attention when we cover these strategies in the private lending chapter, but for now understand that anyone you know with an IRA could be shown how to make that account self-directed and then loan you the money. This assumes you are not in a prohibitive class of people for the IRA owner—meaning your linear chain. If you are in that prohibitive class, there may be ways to do those deals with your family members but they must be structured in a way that makes them compliant. This is where your plan administrator becomes a huge asset.

I want to encourage you to take advantage of the information offered to you for more education on this topic. If you are going to deal in IRAs and show others how to do the same, you will need more education than can be covered here in this book. My only goal here was to expose you to the existence of these accounts and get your mind running and your creativity flowing as to how these accounts can help you grow wealth without stocks or mutual funds. Give a copy of this book to any potential investor and have them read this chapter to get the dialogue started and questions flowing.

The options with your IRA are so much more plentiful than you have been lead to believe. My company has brought in one of the foremost experts in Self-Directed IRAs to give you options:

A) A company to help you roll over all or part of your IRA so you can quickly be ready to start using those funds for your nontraditional investments. This company has been doing these kinds of things for investors for almost 4 decades and is one of the recognized leaders in this very little known niche.

B) Additional training is available through Wealth Without Stocks website on using Self-Directed IRAs to grow wealth. Visit our site and take advantage of what we have taken the time to set up for you as our reader.

© Randy Glasbergen
www.glasbergen.com

"In yet another political scandal, Freddie Mac has
confessed to having an affair with Fannie Mae…"

Chapter 7

Private Lending—No Banks Required

When I do seminars all over the country this is one of the top 3 topics each and every time without fail. I don't care if the group is a bunch of beginning investors just starting out with limited cash or a group of millionaire business people. The people just starting out want to know how to access capital without all the red tape and ridiculous demands made by a traditional bank. The millionaires want to know how to loan out their own capital safely and at high rates of return. The truth is the banker you are trying to obtain money from has no idea how investment real estate or most businesses really work. You would be surprised to learn how little income most bankers actually make performing their jobs. Most people in these positions really care more about the prestige, titles, and their standing in the community than their actual incomes.

It can be very frustrating dealing with a traditional banker when you are trying to achieve nontraditional goals via nontraditional methods. This is very similar to the frustration if you spent 30 days trying to put your round peg through the square hole. Most bankers are NOT business people and are governed by an old style economy way of thinking. If you want to make your entrepreneurial endeavors as easy as possible, you will need to start developing private sources of funds.

Contrary to popular belief, banks don't hold a monopoly on financing projects. There are many other sources to fund properties and projects. Just a few alternatives are:

B) Finance companies

2) Insurance companies

3) Government entities (national, state, and local)

4) Sellers of the properties and businesses (loaning you all or some of their equity by taking back a note and payments over a period of time)

5) Venture capital firms

6) Online financing options that act as a type of clearing house for all types of lenders

There is also a huge pool of billions of dollars that already exists of individuals and hedge funds that loan money to fund all sorts of projects. In our examples, we are going to talk about private individuals loaning money to fund our projects. There are people all over the country who are making private loans right now and you want to start knowing how and where to find these people.

We also have an agreement with a national private lender who would love to fund your deals if the deal meets their criteria, which are very different than your local bank's criteria. After you read the chapter and would like more information, go to our website at www.wealthwithoutstocks.com and click on our US Private Lending tab. Reach out to us via the form provided and we will give you information on what you would need to submit requests to borrow money from this lender.

Why Not the Banks?

Banks require a huge amount of documentation and proof of everything to fund deals. This is especially true now after the last financial and banking collapse ushered in an era of even more regulations and hoops to jump through to get deals financed. Now, even simple straight-forward deals require loads of paperwork and much of it redundant. Many banks are looking for reasons not to do the deals instead of why they should do the deals.

When you are talking about buying properties in the 1-4 unit category, almost every bank or mortgage company loan will be underwritten to Fannie Mae standards (FNMA) which are basically controlled by the government. If you are looking to do anything creative, but yet safe with a financing package, you're out of luck. Investors unfairly received much of the blame during the last banking crisis. The fact is that most of the bad loans and way out mortgage programs such as "120% financing" and the "negative amortization loans" were approved for regular homeowners and not for investors. Investors are mainly responsible for stabilizing the real estate markets when they were in free fall. Investors pumped in many billions of dollars of their money to buy in at reduced prices. They have since been responsible for taking much of the bulk inventory off of the market so prices had a chance to stabilize and even increase off of their lows.

Even with all of this, investors are many times frowned upon by FNMA underwriting standards and it becomes more and more difficult to obtain financing, even on great, safe deals. If I had a deal on my desk now that I could buy for $100,000 and was worth $200,000, and only wanted to borrow $80,000 from the bank, does that sound like a high risk loan to you? The lender should verify the true value, repairs needed, a little credit (but more character), and obtain a title commitment. After that, they should be ready to close quickly. This is not the case when dealing with traditional banks and mortgage companies. They will want a never-ending list of documents from me to prove I am good for the money. So let's just not deal with banks to make profitable deals.

Get involved with your local REA groups and find out who those investors are using to fund their deals. That's a great first step to find money that is already available and looking to be loaned out for solid, safe investment properties. You can expect to pay higher interest and upfront costs than you might pay dealing with a traditional lender. The consumer in us says we should get the lowest rate possible. The only problem is the average consumer dies broke because of that mentality. It's not the cost of the capital that's important, but rather the easy access to it that is critical.

You will pay more money for these loans but you will get them far easier (if your deals are solid, good deals) and more often, creating more profits. How much more you will pay will depend on the lenders you are able to find to fund your deals. There are basically 3 types of lenders in this arena.

A) Hard money lenders

B) High interest private lenders

C) Low (in comparison) interest private lenders

Hard money lenders are generally loans that are made by brokers with hedge funds as the actual lender of the money. These loans will have high points up front (a point is 1% of the loan amount. For example: if you are borrowing $100,000 and pay 3 points you are paying $3,000 for the privilege of borrowing that money.) They also have high interest rates. I was just called about 3 weeks ago from one such broker and they had money available at 5 points up front and 15% interest. I have also seen 10 points up front and 18% annual interest. When you're paying those kind of rates you better have a great deal because you're basically taking on a partner in the transaction. That partner calls themselves a hard money lender. Many times it is still less expensive to use one of these loans rather than pay a money partner half of the profits.

This begs the question: is the deal really good enough to be able to support this expensive debt and still make a nice profit? If the answer is yes, then the question should be: is this loan the only way I can fund this deal and get it closed inside of the time allotted via the purchase agreement?

If you have other sources that are less expensive that can get the deal completed you should use those before agreeing to such high rates and terms. However, if you had to pay this rate and still made a $40,000 net profit would that be alright? Absolutely! I have paid high rates on loans in the past and still made nice profits.

High interest private lenders: These are private investors either lending their own money or possibly pooling a few investors money to loan out funds and make profits for themselves. The rates and terms will generally be less than the hard money lender mentioned earlier. You might pay 2 to 3 points up front and 11% on the note. This is much less and more attractive than a pure hard money loan, but still not considered cheap by any means. These lenders are usually established and have been loaning money for a period of years and have identified their sweet spot for loans. You will find these types of lenders at many of your REA groups. Loans from this group and the first group will generally have short pay off periods of 12 to 24 months. You might make interest payments and then have the entire loan balance due in full within 24 months.

Low interest rate private lenders: These will be your most important source of funds as you move through your career. They will also take the most work initially to borrow their money. These are individual lenders who are not yet loaning out money and most don't even know they can loan out money! These are the lenders you will actively seek out and show why they should loan you money to do deals.

The simple question you should ask everyone you come in contact with that you believe has some available investment capital is "do you currently have any capital you are not earning at least a 7% safe and secure rate of return on but would like to?" If they say yes they do and would be interested in learning more, you simply set up a time for a presentation either face to face or use an online service such as GoToMeeting®. If 7% doesn't get people excited, try 8% but there are many people out there right now that are getting long-term rates of returns in CDs at .5% and a 7% rate of return sounds fantastic.

In real dollars and cents the difference results between $100,000 sitting in a .5% bank account and in a 7% private loan are staggering. After 10 years with the .5% rate your $100,000 has grown to a little over $105,000. The same money and time period growing at 7% will grow to almost $201,000. Would you like an extra $95,000 and not having to work any harder for it Mr. or Mrs. Investor? We will be talking about you being the actual private lender as well but since you will be educated on how this works you will loan your money out at no less than 13% which would grow your $100,000 to almost $365,000 over that same 10 year period.

Private lending is a multibillion dollar industry that almost nobody has ever heard of and it's going on every day all over the country. You just need some education and the willingness to get involved. Private lending is important if you have no funds and want to get started in business, and is also important if you have significant investment dollars you would like to grow safely and with as few headaches as possible.

The Rules if you Borrow Private Money

There is a set of standards you must adhere to if you would like to success-fully borrow private capital and use it to grow your wealth. This book talks about using the loans to fund real estate investments but the rules don't change much if you're using the loans to fund a business venture. The most critical factor in obtaining a private loan is understanding what the lender is hoping for with this loan. The lender wants a very safe loan and very few headaches with this investment. The main factor that makes a loan safe is the collateral with all other factors being secondary.

The lender will look at this loan from a worst case scenario. What if you don't pay them and they need to call the loan due and payable? The only thing that matters at that point is the equity in the project. If the property has a repaired value of $200,000 and the lender loaned $180,000 on that proj-ect, the private lender is almost guaranteed to lose money on that loan after they pay all expenses and try to resell the collateral to get their investment returned. They loaned 90% loan to value or (LTV), which is a foolish loan.

How much safer do you think the lender would feel if they only loaned $100,000 on this project? Now they would be hard-pressed to lose money on this deal even if the house is beat up and they must make repairs before reselling the collateral. They could repair the property and spend $40,000 making it a palace and resell it for a nice profit. The fact is the lender would make more on the property if they have to foreclose.

This is how you know you have a very safe loan as the investor. As the borrower, don't ask lenders to loan an amount of money that is more than 65% LTV and you will be very successful obtaining private funds. Some lenders will ask you to make a down payment with your own funds to add additional equity in the deal and to give you "skin in the game." It's always harder to walk away from an investment in which you have some of your own cash invested than it is to walk away from a deal in which you have none of your own equity in the deal. The down payment is open to nego-tiation depending on the private lender. Many private lenders are happy to make the 65% LTV and don't care if you put up money or not because they feel protected by the pure equity in the deal.

I have, at times, borrowed up to 70% from a private lender, but only in very strong resale markets and in very solid areas. Just use some common sense and make sure there is plenty of equity in the deal to keep everyone safe. The only reason to use private money is because the cash price is exceptional and is worth the headaches of lining up funding.

Some other key factors for these deals:

1) Make sure the private loan is treated as a normal bank which means the lender receives a title insurance policy, hazard insurance policy, and in some cases a flood insurance policy. This will make the lender feel very secure.

2) Have a title company or attorney close all these deals so everything is on the table and above board.

3) Get appraisals back to the private lender for their approval quickly.

4) Have the purchase price loaned out at closing with the first draw for repairs. Keep all future repair money escrowed until repairs are made and verified by the appraiser

5) Make sure you borrow money as an entity and lend money as an entity (LLC or corporation). This will mean you are not dealing with individuals but companies, which is preferred due to the fact that many regulations that exist for individuals do not exist or are greatly diminished for companies.

6) Always get advice from a true real estate attorney with a background in these matters.

When you are the lender

Making private loans is a fantastic way to diversify and grow any investment portfolio. However, with most other subjects in this book it will require a little more effort than just writing a check to your broker or going online and making a trade. You must be prepared to do a little research and a little marketing to make successful loans. Re-read the points above about how to have a safe loan and make sure they are followed on each and every loan.

Once you have successfully made a couple loans you will understand how simple this business really is and the time needed to successfully close a loan will be dramatically reduced. The good news is that once you have performed some due diligence and actually closed a loan successfully there will be almost no time required from you after that point for many months or even years.

Pay attention to the foreclosure process in the state in which you'll be loaning money. Some states have very lengthy timeframes before you get the house back on the rare occasion you might have to foreclose the loan. You may want to talk to your attorney about alternatives to a straight loan.

One example might be that the property you loan on gets put into a land trust with your attorney as the trustee and borrower as the beneficiary of the trust. You have an agreement with the borrower (beneficiary in this kind of deal) that if they ever become 60 days delinquent, your attorney will immediately designate you as the beneficiary of the trust, thus making you owner of the trust that owns the subject property. This is just a suggestion and one of several options that might make it far quicker and easier to take back the house in long foreclosure period states.

I am afraid of not getting paid and having to foreclose!

The reality is that if you loan no more than 60 to 65% LTV on these properties, you will almost never have to foreclose. Most borrowers will not walk away from that kind of equity position. If they have trouble making the payment, for whatever reason, or cannot make the time table set for pay off then it might be time to have a chat with them and work out something until they can get the property sold, refinanced, rented, partner brought in, or any other options they are working on to get you paid.

It's always advisable to run a credit report and criminal background check on your prospective buyer and have them pay for those services in advance along with an appraisal fee. This will scare off many of the riff raff hucksters trying to possibly take advantage of you in the transaction. I am not that concerned about credit scoring, unlike a traditional lender. I am much more concerned about the overall credit background of the potential borrower. After all, many of us will get in a financial pinch once or twice in our lifetimes but emerge out of those dark times. This does not make us losers or bad risks just because of that fact. If I see a chronic dead beat with many creditors chasing them at different periods of time I will probably pass on this borrower and wait for lower hanging fruit as a customer. Take steps to verify the identity they're giving you truly belongs to them. Make sure to make a copy of their driver's license and/or passport to make sure they are who they claim to be when asking to borrow your money. You might in fact do a criminal background check and credit check on John Smith and it comes back great. The only problem is the person you loaned the money knew John Smith's information but was not in fact John Smith. Verifying identities is just sound business.

On the rare occasion that someone cannot pay you back, the collateral in the property should be more than sufficient to keep your money safe and assure the safe return of your capital. Most deals will consist of the borrower doing what they said they would do in a reasonable timeframe and you getting paid off as agreed.

You can also request as the lender that the borrower gives you more collateral or "cross collateralize" the note. Maybe they can give you a first or second lien on another property that has significant equity. This means that if you have to foreclose, you foreclose on two pieces of property with more equity to protect your loan. This will also make the borrower work that much harder to get you paid in full.

Self-Directed IRAs

Make sure you read the chapter in this book about self-directed IRAs because these private loans can be a great place to invest your retirement money and receive great returns on a tax-deferred or tax-free (in the case of a Roth IRA) basis.

Consider a longer pay off period if you are comfortable with the borrower and the property if you are a less hands on investor. We already talked about interest volume and velocity in the chapter on being your own bank. The velocity of money says that the more times you can rotate that money and charge points and fees, the more money you will make on the investment. This is true but this will also require you to do more loans and turn over your money as quickly as possible. If you have the time to handle due diligence on several loans over a couple year period, you may want to keep your paybacks at 12 to 24 months maximum. However, if you would just like to make a solid loan (or a few of them) and then not have to worry about pay offs and re-loaning the money out, then consider loaning the money out for 24 to 60 months.

If you're using private money as the borrower and can secure a decently low interest rate (in the 7 to 8% range) and a 4 or 5 year loan term, you are optimally positioned to have an easier time selling all of your properties. Imagine you have borrowed money with the terms we just described and you are selling the property. You have a buyer that can put 20% down and is willing to pay you top dollar or better for the property. The problem is that their credit needs some time to heal after some hard times the buyer had in the past.

You can sell that house with seller financing on a wraparound mortgage and give the new buyer 2 to 3 years to be able to refinance the home through you before they have to worry about obtaining more traditional financing. This is why obtaining your own private lenders and educating them will be critical to your long-term success.

Finding Private Lenders and Borrowers

If you would like to find people with money who would like to know more about this kind of investing there are many ways to market for them but the easiest and quickest is to have your own workshop. Invite business associates and get a mailing list from a good list broker of people in your area with a certain amount of investable assets (I am partial to $500,000 and up) and you can mail them invitations to attend your workshop.

Be prepared to discuss private lending and then also tell them about a self-directed IRA and how they can use retirement money to fund their loans to you. This is of course self-serving but if you were going to put on one of these events and wanted to add more credibility to the workshop, why not give them a copy of this book to take home with them to read more about private lending and self-directed IRAs? This book will help you explain and sell the program along with giving the concepts more credibility because they are in a book by a bestselling author and nationally recognized expert and trainer. We have bulk purchase plans available so contact us today and order a case or two for your upcoming workshops. You can also just loan out this book on an individual basis or any other way you see fit. Reach out to us via email at info@wealthwithoutstocks.com and put in the subject line "bulk books" and we will help get you started.

You only need a few good private lenders to launch your investment career so don't be afraid to spend a little money up front on lists, mailers, and books to get people in your room. If you're afraid to speak to a group, do a one-on-one appointment with any leads generated instead of the workshop. I would also recommend you overcome the fear of talking in front of groups. Being able to communicate effectively to groups of people makes you very valuable in the marketplace. Consider taking some speaking training course and start small to grow your confidence. The most important part of speaking is to know your material cold. Prepare a power point presentation in advance and practice it before your live show.

Put out the word to your spheres of influence and let them know you're looking for private investors to make safe loans with attractive returns. Make sure you have some cards that might say on them "do you have any investment capital or an IRA that you would like to earn at least a 7% rate of return on safely and securely? Call or visit us online today." Just start getting active because activity breeds success.

As the private money investor looking to loan money, your best source will be getting involved with a local REA club in your area. There are many of these spread throughout the country and depending on where you live, you might have several in your area. Be prepared to attend with some flyers and cards and let people know you have "x" number of dollars you would like to loan out in the next 60 days; and don't be surprised if the demand is more than your amount to loan. That is a good problem to have as the lender!

You can also search online and in the local papers for obvious real estate investors and reach out to them to see if you might be a fit to work together. Even if they won't borrow your money they might know someone who would love access to the funds. It will not be difficult finding investors in search of capital once you begin your search.

Don't I need a license to make loans?

This will be dependent on your state and its regulations. As a general rule, if you are loaning out your own money for our own investment accounts the answer is no, you will most likely not need a license to do those few transactions every few years. If you intend on loaning other people's money, then you will most definitely need a license. If you pool money to loan out you better get a good attorney and check with the Securities and Exchange Commission (SEC) because you may be creating an investment instrument which comes along with its own complicated set of rules and regulations. As always, consult with a good attorney who is well schooled in this arena.

LAW FIRM

"My fleas don't pay any rent and they have loud parties that keep me awake all night. I want to have them evicted!"

Chapter 8

Nationwide Turn-key Income Properties

When I wrote my first book *The Perpetual Wealth System*, the real estate markets all across the country were all experiencing huge downturns in the market prices of single family homes. This created an opportunity for savvy investors who either had cash or could raise cash to pick up fantastic bargains that produced great cash flow.

In many areas of the country you were able to suddenly buy homes at 1960s or 1970s prices while at the same time renting them out for modern day rents. This created a cash buying frenzy in many areas of the country. The mortgage market was so difficult to operate in that many people decided to reallocate other funds and buy these bargains with cash.

Several years have passed and a few things have changed. Almost every market in the country has seen a significant increase in pricing off of their lows from several years ago. In most areas the prices are still far less than the highs of the markets around 2006. Mortgages are now easier to get than they were a few years ago. Foreclosures have come off of their highs from a few short years ago and much of that inventory has been absorbed back into private hands (thus the huge price drops when the market flooded with properties) lowering the glut of properties.

There are also many things that are still true of this market that were true of the former market. Properties are still far off of their highs and available for solid cash flow purchases. Rents have remained high and in some areas have even gone higher than a few years ago. There is still a huge opportunity in solid cash flow real estate if done in the proper markets with trustworthy solid boots on the ground. It's still possible to own properties in great areas across the country even if you live elsewhere. There are still many foreclosure properties that can be bought at nice discounts all over the country.

When I wrote my last book I spent all my time in the real estate chapters describing why Metro Detroit was the cash flow capital of the world and what a golden opportunity it was to acquire heavy cash flow properties in nice areas for less than a decent automobile. It also won't surprise any of you to know that I run a real estate brokerage and investment company in Metro Detroit and have been in the real estate business there for well over two decades. It seemed like a perfect fit: top cash flow market in the country and my expertise covering investment real estate in that same market. I created the Perpetual Real Estate Machine to service investors from all over the world to help them acquire these killer deals that exist in my own back yard.

I still have that business running full steam ahead. I am proud to say we have helped dozens of investors acquire well over one hundred properties right here in Metro Detroit. The only thing that has changed is the pricing now compared to when I wrote *The Perpetual Wealth System*. A real estate market is a fluid beast that is always changing so I can only talk about what pricing we have today. We still routinely get investors into these homes for $55,000 to $60,000 all in pricing. This means that the purchase price, our broker fee, and the rehabilitation bill is all included and totals these amounts. These homes in turn rent for between $850.00 and $925.00 per month. These prices represent about a $20,000 to $25,000 increase off the rock bottom lows of several years ago. However, they are also $80,000 to $100,000 lower than the high price range of these same homes just a decade earlier.

When I was speaking all over North America teaching real estate investment seminars, my friend and speaking partner Brian would always have some fun at my expense. He would always introduce me as hailing from the vacation capital of the world . . . Detroit, Michigan! This would of course be met with a chorus of laughter and sneers. Brian actually lived in the vacation capital of the world of Orlando, Florida but he would revel in telling people about the real "vacation capital." That introduction went over so well, that I have stolen that line and use it in almost every presentation I make outside of my hometown. I tell people I am from the vacation capital of the world and ask them where they think that is and the responses are always the same: Las Vegas, Orlando, Hawaii, Los Angeles and about 4 or 5 other answers. When I tell them no, no, no, and then let them know I am from Detroit, we all have a good laugh. I then tell the crowd the following:

Detroit may not be the vacation capital of the world but it is one of the cash flow capitals of the world. You will be hard pressed to find an area that has the same rent to value ratio. There are areas that have similar (even a little lower) pricing but also have much lower rents. There are of course much more expensive areas but most of their rents are not accordingly higher than Metro Detroit's rental rates. This creates a very unique opportunity. I don't want to spend the same amount of time describing why Metro Detroit is such an unknown gem as I did in my first book. I do want to bring up a couple answers to the most common questions I received from the first book and then point you to other places to get more information.

Commonly Asked questions by prospective investors about Metro Detroit and my answers:

A) Isn't Detroit bankrupt and people don't have jobs?

Answer: Detroit has been mismanaged for over 50 years with a huge population loss from about 1.7 million in the city during its highs to just over 700,000 today. However, we don't buy homes in the city itself due to high property taxes and poorly performing school districts. Detroit is more than just the city limits. Metro Detroit is composed of the tri-county area with a population of over 4.5 million people. Metro Detroit has hosted the car industry along with all of the manufacturing this entails for over 100 years. That has created much wealth and high paying jobs. Metro Detroit has some of the highest per capita family income in the nation. There has also been a large shift in the last 15 years to a large medical community to complement the auto and manufacturing industry. There are about a dozen world class medical facilities within 45 minutes of downtown Detroit. These centers draw people from all over the mid-west and the rest of the country as patients. These medical facilities create high paying jobs. Between the auto, manufacturing, and medical industries there are many high paying jobs for the locals to occupy.

B) Isn't Detroit a high crime area?

Answer: Yes the city is a high crime area (some areas much more than others) but we are not investing in the city but rather the suburbs. The city of Detroit has some great places to live and work but unfortunately there are also areas of high crime, blight, and neglect. The city has made great strides over the last 5 years but it must overcome 50 years of mismanagement and that will not happen overnight. The non-homestead taxes in Wayne County (where Detroit resides), are out of line and make property taxes too high when compared to the adjoining counties. When some of these things change, Detroit proper might be a good play for out of area investors but for now, the suburbs are a better investment.

C) What do people do in Detroit?

Along with the answer to the first question you must remember that Detroit is in the state of Michigan. This is a state rich with natural resources from massive amounts of fresh water (California would love the great lakes) and timber. It is estimated that there are more trees in the state of Michigan than in all of Western Europe. This creates a huge travel and vacation industry both in summer and winter. With all that freshwater; swimming, boating, fishing, and hunting are huge past times in the state. It is also said that Michigan has more golf courses than any other state in the union! They don't typically invest millions in golf courses in broke areas. Just something to keep in mind the next time you see all the negative comments about the city on CNN or another news outlet.

For more information on Metro Detroit Real Estate go to www.perpetualrealestatemachine.com and spend some time looking at videos and facts about Metro Detroit. When I wrote the first book, I was just set up to help people in my backyard who wanted to buy real estate. I realize now I wasn't bringing all my assets to bear with that program. This time around I want to give my readers and investors the ability to buy great deals in other market places throughout the country. No matter how great I (and many others) think Metro Detroit is for investing there are certainly other reasons to invest other than the highest cash-on-cash returns.

Because of all my speaking in the US and Canada, I have been fortunate to network with some of the top real estate investors and brokers from all over the country. Many of these people have become friends and business associates who are experts in their own backyards. They are also financing and real estate investment experts. I went to many of them in different markets and asked them if they would take care of investors that I sent them who wanted to invest in their backyards. The response was over-whelmingly positive and I have been able to give you the ability to acquire great properties in these major markets:

1) Detroit, Michigan
2) Orlando, Florida
3) Tampa Bay, Florida
4) Miami, Florida
5) Las Vegas, Nevada
6) Columbia, South Carolina
7) Phoenix, Arizona
8) Charlotte, North Carolina
9) Jersey City, New Jersey/NYC area

This is a fluid list and more areas could be added by the time you read this, so for more up to date information, visit the site at www.weatlhwith-outstocks.com, US Properties tab, to find biographies on the real estate experts and information about what makes these areas potentially good investments. You will be able to download information and reach out to these experts tomorrow if you wish. You will need a special code to access these professionals at our site. This information is only available to people who have invested in this book. Please write this code down because you will need it for a couple different pieces of information at the website. **The code is: WWS15.**

Some of you might be thinking that you could go to Realtor.com and find agents all over these areas to work with you. This seems like a good thought but it's an idea that is majorly flawed. In all my years in real estate investment and sales I have found that it is a rare bird that truly understands both sides of this business. Remember my analogy in the chapter on setting up life insurance policies with your local insurance agent? Real estate investment is the same kind of unique niche and very few Realtors® are savvy real estate investors or understand all the ins and outs that are possible in this side of the business. This is no slam against them by the way it is just a unique niche that they don't receive training on for the most part through traditional real estate channels. They focus much more on the retail home buyers and home sellers instead of investors. The retail world can be a very lucrative market to be involved with as an agent but is a completely different animal than the investment market.

You want to make sure that first and foremost the people you deal with have the highest ethics and can be your trusted "boots on the ground." Then you need to make sure they are experts in the areas (both geographically and types of properties you want) where you want to invest. I have taken all that guess work out of the equation for you and arranged complete turnkey real estate investing programs in all these cities.

When you go to www.weatlhwithoutstocks.com click on the "US Properties" tab for an information package to be downloaded to you immediately with information about the professionals that are just waiting for you to contact them to begin your investment journey in any (or several markets) described in the above paragraph.

Why might you consider one area vs. another area of the country? Detroit is the cash flow capital of the world but it is not in a place a mass of population will be flocking to in the next 10 to 30 years. Many of the areas might not give you the same cash-on-cash return but might give you the chance at substantial back end profits based on appreciation when you sell. You probably won't be able to buy as cheaply or get as high of rents but maybe you could increase your investment 2 or 3 fold down the road. That might be worth sacrificing some immediate cash flow. Everyone has different wants and different goals in their overall investment plan. Our job here in Wealth Without Stocks® is to give you a plug in solution in many solid real estate investment areas all over the country.

Whether you are looking at cash flow real estate across the country or around the corner there are some rules to follow to make it an attractive investment.

1) When you are buying for cash flow and investment, it is not location, location, location, but rather cash flow, profit, location. The cash flow numbers on a piece of property are even more important than its possible future profit or its location. Future profit is great but you need to have a positive cash flowing project to get to that back end profit years down the road.

Nothing will kill your investing career more quickly than negative cash flowing properties. I don't recommend buying in high crime and high unemployment areas. Many times you can get sucked in by the low pricing but understand the price is low for a very good reason. Lousy areas attract lousy tenants who generally will not take care of your property or pay the rent on time and sometimes not at all. Stay away from these areas and don't get conned by "guaranteed section 8 rents," believing you will always get your money. I love the Section 8, Housing Choice Voucher Program. As an investor there are tons of people who qualify for the program who can rent in stronger areas and don't have to live in the run-down part of town. Your target rich areas are in low to upper middle class areas where most people work during the day. You will pay more but the property will rent for more and give you far fewer headaches than the sucker deals in the high crime areas.

2) Get your property professionally managed even if they are in your own backyard. Management is critical to cash flow real estate. Don't be cheap and think you will manage this yourself. Let someone whose full time job it is to manage properties handle the day to day operations. They manage the properties and you manage the management

company. This also frees up your time to do more deals or work on income producing activities.

3) Always run a cash flow analysis and even more so if you are looking at apartments and commercial properties. If you're buying single family homes, the cash flow analysis is usually quite brief and will usually only include gross rents minus taxes, management fees, insurance, and some deferred maintenance. Most single family homes are rented with the tenant paying all utilities and handling all the lawn and snow maintenance. This is very different in apartments so you must always know what you are responsible for paying and make sure it is part of your cash flow analysis. Then ask yourself what could I do to lower these expenses? New insurance carrier? Rebid snow and grass contracts? Fight my property taxes and get them lowered? There may be a dozen other possible cuts to increase your cash flow.

NOTE: Unlike single family homes, apartment buildings and many other commercial property ventures (usually 4 units or more) are not valued by comparable values or "comps." They are evaluated for value based on net income. Therefore if you can cut your expenses and/or raise income from the building your value will go up substantially in proportion. The multiple will vary depending on area but for every $1,000 increase in Net Operating Income (NOI) the value of the building will go up $7,000 to $10,000. So imagine if you could raise rents, (or rent out more apartments making your vacancy factor lower than when you bought) charge for other space or services on the property, (laundry, storage units, vending, vehicle storage etc.) enough to create $10,000 of extra NOI your investment would be worth around $100,000 more if you went to sell the building. This is why management is so critical, especially in multifamily deals. If you think you would prefer to buy apartment buildings or some other commercial cash flowing property, both my company and our joint venture partners can help you with those investments as well.

4) Remember to check to see what your new property taxes will be after the sale. Many municipalities could raise your taxes once they have a new sale recorded. Make sure to look ahead and not just behind for your numbers.

5) Consider offering lease options or rent to own terms on your single family homes. This will only be effective in middle or upper middle class properties. Many times you can get more monthly rent, turn over more expenses to the tenant, and have a built in buyer down the road. This might be more beneficial than a straight rental. One of the exceptions would be if the area you are buying in is predicted to have really strong appreciation. You may be better to hold on to the property as a straight rental.

6) Don't trade good cash flow for potential equity. I have seen many investors lose their shirts by buying properties that had strong negative cash flow but had the chance for huge appreciation. This is the old "pig in a poke" routine. It has a positive cash flow or you don't buy it for income. Violate this at your own risk.

7) Pay attention to your numbers and review every quarter to make sure expenses are staying in line and rents are as regular as possible. If you are having a problem with a tenant who is not paying and you are getting ready to evict them, try offering the tenant cash for keys before the eviction. I would offer them their entire deposit back if they could be out in 2 weeks and leave the house in broom swept condition. Yes they may owe you a couple thousand dollars of back rent but now is the time for common sense. If you have to go to court to evict the tenants they almost always will leave your property in lousy condition requiring you to finish cleaning out the debris but also cleaning the home. This will take an extra 30 to 60 days instead of just giving them say $1,000 cash to be out in two weeks but leaving the house in decent condition. I have asked tenants to pay for the carpet cleaning and some spot painting (usually no more than $150.00 of expenses)

before I give them their money. If they live up to the agreement you get the house back in rentable shape far more quickly than a full eviction. Don't take it personally or feel like you're getting duped by the tenant. Business is business and this situation is about minimizing losses from repairs and too much holding costs. Let the management company know to follow this protocol every time they have a problem tenant.

Calculating returns on these investments

Real estate is a little more difficult to calculate returns on investment than your traditional cash-in-cash-out scenario as with stocks or funds. There are several areas to be calculated when figuring an overall rate of return. We will use a hypothetical example of what a prospective investment might return. We will be looking at a rate of return in all of these areas:

A) Cash-on-cash return is how much annual income will be received in relation to the cash investment.

B) Equity acquired at initial investment is how much the current value is compared to the price paid.

C) Debt pay down will calculate the rate at which any debt used to purchase the property will be repaid thus building your equity position and increasing the rate of return on your investment.

D) Tax benefits will be any depreciation we might be able to take on our income taxes or other expenses we may incur. These expenses can usually be written off against other income thus increasing your net income from other sources. (Check with your tax attorney.)

E) Future appreciation in the project that will dramatically alter the overall rate of return.

Say we are buying a 10 unit apartment building for $500,000 and putting $100,000 down plus another $20,000 in costs and minor upgrades immediately after closing, for a total cash outlay from us (or one of our cash partners) of $120,000.

After a cash flow analysis we figure the building will have $80,000 in adjusted gross income. (Gross income from rents and other income from the property minus vacancy allowance.)

We also figure that all the expenses on the building will be about 50% of the adjusted gross income, leaving $40,000 behind in Net operating income before any debt service. Remember this is just an example so don't assume expenses will be at 50% but for the ease of an example we will use that figure for the calculation. Your actual investment will vary. We will have borrowed $400,000 @ 5% for 30 years for a total payment of almost $26,000 annually ($2,147 monthly).

When you subtract out your debt service from your NOI this leaves you your pretax profit of $14,000 cash-on-cash return. You laid out $120,000 of your own money so this would represent 12% cash-on-cash return (sometimes referred to as a cap rate). This would be considered a very high return in normal investment fields such as a mutual funds but this is only the beginning of the potential return.

You acquired this building at $50,000 per unit or per door. You quickly determine that other apartment buildings in the area are going for closer to $55,000 per door which means you have acquired about $50,000 in extra equity. This is only paper profit and won't be realized until you sell the property (or possibly refinance and pull cash out) so for now we will just leave that calculation in the final sell price equation.

We will assume this will be a 10 year investment and you will make normal payments on the original loan of $400,000. In 10 years you will owe approximately $325,000, adding $75,000 to your equity position. Remember that was someone else's money (your tenant's) making the payments and building your equity. Also remember to check out the software program we have available to you that is used to pay down debts in record time. This simple piece of technology can be used to help you pay down the building faster without increasing your normal monthly payment. You can find more information with some very easy and quick videos about this software on our website. If you like what you see, reach out to my office for a free analysis to see how fast you can pay off all your debts without increasing your monthly payments.

You have been able to depreciate this property off of your taxes saving you $5,000 a year in personal income tax which means you keep $5,000 more in your pocket, making this an even more attractive investment. This can be figured annually and would represent another 4% return on your $120,000 capital investment.

We sell this building in 10 years and have raised the income from rental increases, maximizing square footage, and leasing more space on the grounds. The new value based on income is $850,000 and we sell for that amount but have some selling expenses netting us $800,000 in proceeds minus the $325,000 in debt netting us $475,000 of which $120,000 was our capital returned to us that was originally invested in the project. This leaves $355,000 of before tax net cash profit.

Let's add all this up over 10 years:

Our 10 year cash flow profit	$140,000
Our 10 year tax savings of	$50,000
Our 10 year equity/cash profit	$355,000

Your total profit on this investment is $545,000 on your $120,000 investment over 10 years. This represents a 450% return over 10 years. This is a game changing investment. Let's compare that to the same $120,000 at 7% in the stock market.

After 10 years, your $120,000 would have grown to $241,000 or a doubling of your original investment. This assumes a 7% compound rate of return in the market which is not likely. This is why everyone who is serious about wealth creation needs to start understanding that there are other alternatives to the stock market and mutual funds. The above example is not void of any risk. Many variables will affect the actual return. Remember that this apartment building is also producing monthly positive cash flow so you are able to access some of your profits on an ongoing basis instead of having to wait to sell the asset as you would do with a stock or fund.

Investing in long-term cash flow properties can be a tremendous way to grow wealth at an accelerated rate for the right investor. This won't be for everyone right now but I would suggest to you that if you don't have the money to do a deal like this, you probably know of someone who does have the money. Their weakness is they have no idea how to find these deals, analyze them, and profit from them. You, on the other hand, are getting strong in that area with your knowledge base and access to professionals who can help you along your journey. You might consider bringing in a partner and splitting profits. This is how I got started with no money, no job, and no credit. I wish you well in your new ventures and if my team and I can help, just give us a call or an email.

Lastly, there are different kinds of income properties you might want to take advantage of depending on the area of the country in which you're going to invest. Some alternatives include self-storage units, group homes, and assisted living facilities, just to name a few. You can also invest in mobile home parks and we have a chapter included on that very topic. When you decide what area of the country interests you the most, connect with one of our professionals through our website and discuss what you both feel might be the best fit for your situation.

"I'd like to make enough money
to be hated, but not despised."

Chapter 9

Million Dollar Marketing to Launch and Grow Your Business

Marketing is the most important part of any business. I don't care how good of a widget or service you have if the right people don't know about it at the right time you are doomed to mediocrity or failure in your venture. Far too many businesses get hung up on their product or service and pay too little attention to how they are going to get the word out about their offering. You can get away with an average product or service but you cannot get away with an average marketing plan. You will of course strive for a great product or service because marketing can get you launched and making money with an average product but success will be short lived without a true quality offering.

Most people believe marketing and advertising are actually the same function for a business. Nothing can be further from the truth. Advertising is much more of a shotgun approach to getting your message out to the public. The approach is usually quantity and not quality of prospects engaged or eye balls reached. Advertising might be a billboard on a main street in your town seen by thousands of people every day. These people are all traveling the same road but are very different in location, work, interests, age, sex, income, and dozens of other factors. You're hoping the sheer number of people who see your billboard will make this a successful strategy.

Marketing is more pre-determining who the ideal prospect would be for your business and trying to reach that perfect group and preferably at the right time. This message would also tell a particular group what's in it for them to do business with the company. This is a much more laser-like approach to business building and will require more thought and effort on your part as the business owner. Who would want your widget? Who would be perfect for it—if they only knew it, and you, existed? I am going to use my businesses as well as others as examples of this so you can start your own mind spitting out ideas.

Your heating and cooling company could invest money in those billboards and might do well but unless you have some kind of tracking mechanism in place you would have no idea where that call or eventual customer actually came from in your advertising efforts. Instead of the billboards, you could ask yourself who your perfect customer is for your business. If you are looking for new installation business you could be wasting much of your marketing dollars if your billboard is primarily seen by people who live in homes that are 10 years old or newer. Maybe even up to 20 years might not be the best.

What if we could find a list of 5,000 homeowners within 50 miles who have houses that were built 20 to 25 years ago and did a mailing to that list? What if we kept mailing to that list every quarter with a great offer of a free carbon monoxide test on their furnace and other safety and efficiency inspections? Since we know that most residential heating units are usually good for between 20 and 25 years that is a target rich environment. Marketing is not just about finding the perfect prospect but is also about finding the perfect prospect at THE RIGHT TIME! Since this is nearly impossible, you must be on that prospects mind when they need you. Early last year when the weather started to turn cold my furnace went out and we woke up to 55 degree temperatures in the house. There is not a heating and cooling company in my town that would not have loved that information the morning the furnace would not work. There was no way for them to know, so we called the first company that came to mind and they got the job. The repair was made and a sale was generated for their company but with nothing more on their part than dumb luck.

Since then I have received no further correspondence from that company, so if we have trouble tomorrow or want a new unit, I don't even know who to call unless I want to go digging through old invoices. I have never gotten a thank you card, informational pieces, emails, or any other offers since they repaired my unit. How sad for their business. They received an easy sale and have no idea how to turn that sale into a long-term, loyal, and referring customer. Why has no other heating and cooling company (that I am aware of) in my area sent me something of value at least every quarter? After just a few quarters they might have top of mind consciousness in my household and have a great chance at making the initial sale and then subsequent sales and referrals from me to others in my sphere of influence.

Savvy marketers understand that we don't market just to make a sale. We really market to obtain a customer that could result in many sales and referrals for future easy sales. I have thousands of people in my database, and I wish I could get every one of them into my business in some form or fashion this year. However, I know that is wishful thinking and not reality. I need to constantly drip information to them that has real value in their lives. Many of these prospects will never transact any business with me but many of them will need my help in the future. It's my job to be at the top of their list when they need help with money, real estate, insurance, debt relief, tax mitigation, or business strategies. When it's their perfect time, I will be around to help them and create a long-term client from a prospect.

Good marketing is about capturing some kind of information from a prospect that could be used later to keep in touch with them and make them an occasional offer to do business with my company. This is called direct response two-step marketing. We want a prospect to raise their hand and tell us they might be interested in being involved with our company at a deeper level but they aren't sure yet. We do this by offering loads of free information that can be downloaded or viewed right from our site. The prospect will put in at least their name and email address (some prospect will input all their contact information) to receive valuable information from our site. They are free to use this information as they see fit and even take it to their trusted financial advisors. We know many do just that and we might never hear from them again. We also know many will take the information to their professionals and because those professionals have little experience with the niches we describe we have a good chance of getting that person as a client later. There is still another group that doesn't have a traditional financial advisor or a financial plan. After studying my company's information many will choose to reach out to us and put us on their power team by becoming a client at some level.

If you are reading this chapter, it is a good bet that this is not your first contact with me or my company, so you might be receiving free training and the occasional offer from my company. If you're not, go to our site and download some information that interests you and read our follow-up correspondence. Even if you never intend to transact business with us in any way, you will receive a huge lesson in solid marketing that produces consistent results. This is two-step marketing because we are not looking for a sale on the first contact (of course, we take them when they happen) but rather a prospect to turn into a contact. Then we can keep that contact informed with great information until they either become a client themselves and/or refer clients to us who need help. We are very ok with you not wanting to "buy" right now. We would just like to know that you have some interest by leaving us a trail to follow.

The offline and online worlds of marketing

There is much success to be had in both worlds and you can do two-step direct response marketing offline as well as online. The truth is a successful business should employ both worlds for a killer cohesive marketing strategy that produces results.

In the offline world, good old-fashioned mail or "snail mail" is often overlooked and even forgotten in this fast-paced, online world. This is a serious mistake for any business owner who is serious about success. A good mailing list combined with an actual marketing plan can still be a killer way to generate great returns on your marketing dollars.

Here are the must-haves in a successful campaign:

1) Determine your Unique Selling Proposition (USP). This is what position or angle you have that will separate your product or service from the mass of competition. It could be part of your slogan, but that's not mandatory. Here are some unique selling propositions that have been big successes from businesses, including my own:

    a. Dominos™ - Fresh hot pizza delivered to your door in 30 minutes or less or its free

    b. Beat the bank by becoming the bank

    c. Save big money at Menards®

    d. Subway® sub shops were genius when they made their standard sandwich shop into a weight loss product with the introduction of Jerrod who ate their subs twice per day and lost over 200lbs. Their sales skyrocketed and now they are not just a sub shop but are also a weight loss and health food store.

    e. FedEx®- When it absolutely, positively has to be there overnight.

    f. Create your own Private Pension

    g. Build a real estate cash flow machine

    h. Jimmy John's® Submarine Sandwich Shop - Freaky Fast. Freaky Good.

These are just a few examples of how a USP separates an average business from a successful one by figuring out one or two good USP's to use in their marketing.

1) Buy a solid list of prospects from a reputable mailing list company (visit www.wealthwithoutstocks.com Resource tab for a list of list companies)

2) Make sure the list is updated recently and purged of old mailing addresses

3) Buy at least 1,000 names and addresses

4) Tracking mechanism built into the offer such as its own URL (website extension) or toll free extension number

5) Mail out to the same list until the results don't justify the cost any longer

Number 5 needs some explanation. It's very easy to get caught in the trap of thinking mailing to more names will be the best strategy. It has been proven time and time again that repeated mailing to the same list with different messages will produce far better results. This is because of the timing issue we have already discussed and due to name recognition and brand building. This only can happen after repeated exposures. The secret is to mail to the same list (assuming it's a good list) but mail in different forms. If you have committed to mail that list every 60 days for a year than your mailings might look like this:

Six Month Campaign

1) Introduction letter with offer of free package if they call or go to your website. An offer is a must in every mailing, no matter its form, and you must be able to track success or failure

2) Another offer in a letter with a brochure of your company and testimonials

3) Another offer on a postcard with more testimonial blurbs

4) Another offer of a possible free service, safety check, download, educational audio or video, etc.

5) A special envelop that looks like it is from federal express with something in the envelope that connects to the offer. This is called bumpy mail and almost always gets opened and remembered even if the sale doesn't happen right away

6) A final call to action that might say what do I have to do? I have (then list the offers in mailings 1 to 5 and give them an even better "final offer")

You should track every mailing and its results. These could be your results categories:

A) How many sent

B) How many returned (if too many are returned you have a list with old information)

C) How many leads generated by your free offers

D) How many appointments or conversations booked

E) How many sales generated

F) How much gross income generated from mailing

G) Net gain or loss on this campaign

Don't be surprised if for your next mailing, the numbers tracked all improve, and for each subsequent mailing as well. This will be true until the list runs its course and it will be time to acquire a new list. Also, you might show a loss on this mailing (depending on margins for what you sell) but that doesn't mean it's not a success. Assuming you generated good leads, they might not show this mailing as revenue but very well could during the subsequent mailing cycles. The true numbers for your campaign might take 6 months to a year to judge their total success or failure.

Let's assume you sell something for $3,000 with a 40% margin of gross profit. When you make a sale for $3,000 that equates to $1,200 gross profit on the item. This means that $1,200 goes to your top of the line income to be used in your business. We will work this list for 6 mailings and see what happens.

NOTE: If you sell something far less expensive, your response and sale rates will be much higher than an expensive product. This means it will be important to have a more expensive offering after your entry level product or service.

First mailing costs $0.50 between postage, paper, list cost, and printing. You send out 2,000 mailers at a cost of $1,000. It looks like this:

A) 2,000 mailed

B) 40 returned as undeliverable

C) 30 leads generated or 1.5% for a free offer or service

D) 10 appointments booked (33% of leads)

E) 3 sales made from initial appointments or 30% of appointments set

F) $9,000 gross income from the first month

G) $3,600 gross profit from first month

H) 3.5 to 1 gross profit on dollars spent

I) $2,600 gross profit from campaign

You have invested $1,000 to make $3,600 gross profit, which would be acceptable any day of the week. What happens in mailing number two if your numbers double from response? (It's possible, because they're starting to know who you are and like your message.)

What if just one of those leads generated from the first mailing converts? How about if one more of the appointments that were conducted the month before turns into a sale? You can see the possibility of snowballing due to the focus on not just sales but generating leads. An inexpensive follow up campaign by email and phone calls should be instituted on all leads that didn't buy right away. FOLLOW UP IS THE MOST VIOLATED RULE IN BUSINESS! The lion's share of the profit comes from proper and predictable follow up. I don't mean you should call them every few days and become a pest (unless what you sell has a very short sales cycle); I am talking about an email every two weeks and a call every 30 to 90 days until one of three things happen:

1) They buy from your company
2) They tell you to get lost and are never going to buy from your company
3) Either you or they die!

Even if you don't call them after say 10 tries what harm does it do to send them an email at least every two weeks? Keep giving them good information and you never know when the right time might be for them to do business with your company. You're also setting yourself up for referrals from your leads that might not have even done business with you yet. Just last month I received an email from a couple whose daughter had seen me speak at an event. I was talking about wealth creation through self-banking and using properly designed whole life insurance. Their daughter was not yet ready to set this program up due to a couple short-term issues that needed her attention. However, she told her parents about the information she learned and sent them to one of my websites. Her father proceeded to devour all the videos and training programs I had on the site. After that he reached out to me and shortly thereafter became a very valuable client to my business. The original prospects, sister- and brother-in-law have also become clients before the original prospect! This was all because of proper follow up. Get your follow up program in place today!

This campaign we have been discussing might cost you $6,000 to $8,000 to run for the year but could generate $50,000 of gross revenue or more with sequential mailing and proper follow up strategies. This means you should be mailing even more and reinvesting some of the profits to mail to another list or two. However, make sure you don't just assume those next two lists will get the same response as your first list. Track and test them both before spending big money on the mailings.

Newspapers and Magazines

Many people think print media is old school and all marketing funds should be spent online. I disagree 100% because there are still many millions of people that like print media and read papers and periodicals very often. When you spend marketing dollars in print media the same rules still apply as above. Use direct response two-step marketing with a free offer of something of value to anyone who responds. Put a tracking mechanism in the ad so you know where the leads are coming from and how the ad is pulling. This could be as simple as having an order form online that asks for the offer code. You would include a different offer code in every different kind of marketing. Newspapers might be offer code 1 and magazines might be 2, etc.

Remember you should always have multiple fishing lines in the water when you're fishing for leads and sales. If you just have them call one number without even an ad code, then you will never know what ads are working well and which ones are a flop. Every ad you run in every form must differentiate itself with an ad code, offer number, toll free extension, URL, and alike. After 30 days, if you see that your ad in a certain newspaper isn't pulling well, you can pull that ad or change the ad itself to see if you can get it to pull. If you change the ad and it still doesn't draw a good response, pull the ad and invest your marketing dollars in areas where they are working.

Headlines are key in all your ads, whether online or offline!

The headline of your ad better be a grabber or your dollars are wasted. No boring or humdrum headlines allowed. If I owned the heating and cooling company, the headline might read something like this:

"Government Estimates that 4 million Furnaces may Leak Small Amounts of Carbon Monoxide—We would like to make sure yours is not one of them for FREE!"

"Last Year 200 families Buried Loved ones due to Faulty Furnaces" (or whatever the real number might be) **"Please let us keep your family safe."**

Of course, whatever you source should be credible and only use real numbers, but I hope you get the point. Always think of a headline that talks about trouble or something fantastic; solve a problem they might or might not know they have. I also like anti-establishment headlines. The above example is a headline and sub-headline working together to grab and make a soft offer at the same time.

"Find out why your 401k is a sucker's bet and how you are getting hosed without even knowing it."

This flies in the face of conventional wisdom and makes many people stand up and give you a second look. Then I would put something like "Get this valuable free report" or "free video," "audio," etc. This will force people who have some interest to leave a trail for you to begin the marketing sequence to convert them from a lead to a customer or client.

When your headline is complete, ask yourself this question "Could the National Enquirer® use this headline?" and if the answer is yes, you probably have a winner! Those kinds of papers and magazines sell very well and are always put at checkout counters in grocery stores. Their headlines (and pictures) only have a brief second to grab someone's attention to at least pick up the magazine and decide to put it in the basket or not. They have mastered the headline and sub-headline game, so pay special attention next time you are checking out at the grocery store.

Not just any publication but the right publications

You want to take the same approach with your publications that you do with your mailing campaign. If I have a great product or service for the outdoorsman, then Better Homes and Gardens® might not be the place to spend money, regardless of how many people read this publication. (By the way it might be a good spot but gear the ad to "hunting widows" or some spin for the men in their lives). There are many publications that just won't be a fit for your business no matter how many people they might reach. Tailor your message to your perfect prospect and then get it in the right place where many of those perfect prospects gather to read about things that capture their interest and imagination.

Niche publications

One of my niches for my business is Realtors® so I spend time soliciting Realtors® and brokers at all levels to see about speaking at their events or writing articles in their publications. I can run ads in national magazines, state magazines, local magazines, and local periodicals or newsletters. The difference will be the pricing in each magazine and the number of potential eyeballs for my advertisement. I can also tailor make my message to speak to Realtors® strengths and weaknesses and what might push their hot buttons.

Depending on what niche you pursue, there are also more than likely many associations that represent your group of ideal prospects. You can also solicit them to see about speaking, writing articles, and advertising in their papers. Start locally with small associations and get letters of reference assuming your talk went well. Then use those to ladder up the chain and get booked at bigger, more prestigious events or written up in publications. Using this same strategy I was able to take an idea to operate in that niche to speaking at high level events and writing articles for state-wide magazines for Realtors®.

This part of the chapter ties in great with the chapter on becoming famous in your niche. The more niche friendly your product or service is the easier and less expensive your ideal customer is to reach. When possible, niche all or part of your business instead of just catering to the masses. My main company is Perpetual Wealth Systems, which has mass appeal to anyone who is trying to get ahead financially. This means that I have the benefit and curse of having mass appeal and being able to service almost anyone who wants to get ahead financially. However, how can I effectively find these people and try to make them feel special? How can I tailor my message to hit their hot buttons? I can only do it in the most general of terms and usually at a maximum of cost.

This is why if you go to www.johnjamieson.com you will see several big links to niches I serve: Realtors®, Doctors, Retirement age people, real estate investors, and even younger people just starting out. This means that I can have a mass message but can also craft more specific messages that will have more appeal to each group. Does your product or service allow you to service a couple different niches? If so, don't be afraid to build some custom marketing messages for those groups. Maybe start out with marketing material for the masses (if you can service the masses) and one specific niche.

What I just described to you and what you will witness online did not happen overnight. It began with a decision that I wanted to get my message and business out to as many people as possible. I started with one site and one message and built more as I moved forward. You can do the same. Don't get intimidated and go into "no action" mode. Just begin from wherever you are and start to get your message and business out into public consciousness.

Invest in Marketing

Don't be afraid to invest in your business by spending some targeted marketing dollars. Marketing is the gasoline for your business engine. With no gasoline or poor quality gasoline it will be almost impossible to get your venture off the ground, let alone humming along spitting out income for you and your family.

Just don't spend recklessly but rather with a goal in mind and with way to track your marketing dollars effectiveness. If you spent $5,000 on marketing but could track $30,000 in sales from that investment what would that mean? It means next time spend $10,000 and see if you equates to $60,000!

Test, Test, Test

Never roll out a full marketing campaign unless you have first tested it on a smaller scale and received positive results from the test. In mailing you need to at least send out 1,000 mailers from your list to give the test a decent shot at success. The law of averages in all things is a powerful fact to always keep in mind. If I only send out 100 mailers (assuming as above to a totally cold list that has no current relationship with you) then the law of averages is working hard against me and the results will be skewed. If your periodical or print ad works well in one magazine or newspaper try rolling it out in 5 or 10 and if results are still good, you know you have a winner and you should invest more dollars to get bigger results. This all begins with a decent test.

Spend some time on the web and research print publications for your niches. I just Googled® periodicals for real estate agents and then periodicals for doctors and received more information than I could possibly ever use. You can do the same and then spend a little time finding what you believe would be the top 5 periodicals for marketing your business. Get some pricing, make a budget, and design a simple marketing campaign.

Joint Ventures

I also want you to start asking yourself what other businesses could help get your message out to the public to the benefit of all involved. Consider starting your own little consortium of like-minded business owners who are committed to helping each other grow profits. I am not talking about the many local networking companies that are located all over the country where you meet every week and exchange referrals. I see nothing wrong with these organizations and have been a part of them myself in the past, but this is the next level or two up from these groups.

What I'm really talking about is growing a distribution network for your product or service; this is more strategic and long term. If you joint venture partnered with the right business or businesses you could take years of the marketing and distribution of your business. One of my niches, as I already mentioned, is Real Estate Agents. There are several reasons for this:

1) This is a group I know at their DNA level from being in that industry in some form or fashion for 25 years.

2) There is a huge need for a true financial solution for Realtors® to grow and protect wealth. They are famous for high income and low net worth. I have a real solution for those agents that are looking for answers in their own financial lives.

3) Realtors® have a huge distribution potential. I could help their customers and clients with their wealth creation efforts as well as the Realtor®. I could also get referred to other real estate offices, real estate franchises, and real estate associations. This has all happened but only because I envisioned it and set up a plan to make it happen over time.

4) The same is true for Doctors, except the part of being a part of their industry for 25 years. This brand was started because of its enormous potential and my experience with doctors on a professional level. I was teaching real estate investment seminars all over the country and many of my classes had one or two doctors as attendees. I got to know many of their problems when it came to investing and money. I created a unique selling proposition (USP) designed for that niche (How to Become a 6-Million-Dollar Doctor). Then I took steps to enter that industry as a consultant. This has taken longer but has paid great dividends for my business that will get bigger in the next few years.

What other types of business could you joint venture with to help your business and the host business? Could you set up a revenue sharing plan for the host business? If you're dealing with licensed services, many industries will not legally allow commissions or income of any kind to be paid to non-licensed people or entities. If there are no licensing issues many times you can set up a revenue stream for the host business. If the host company does need a license of some sort to share in revenue it might be worth their time to obtain the license as it could mean ongoing revenue for years to come.

What if you had a jewelry store and you wanted to run a special Valentine's Day promotion? Couldn't you seek out a joint venture partner who might have access to a large email or regular mailing list? What about a pizza store, auto repair, insurance, real estate, or any one of dozens of other businesses? Reach out to them with a phone call and propose that they help you promote your special offering in the weeks leading up to Valentine's Day. You will be offering a great deal and they can bring value to their client base and keep in their client's minds. Tell them that anyone that comes into your store with their special coupon from the joint venture partner that makes a purchase will receive a commission on the sale. Maybe these businesses get the word out to many thousands of people on your behalf and you end up with 50 solid sales of a $1000.00 package that you would not have had otherwise. This generates $50,000 in sales and you pay out a 10% commission to your JV partners of $5,000. This leaves you $45,000 of Gross Sales with no other marketing expense. You can reciprocate with those businesses by making special offers for them as well and also participating in sales.

This is one of many dozens of possibilities both offline and online that you should put into your overall marketing plan. My company would like to Joint Venture with you in several different areas. Some of these areas will require you to have or obtain a license (not hard to obtain and once you have it you have it), and some will not require licensing, so feel free to reach out to us to see how we can help you increase your income by working with Wealth Without Stocks® and Perpetual Wealth Systems.

EDITORIAL DEPT.

"We'd like you to condense your novel into something that younger people will want to read...in 140 characters or less."

Chapter 10

Million Dollar Internet Marketing

I have asked my friend Brian to help out with this chapter because he works with people to help them create brands, businesses, and sales on the internet. I also want to mention a few things myself on the power of the internet and how it has helped me launch my brand and help grow my business.

You have a potential for a worldwide marketplace at your fingertips. You have the ability to reach your ideal prospect for very reasonable fees and then add that prospect to your database and follow up for almost free! (I say almost because you will need to spend a little money on some basic technology to help you run your online business, but the cost is usually very low.) Once your prospect is obtained, you can offer them information and opportunities to do business with you until they opt out of your list.

When I became a true believer in the web

In 2007 I began working with a company who showed people how to reduce their debts and mortgages by utilizing very unique personal finance software. This is a relationship that continues to this day. The man who brought me into that business is named Juan and we became friends and business associates. The company was made aware of my ability to market and train others how to do the same so they asked me to do a series of webinars to train their field sales representatives. I agreed to do the training for free which was fine with me as long as I could have the names and email addresses of everyone who attended my trainings. They agreed to this arrangement and it was great for both our interests. During the next

9 months I held trainings on all kinds of marketing topics including copy writing sales letters for this product. Hosting these trainings or "webinars" I was able to obtain over 8,000 names and email addresses of business and sales minded individuals. I was also able to help their sales force create more sales. I met a lady at a live seminar I was speaking at and she shared with me she had used my sales letter and made an extra $10,000 of income she could directly attribute to my trainings. It's very gratifying to find out when people use your teachings and create great results!

After 9 months of free training I decided to start to market products and services I thought would be a good fit for this kind of list. I have a joint venture partner (sound familiar) who has a fantastic course on money and taxes. I had invested in it myself years earlier and had received many times my investment back in actual value. I really did not know what to expect when we started to advertise the webinar to the list. We sent out a series of 4 email invitations to the 8,000 person list and ended up with a little over 1,000 people signing up for this free information webinar. (This is better than the average percentages but because I had never offered them anything for sale in the past and had given incredible value, I had a very receptive list.)

We actually had a little over 500 people show up on the webinar for this presentation, which is considered a high percentage for a free webinar. We offered a $1,295 killer training package at the end of the call and within 3 days, had sold over $50,000 in product to the attendees on that list! We were all very excited and decided to repeat that webinar again in 3 more weeks.

If you remember we had 500 people not show up on the call so there was still a huge demand for this information. To make a long story as short as possible, we offered other products and services to that list for the next 8 months and did over $250,000 in sales. However, if that sounds awesome (and it was) I wish I would have known more about list building. You see, what I have figured out since then is that you can't just pitch people constant products and services or you'll burn your list out. What I should have done is put on a webinar with something to sell every quarter. The other times I would have given the list loads of free valuable content that would have helped their business. I had violated a rule I don't want you to forget: People don't care if you sell to them but they do care if that's all you do is sell to them. So now when you get emails from us, you will see a 90/10 ratio. This means that 90% of the time we will just give you great training with no sales pitches. Every once in a while, when we have a great program we think you should have, we will do a sales presentation and a pitch.

This makes my list much more valuable and stable to me over time instead of just constantly pitching to my list. It also creates much more value for my email list subscribers. I have stayed on some people's email list for many years because they offer much value. I even buy something from them once in a while and that is fine with me as long as there is much value of being on their list. Whenever I am just pitched by a company I opt out quickly and my guess is you are much the same way.

Page #1 of Google®

When you Google® or Bing® my name it will come up page 1 #1 on both search engines. Google® will show you the link to AOL's DailyFinance website where I wrote about 36 articles. That site has loads of followers and links attached to it so the search engine gives it huge rankings and gives me clout for being in it so many times. Also when you Google® "whole life insurance, 770 accounts," and several other article topics, my articles appear on the first page and sometimes are the first actual article just behind the paid ads that pop up first!

I tell you this because a couple of years ago I wouldn't have appeared anywhere near page one, #1 and in fact you would have had to go down many pages to find me because I was not "important" in the search engine rankings. Writing those articles and other concentrated efforts over the last two years has catapulted me and my brand for online search engines. That has translated into great exposure and verifiable monies earned by my company. My first book, *The Perpetual Wealth System,* takes up about the first 5 pages of Google® and Bing®. Just a few short years ago, they would have not appeared on those search engines until you were well past 10 pages and how many people search past even two pages? This was achieved by appearing as a guest on radio shows, podcasts, magazine interviews, and various other methods.

I would highly recommend you start writing articles about your business and industry. Post them on your blog but also look for other sites that would love to have your articles. There is a massive need for constant online content and you can benefit from providing some of that content. Writing and appearing on radio and television shows also gives you more credibility than your competition. This is also true of writing a book about your business. A book is a big undertaking but I would highly recommend you start on even a small book as soon as you can. However, you can start writing articles (maybe 500 to 1,000 words) and find some people out there who want content on what your expertise is and then provide them a steady stream of information.

One more thing before I turn it over to Brian. I highly recommend you start to shoot videos and upload them to YouTube® and other video sites. With high speed internet, videos are taking over the web and you should put them in your arsenal. They don't have to be fancy. Most of my videos are me in front of a whiteboard training and teaching. However, the video always gives the viewer the information to go to my websites at the bottom of the video.

Even if you aren't a great speaker, don't be intimidated. Simply get started doing 3 and 4 minute videos and you will get much better at your delivery. This will also prepare you for giving live speeches, which is also a powerful way to deliver your message to many people very quickly. Videos can also be placed in many online magazines because it helps in search engine recognition as well. If you would like to see my videos that I post on You Tube® just go to www.multiplewealthstreams.com and sign up to watch our You Tube® channel. Any article can also be a video! Let's bring in Brian to talk about more online marketing and money-making strategies.

My name is Brian and I have been helping people and businesses build online businesses for more than a decade. I am very excited to be a part of this project and know me and John can help you create income and wealth online.

> "Give me a lever long enough and a fulcrum on which to place it, and I shall move the world." You may already be familiar with that famous quote by Ancient Greek mathematician, scientist, and inventor - Archimedes.

Here Archimedes is referring to the power of a lever and more importantly the principle of leverage. In science leverage refers to the concept of moving an object with less force, but there are many ways we can apply this simple, yet powerful concept outside the field of science.

Many people in the financial world are very familiar with using leverage in financial situations to get higher returns with a lower investment risk; such as using debt to finance an investment or using an option to control a stock.

Simply put, I think the most general way of thinking about leverage is as a way of getting more with less. When it comes to business and marketing, I think one of the most powerful forms of leverage available to you is an effective Internet marketing strategy. Think of the Internet as your personal lever and fulcrum for your business.

The Power of Automation

So why am I so bullish on Internet marketing? One word: automation.

With an effective online presence your prospects find you. Once they do, your website or landing page does the selling. If they don't buy, you can follow up with them automatically through email marketing. And once they do buy, the transaction can be made without you even knowing about it or being involved. Product delivery is handled instantly and digitally (even physical products can be fully outsourced). And this all happens 24 hours a day, 365 days a year, rain or shine, whether it's 2PM or 2AM, whether you're sleeping or awake.

After the initial set-up, your involvement in maintaining it all can be minimal; leaving you more time to focus on working on your business rather than in it.

Automation is the reality of Internet marketing. And if all of this sounds good at a "big picture" level you'd be truly surprised at what you can automate and systematize using the power of the Internet.

So with that said, let's get into the specifics on how you actually do all of this.

Internet Marketing—The 30,000 Foot Overview

In business and marketing, there are three main things a business must do well in order to be successful; it has to be able to (1) generate leads, (2) capture those leads, and (3) convert those leads into sales.

When it comes to online marketing these translate into:

- Traffic Generation (lead generation)
- List Building (lead capture)
- Sales Conversion (lead conversion)

From a "big picture" standpoint, all you have to do to be successful online is get traffic; build your list, and follow-up to generate sales.

Of the three points listed above, usually most people are interested in getting more traffic to their website, overlooking either the importance of list building or the opportunity it has to increase sales.

If a website is underperforming, there are usually other things you can do to get it to convert better and produce more sales (which we'll talk about in a bit). To put it bluntly, if you have a website that is underperforming, then adding more traffic to it will just make it underperform at a higher level.

Now once you have a website that is fully optimized to capture leads and convert those leads into sales, by all means you'll want to drive as much traffic to it as possible; since you are able to maximize the visitor value and customer value.

With that said, we'll explore each of these areas in more detail. First I'll share with you my favorite methods of driving traffic, then we'll take a look at how you can optimize your website to capture leads, and finally we'll talk about the best ways to increase the amount of sales from your website.

Let's go ahead and start with the most popular topic, how to get more traffic to your website.

How to Drive Traffic to Your Website

Whenever I'm coaching or consulting with a new client usually one of the first questions they ask is, "How do I get more traffic to my website?" This is understandable, as all things being equal, the more traffic you get to your website the more money it will make.

Though there are literally hundreds, if not thousands of different ways to drive traffic to your website, all of those methods can be categorized into two main categories; free traffic and paid traffic.

Free traffic—the benefits of free traffic is that it's, well, free. Usually though most free traffic methods will involve some type of time investment and you may not see results immediately.

Paid traffic—the benefit of paid traffic is that in most cases it's immediate. You can pay to run an ad and start driving traffic within minutes. You usually won't be profitable with paid traffic immediately and will have to do some testing to find a winning offer.

When I first meet with new coaching and consulting clients the area that they are most interested in is how to get free traffic. With that said let me share my top 3 methods for getting free traffic to your website.

Free Traffic with Content Marketing

When it comes to generating free traffic to your website usually you will be engaging in some type of content marketing. The idea is that you create content and people find that content through search engines, links on websites, and social sharing. Let's take a look at what I consider to be the three best content marketing strategies.

Guest Blogging

Guest blogging is hands down my favorite way of generating free website traffic. There are several reasons why this is such a powerful method. If you think about it, there are a lot of websites and blogs out there that already have a lot of traffic and attract your ideal customer. With guest blogging you can tap right into that traffic and reach your audience.

You probably already know a handful of influential experts, websites, and blogs in your market. You could always do some Google® searches to find other websites and discover new blogs in your market that you may not know already exist.

Once you find and identify these websites, start contacting them and offer to do a guest post or write an article for them. They key that I've found when contacting websites is to introduce myself, compliment their website and what they do, and offer to write some original content for their website. Of course, you'll get an author byline with a link back to your website and/or squeeze page.

The great thing about guest posting is that it's free and can drive a lot of traffic to your website quickly. You just have to put some time in to identify relevant blogs in your market and reach out to make those connections.

Video Marketing

Another extremely powerful method to getting free traffic to your website is through video marketing. The reason why video marketing works so well is that there is not as much competition relative to other content creation methods. In addition to that, YouTube® happens to be the second largest search engine; with Google® being number one of course. A high number of searches for video with a low number of competing videos make for a great opportunity of getting free traffic from videos.

The good news about video is that (1) they don't have to be very long and (2) they can be made with relatively inexpensive equipment; in some cases right from your Smartphone. Let's take a look at some ways you can quickly and easily create video content.

Talking Head Video—With this type of video, you just stand or sit in front of a camera and speak your message. These days most smartphones can record HD quality video; all you need to add is an inexpensive lavaliere microphone to get good audio quality and a tripod to hold the phone.

Screen Capture Video—If you're not comfortable standing in front of a camera and talking then another option is to do a screen capture video. With this type of video you can record what's on your computer screen (a PowerPoint or Keynote presentation or software / website demo) and use a microphone to record the audio. I like using a screen capture recording and editing software suite called Camtasia from Techsmith and using an inexpensive USB Condenser Microphone to capture good quality audio.

Live Video Recordings—Another option is to simply take video footage of you speaking at a live event or any other type of recordings you may have. If you have longer videos you can break them down into shorter segments.

As I mentioned above, YouTube® is the second largest search engine and the 800lb. gorilla when it comes to video marketing. I recommend uploading your videos to YouTube® so people can find your video content there. A best practice is to include a link to your website as a watermark on the video and also in the description of the video when you upload it to YouTube®.

Though video marketing isn't for everyone, it's a huge opportunity for those who wish to capitalize on a free traffic method with relatively little competition.

Building Authority with Your Own Blog

The final method of content marketing I recommend is to regularly add content to your own website/blog. In most cases you won't get traffic immediately like you will with guest posting and you won't even get traffic as quickly as by uploading videos to YouTube®; but you will be building your own asset and web presence that you have full and complete control over.

Though it takes time to develop high levels of traffic and an authority website, there is nothing better than getting free traffic to your own on a regular and consistent basis.

It doesn't seem that a day goes by that the Search Engine experts are coming up with new ways to "game" the system, touting the latest and greatest tactics to get higher traffic in the search engines. While these tactics may work temporarily in the short run; the usually don't work long-term, and in some cases can hurt you in the long run.

The best advice I can give when it comes to getting your own blog ranked highly in the search engines and attracting a large amount of free traffic is this: regularly update your blog with **good quality original content that is useful to your audience.**

Each of those things I mentioned in that sentence above is important, and you do have to do all of them; let's take a look at it again:

- **Regularly update your blog**—the more consistent you can be the better. The more you can do it the better; but for many people it's tough to stick to a multiple time per day, or even daily schedule. I'd say if you're serious about bogging as content marketing strategy, you'll want to update your blog at least on a weekly basis when you're just starting out.
- **Good quality original content**—more important than quantity, many will argue, is the quality of your content. Though it's okay to curate other content for your audience, your main focus should be on producing good quality original content.
- **Useful to your audience**—this one should go without saying. Of course you want your content to be useful to your audience. The more useful it is, the better you'll position yourself as an expert and authority; and the more people that will link back to and share your content.

That's all there is to it. If you focus on doing just that, you'll get found for the keywords and topics that are important to your audience. Other websites will link back to your website. And Google® (and other search engines) will rank your website favorably.

Now that we've covered some of the top methods of driving traffic to your website, let's talk about the second step in this process, building your list.

Building Your List

Out of all of the thousands of websites that I've reviewed and critiqued for my coaching and consulting clients, without fail, the biggest opportunity for improvement has been with their list building efforts.

List building is simply the idea of capturing the information of the visitors who are visiting your website so that you can follow up with them to make sales.

Let's talk about why this is such a big opportunity and why it's so important.

Simply put, the first time somebody visits your website they're probably not going to do what you want them to do. First time visitors have either somehow stumbled upon your website (most likely through a Google® search) or are coming to your website from a direct source (like a link from another website, advertisement, etc.) just to get a little more information and learn more about you and what you have to offer. Only a small percentage, less than 5%, will make a decision to purchase your products or services on the first visit.

The problem is, once they leave your website the chances of them coming back on their own accord is very small.

The reality is, as a website owner, you're spending a lot of time, energy, effort, and money to reach your audience, promote your website, and get traffic to your website; so it would be unfortunate to have it all go to waste.

That's the reason why focusing on building your list is so important. By simply giving your visitors some type of free offer / incentive to give you their email address, you can now follow up with your visitors and bring them back to your website multiple times to see your offers. The more times they come back to your site and see your offers the more sales you'll make.

Not only that, but through effective email follow-up you can provide additional information that will get your prospects to know, like, and trust you, build your authority in the marketplace, and not only increase first time sales; but have the opportunity to get repeat sales.

Through effective list building and email follow-up, most businesses can increase sales by 2 to 3 times, and in some markets / industries that have a more robust product funnel or high ticket offers can see an improvement of up to 10X or more. John's story about how he was able to capture the email addresses of those attending his webinar trainings and following up to do additional webinar trainings is a perfect example of the power of building your list.

Now that you know the importance of list building and how you can benefit from it; let's talk about how you can implement it into your online strategy.

Powerful Free Offer

List building can be broken down into this simple mantra: **Offer something valuable, for free, in exchange for contact information.**

Overall, this is a simple concept, but let's gets into a little more detail.

First, let's talk about the free offer. You may already notice that many websites ask people for their contact information, usually their name and email address. In most cases they are simply asking people to "get blog updates," or sign up for their "email newsletter." While I do commend them for capturing leads (any list building is better than no list building at all); there are better ways you can get more people to opt-in to your list. Keep in mind that, all things equal, the bigger your list the more money you will make.

A better way to get more people interested in and excited about your free offer is to offer something more specific and tangible; something that they can download immediately for instant gratification. Some examples of this include a:

- Free eBook or special report (commonly known as a "white paper" in certain industries)
- Downloadable audio MP3 (interview, audio narration, etc.)
- Video training / presentation

It really doesn't matter what the free offer is; so long as that it promises a benefit that your visitor and prospect would be interested in receiving.

Something that they would gladly give your their contact information to get access to.

I personally believe that the easiest thing to create and offer is a downloadable PDF, which could be a longer article, short report, or some type of tips, checklist, or cheat sheet.

Another best practice for maximizing the amount of people who download your free offer is to have a graphic image that represents the free offer. Even if it's a digital download, you'll want to show a picture of your free offer. This would be a cover with title for a free report, maybe a CD or iPod with title of your audio interview, or a screenshot of your video.

Ways to Build Your List

Now that you know how to build your list let's discuss some of the best places and ways for you to let people know about your free offer; specifically where on your website you can build your list.

Website Opt-In Forms

The most common way to let people know about your free offer and build your list is with an opt-in form on your website. You've probably seen these plenty of times on other websites you've visited. Usually on the sidebar of a website or at the end of an article you'll see a space where you can enter your name and email address to subscribe.

You absolutely want to be sure you have your opt-in form for your free offer (along with the graphic representation of it) on the Home page of your website; as that will be the most visited page of your website. As a best practice, you should include your opt-in form / free offer on every regular page (more on that in a bit) of your website, including your About page, Contact page, Blog post pages, etc.

You can create opt-in forms for your website using a simple tool called an email auto responder, which we'll talk about later in this chapter.

Pop-Ups

The pop-up has to be, hands down, one of the most controversial online marketing methods ever devised. There's no doubt that you encounter pop-ups on a daily basis as you surf the Internet from site to site. If so many people openly admit their disdain of pop-ups why do so many websites and online marketer's use? Simple: they work extremely well.

The reality is, if you use them properly, a pop-up can actually add value to and enhance the experience of your website visitor's. While many online marketer's will use pop-ups to show unrelated ads that are irrelevant to their website (hence why so many people dislike them); you can effectively use pop-ups to show free offers that are highly valuable, relevant, and interesting to your prospects and website visitors and build your list.

The way this works is fairly straightforward. When a visitor comes to your website, you would have your website pop-up a separate window that would show a picture of your free offer, include a headline that stated the benefit of the free offer, and finally an opt-in form for them to enter their contact information.

As mentioned above, you'll already have your free opt-in offer on all of the pages of your website; but if you utilize a pop-up on your website you'll find that it can result in a significant increase in the amount of people who subscribe to your email list.

Most email auto responder services will allow you to create pop-up forms for your website.

Squeeze Pages

Without question, a squeeze page is one of the most powerful ways for you to build your list. In fact it's so powerful, that if I could only have ONE page on my website, I would make that page a squeeze page for the sole purpose of building my list.

For those of you who may not know, let's cover exactly what a squeeze page is.

Simply put, a squeeze page is single page on your website whose sole purpose is to capture the information of the person visiting that page. Generally speaking, this page will fall outside the normal template or design of your website.

A regular page on your website, such as the Home page or About page, will usually have a navigation bar at the top with links to your other pages, a sidebar on the side with advertising links, banner ads, links to other pages and websites; and probably even more links at the bottom of your website to various pages and resources.

In other words, there are A LOT of options and things for someone to do other than entering their information into the opt-in form to get your free offer.

With a squeeze page, we basically take away all of the navigation links, the sidebar, links to other pages, and all of the other distractions so that there is a singular focus on the free offer and opt-in. Because of this singular focus the conversion rate on a squeeze page is significantly higher than a regular opt-in form, and in many cases higher than a pop-up as well.

Creating a squeeze page is pretty straightforward; all you really need is:

- An attention getting / benefit driven headline
- A picture of the free offer / graphical representation
- Some bullet points that further describe additional benefits of the free offer
- An opt-in form to capture their name and email address

That's all there is to it!

Generally speaking, whenever you are doing any type of paid advertising (offline or online) using the direct response two-step method you already learned about; you'll want to send that traffic directly to your squeeze page instead of your Home page or any other regular page. This will give you the highest amount of opt-ins and give you the highest amount of ROI on any advertising dollars spent through your follow-up marketing efforts.

I'll discuss some of the tools and services you can use to create squeeze pages later in this chapter.

In-Content Call-to-Action to Your Squeeze Page

The final method of building your list I want to mention is to include calls-to-action within the content of your own website letting people know about your free offer and directing them to your squeeze page.

You can include this call-to-action in various places on your website and really anywhere that it would make sense to offer. For instance, if you have a blog post that happens to be covering information that is similar or related to your free offer; you might let them know that you have a free special report that goes into more detail or covers another aspect of the information you just covered with a link to the squeeze page where they can opt-in to get the report.

Another option is that you can include a call-to-action in your author by-line at the end of each of your blog posts that quickly lets them know the benefit of your free offer along with a link to the squeeze page.

With many of my coaching and consulting clients, I advise them to include a short "welcome letter" on the Home page of their website that includes, among other things, a call-to-action for new visitors to get their free offer with a link to the squeeze page.

You can probably place several website pages or blog posts on your website where it would not only make sense, but benefit the visitor. You simply let them know about the additional free resource you have available along with a link to your squeeze page where they can get it.

Tools of the List Building Trade

Up to this point we've covered the importance and benefits of list building. I've also shared some of the best ways you can go about building your list on your website using opt-in forms, pop-ups, squeeze pages, and in-content calls-to-action.

The final things I need to share with you are the actual tools and technology you can use to implement these list building strategies into your online presence.

List Building and Email Marketing Tools

When it comes to actually capturing the information of the people visiting your website and following up with email marketing, I highly recommend you use what's referred to as a "third party auto responder service."

In a nutshell, an auto responder is a tool that you will use to create the forms you put on your website, store the contacts in a database, handles your email marketing and (my favorite part) automate most of the process.

There are several reasons you should use an auto responder service to handle your list building and email marketing rather than doing yourself, including:

Email Deliverability—Arguably the most important reason to use an email auto responder service. The main job of an email auto responder service provider is to maintain relationships with Internet Service Providers to ensure that your emails actually get delivered. If your emails are getting blocked and filtered to the SPAM filters there's no point in sending them at all. This will surely happen if you attempt to send mass commercial messages on your own.

Legal Compliance—As you may be aware, there are very strict laws in place to protect consumers against SPAM and unsolicited commercial emails. Email auto responders help you stay in compliance by automating opt-out requests.

Marketing Automation—My favorite part of using an auto responder is the ability to pre-program automated messages to go out in a specific sequence and have each message automatically personalized with the recipient's name or other personal information I may have collected.

There are several companies that offer third party auto responder services either as a standalone service or part of an entire Shopping Cart or CRM solution. Though everyone's situation is unique, for the most part if you're just getting started or doing up to $250,000 to $500,000 in sales you can probably get by using a standalone service; anything beyond that you may need to look into a more comprehensive solution such as a Shopping Cart or CRM as I already mentioned.

At the time of this writing I recommend iContact® (icontact.com), or GetResponse® (getresponse.com) as a standalone auto responder service and 1ShoppingCart™ (1shoppingcart.com) or InfusionSoft® (infusionsoft.com) if you're looking for a Shopping Cart / CRM solution.

Squeeze Page Tools

When it comes to creating squeeze pages for list building purposes, it's never been easier and more available to people who are more interested in business and marketing and less interested in the technology behind it.

I remember the days of having to hand code web pages using HTML and spending several hours on end learning how to piece everything together. Luckily those days are over and there is special software, tools, and technology dedicated to making creating things like squeeze pages relatively easy.

If you're using the WordPress® platform there are WordPress® plugins that you can install that will turn any of your pages from a "regular" page to a squeeze page. One of my favorite plugins that can create squeeze pages (along with sales pages and other advanced features) is Optimize Press (optimizepress.com).

If you're not using the WordPress platform, you may want to consider a squeeze page creation and hosting service like LeadPages (leadpages.net).

A final option would be to hire a web designer / programmer to create a customized squeeze page for you.

Usually the next question I get after covering List Building is, "Now that I have a list, what do I do with it?" That's a great question and leads us into the final piece of the formula, how to increase sales with follow-up email marketing.

Increasing Sales—The Fortune is in the Email Follow-up

You may already be familiar with the phrase, "the fortune is in the follow-up." With the relatively low cost of email marketing and the huge responses you can get from email relative to other channels, you may find that a good email marketing follow-up campaign can be the highest ROI marketing activity you could do in your business.

You may have also heard that a prospect needs to see your message and offer anywhere from 8 to 12 times or more before they make a decision to buy. All things equal, the more times a prospect sees your message and offer the more likely they will convert into a sale.

When it comes to online marketing, I truly believe that email marketing is the most cost effective and highest ROI way to bring prospects back to your website and convert them into sales.

With that said, there is a right way and wrong way to do follow-up email marketing. It's not just about constantly sending "pitches" and sales offers. That is a surefire way to actually turn potential customers away and get them to unsubscribe from your list.

As mentioned in our discussion about list building, email marketing offers an opportunity for you to get your subscribers to "know, like, and trust" you, build your authority and prove your expertise, and develop a relationship that not only leads to one sale, but multiple and repeat sales.

When it comes to email marketing and follow-up and maximizing your results, there are two things I recommend you do. First I recommend that you put all of your new subscribers into an email "welcome series." Second I recommend is that you maintain regular email communication with your email list. Let's explore each of these in more detail.

Your Email Welcome Series

If you remember, one of the benefits of using an email auto responder is the ability to preprogram and automate a sequence of emails. Using this ability to put all of your new subscribers through a "welcome series" is one of the most powerful uses of that feature.

At the risk of sounding redundant, an email "welcome series" is simply a series of emails that you send to all of your new subscribers to welcome them to your email list. Not only that, but a good welcome series:

- Delivers the free offer that you promised which establishes and builds trust
- Provides additional free content that build good will and establishes your expertise and authority in the market
- Brings the prospect back to your offer multiples times to convert new prospects into customers

Your welcome series should be a series of 3 to 5 emails that you deliver over the course of one to two weeks (depending on the frequency you choose) that accomplishes all of the above goals.

To make this task easy for you, John and I have put together an agreement where you can get free access to my **"5 Part Email Follow-up 'Welcome Series' Templates"** which are five fill-in-the-blank email templates that you can use to create an automated "welcome series" that will help you build trust, increase your expert status, and convert your new prospects into sales.

Usually these templates are only available to my one-on-one coaching clients or those who see me speak at live events and trainings; but John and I have decided to make them available to you as a bonus for purchasing this book. You can get free instant access to the templates at: www.wealthwithoutstocks.com and visit the Million Dollar Internet Marketing page.

I've had many coaching and consulting clients use these templates successfully across many different industries and encourage you to implement them into your online marketing strategy.

Now that we've covered the "welcome series" let's talk about what happens after that.

Regular Email Communication

When it comes to internet marketing, the biggest mistake I see people making is that they are not building their email list, or building it as effectively as they could be. After reading this chapter, hopefully you won't fall into that category.

For those who are building their list, the second most common mistake I see is that they are not emailing their list enough. I've been on countless coaching and consulting calls where the website owner reports to me that it's been several months since they've sent an email and that they don't have any type of "regular" email schedule.

An important thing that you should remember is that, all things equal, the more emails you send, the more money you will make. That's such an important point that I will repeat it in bold: **the more emails you send, the more money you will make.**

Does that mean that you should send multiple emails a day with nothing but sales pitches? Of course not, and we've talked about the importance of using emails not just as a sales tool; but a vehicle to provide value, build trust, and develop relationships.

But the reason why I stress this point is that the majority of people that I work with are not using email to its true potential to maximize the amount of sales and revenues that it can generate.

My advice is that you should email your list at least one time a week.

If one time a week seems like a lot, I would point out that the most successful companies in the world email their lists multiple times per week, and in some cases multiple times per day!

However for most people just getting started with an online presence, sending multiple emails a week (or day) just isn't possible; but managing a weekly email schedule is feasible.

When I say you should email your list one time per week, that doesn't necessarily mean that your email has to be a full blown newsletter or article; it can simply be a quick update, shared resource, or piece of information that your audience would find interesting or useful.

If you're already committed to doing a weekly blog post; that can be the reason you are sending an email; to let them know about your most blog post, guest post, video, etc.

Really, any reason is a good reason to email your list; the key is that you just want to do it regularly and consistently so that you always have top-of-mind awareness with your prospects and customers.

An easy way to double the amount of email you send to two emails a week is to simply send your regular email on one day of the week, and send a simple "reminder" email or "did you miss this" email as a follow-up.

As long as the emails that you are sending are useful and relevant to your audience, your emails will be viewed as welcome content that adds value to your prospects and customers.

Feel free to use the email templates I've given you from the "welcome series" to repurpose for your weekly emails.

Conclusion

You've gotten this far, congratulations!

What I've give you here is the exact 3-Step Formula I give to all of my coaching and consulting clients who are looking to start, build, or grow a business using the internet. It really just boils down to three things: get traffic to your website, build your email list, follow-up and make sales.

I've shared with you my favorite methods of driving free traffic to your website, my best strategies for building your list, and the actual email follow-up templates that I give to my private clients to follow-up and generate sales online.

I hope you have found this information useful and valuable and more importantly hope you take action and apply these strategies into your online marketing efforts.

I'd like nothing more to hear your success story.

I want to thank Brian for putting together such a comprehensive look at getting started online and maximizing the results. Many people reading this may have been "online with their business" for years but not really using the web as the massive marketing tool it has become. Many business owners have a glorified brochure as their website and that is totally missing the golden opportunity at your feet.

I would like to finish this chapter by talking about some paid online marketing sources. You could have an entire chapter just on sources for online marketing so always check our site for new tools and the latest when it comes to online marketing. However, no online marketing chapter would be complete without talking about the power of Facebook®. Most people only know Facebook® as a way to post updates and pictures about their lives to friends and families. This is certainly one way to use Facebook® but if you're an existing business owner or would like to launch your own business after reading this book, pay close attention.

You can and should use Facebook® as the great business tool it has become. First, start a business page on Facebook®, which is free of charge.

Most people think that if they launch this page and tell their friends and family about the page everyone will "like" the page and they will get business. This may be true in the initial stages of your launch but you will need to do more than just post stuff on your business page to actually make great money from your efforts.

You have the ability to have your marketing message appear in people's newsfeed on their Facebook® page that don't even know who you are or what you do for a living. When you click on "create ads" you will be asked what you're trying to accomplish with your advertisement. Once you choose from a menu of about 10 options you will be walked through a very simple ad set up screen. Pay special attention to your targeted market because you can market to many different broad categories and sub-categories. Remember when I asked you to determine who your ideal prospect would be for your business in the marketing chapter? It's during times like these when that knowledge and information about your business is critical. Let me walk you through an example from one of my own businesses.

As you probably already know, I have a complete turnkey real estate investment solution for people that would like to own income properties. I have that solution set up in my hometown of Metro Detroit but also have experienced associates in many other areas of the country who can help investors in those locales. Let's assume I wanted to attract investors to buy properties using my services in Metro Detroit. Who is my perfect potential customer and what traits do they possess?

1) They have a desire to diversify their income and asset base and are interested in learning more about real estate.

2) They have money to invest (you don't need any money to invest in many kinds of real estate because I started with no money, no job, no credit, and no experience and bought many millions of dollars of real estate from that position) because these deals will be all cash transactions.

3) They have either owned investment real estate in the past or have expressed an interest in learning more about the business.

4) They are living in a very expensive marketplace where they can't make income from a single family home (for example, San Francisco, Los Angeles, Seattle, New York, Vancouver and about a dozen other major cities in the United States and Canada).

5) They have over $300,000 in an IRA or elsewhere and are interested in making nontraditional investments

6) They are actual doers and not just thinkers.

In this scenario, this would be the perfect prospect I am trying to reach. I can dictate many of those perfect traits to the Facebook® ads page. This will assure that my message will go to the people who are most likely to be looking for a solution my company offers.

You will also be setting a budget for your campaign. If I was prepared to spend $2,000 for the month, I could tell the ads page that was my budget and I wanted it spread out over the next 30 days. By the way, you can spend much less and much more as your budget and profit margins allow. You can also run a campaign over a few days instead of over a whole month. This is a very flexible and targeted marketing platform. If you remember from above, our main goal is to obtain a legitimate name and email address from the prospect so we can continue to market to and educate them over the coming weeks, months, and even years. This will equate to eventual sales and referrals from a certain number of our new prospects.

With this in mind, it's every bit as important (and maybe more) as picking the right target market as to where you're going to send them and what you are going to offer them when they click through your advertisement. I would highly recommend that you first take the time to build your offer, landing page, and the start of a follow up campaign. This sounds harder than it actually is in practice. Let's go back to my real estate business and get some ideas flowing.

A) I could offer prospects a free chapter of one of my books (you could write a report or chapter in about an hour).

B) I could offer the prospect a free video and training that is recorded.

C) I could offer to walk that prospect with live video through actual houses and neighborhoods and can use my Smartphone to shoot the video (because of the physical nature of real estate and this prospect not being from Detroit, this could have a huge draw).

D) I could send them to a webinar about investing in Metro Detroit Real Estate.

E) And any other thing that would have highly perceived value or "hook" but that is free to deliver via the web for my company.

So I would make this simple:

1) Set up (or pay someone on Elance.com to do it for you which goes for all techie stuff) a simple landing page that will tell them the benefits they're going to receive from my free offer. Put big arrows that point to a sign in box use one of Brian's sources above and ask the prospect to put in their first name and email. Make it clear in your writing on the landing page that your report, link, etc. will be emailed immediately to their email address which will force them to give you their correct email address as opposed to a phony one to get your information.

2) Now create your advertisement on Facebook® described above and decide when you want it to launch. IMPORTANT: YOUR LANDING PAGE DESCRIBED ABOVE IS DIFFFERENT THAN YOUR FACEBOOK® BUSINESS PAGE. IF YOUR GOAL IS TO GENERATE AN EMAIL OF A PROSPECT YOUR BUSINESS PAGE WON'T ACCOMPLISH THAT GOAL! WHAT YOU SHOULD DO IS CREATE A LINK AND ANOTHER TAG LINE INSIDE OF YOUR FACEBOOK® PAGE THAT MAKES THAT OFFFER AND DIRECTS THEM TO YOUR OUTSIDE LANDING PAGE SO THEY CAN LEAVE AN EMAIL AND HOPEFULLY LIKE YOUR PAGE AS WELL. OBTAINING "LIKES' ON YOUR BUSINESS PAGE IS FINE BUT NOT NEARLY AS IMPORTANT AS OBTAINING A DIRECT WAY TO COMMUNICATE WITH THAT PROSPECT.

3) Implement Brian's and my free gift to you (sound familiar) above called the 5 Part Email Follow-up 'Welcome Series' Template. Simply fill in the blanks and you now have a simple follow up system that you can expand on as you see fit. Always take the time to educate your prospect in those emails and offer them the ability transact business with them as they become ready for your service

You now know more about marketing successfully on Facebook® than 99% of the public does and you can learn more. Pay attention to some of the ads you see on Facebook® and actually become a prospect for the ones that interest you so you can see what other companies are doing to attract prospects and drive sales. Only pay attention to the ones that implement the direct response two-step marketing blueprint we have laid out extensively here in this chapter and the offline marketing chapter.

This same basic program can be implemented on Twitter® but I would stick with Facebook® to get up and running before branching out to other platforms. There are millions of prospects already waiting for you on Facebook®.

Driving more paid traffic to your marketing system

You should also look into testing your results with Google Ad Words®. Google®, as you probably already know, is the king of online searching. Millions of people "Google®" what they're looking for every day and you can pay to have them find your ad first (or close to first). This is done by using the same structure we talked about before with a landing page, offer, and follow up. You can find out how much it will cost you "per click" for certain key words and phrases.

You might decide you can invest $20.00 per day to market on Google® and you find out after researching tag words that you will spend about 10 cents per click. This would mean you could get 200 clicks per day to your landing page from people who are searching for what you have to offer (or something similar).

Using any website analytics you can see how many unique visitors you have to your landing page per day. If it's 200 unique visitors that day and

10 of them requested your free information, that means you spent $2.00 for every email address you received. Now you can scale that model up or down from there and begin your follow up campaign as already described.

There is of course more you can learn about Facebook® and Google® marketing, but now you have enough to go out and start building your online infrastructure and then start driving traffic to your spider web. You also can take a look at my "spider web" at www.theperpetualwealthsystem.com and click on Video of the Week. Then scroll down just a bit and see all the free reports and offers I have for people who land on that page. Just to give you an idea of a little more advanced spider web with multiple offers.

To help you out I have created a list of the recommended companies on my website, www.wealthwithoutstocks.com under the Resources tab.

"Looks like it might be a busy week. They made the coffee with Red Bull instead of water!"

Chapter 11

Million Dollar Media Strategies

You have probably figured out by now that this entire book is not just about investing money and growing the investment. We certainly cover many ways to achieve that goal but I also wanted to include information that can help you create wealth through your own business efforts. Have you ever heard of a company started on a shoestring that just a few years later was worth millions of dollars? Maybe you have heard the stories of selling out companies for tens or hundreds of millions of dollars? Have you ever thought that you would like to have that kind of luck?

The good news is that luck has very little to do with such success stories. There is always the helping hand of being in the right place at the right time, but again that's a very small part of most success stories. Take a business such as heating and cooling for just one example. Is this business in the right place at the right time? No, it just needs weather to succeed or fail. Perform a quick Google® search, put in your city and heating and cooling, and see what companies pop up in your search. If they're showing up in your search, there is a good bet they are a very successful heating and cooling company and have figured out how to have potential customers easily find them online. This in itself does not guarantee success but it's a solid point in their favor. I have met several millionaires who owned heating and cooling companies and I have also met people in the exact same industry that lived pay check to pay check and struggled financially.

If you analyze what the successful company does vs. the company that just squeaks by, there are usually several big differences in those two companies. The biggest will always be the attitude of the person or teams running the companies. The successful company has leaders who believe they will dominate the market in heating and cooling and are determined to gain a large market share for their business. I bring up a seemingly humdrum heating and cooling company to dispel the myth that creating a successful company is all about timing. Timing certainly has its place but so do marketing, branding, hard work, developing a unique selling proposition, and promotion.

We have an entire chapter in this book about successfully marketing any venture you choose to take on and use to create wealth. This chapter is all about using the media to help build your wealth. Someone that owns a traditional or what some might consider a "humdrum" business might not think the media would like to cover them or their business. They would be wrong!

The fact is the media is so massive and needs so much material that anyone reading this chapter has the ability to become famous in their niche to create wealth. When I started my wealth strategy company Perpetual Wealth Systems, I had no media exposure in my past. I had extensive marketing and speaking experience and had made some important contacts, but had never been covered with one bit of media exposure.

I always wondered how people in my industry or similar industries appeared in stories in newspapers, magazine articles, radio interviews, television interviews, internet articles and other media outlets. I knew that appearing in such things gave you instant credentials and a leg up on much of your competition. I knew I had to figure out how to crack this code for my business and brand so I went and hired some help.

In just a few years and as of this writing I have been featured in numerous newspaper articles, magazine articles, radio shows, online articles, and other media outlets. What a difference a few years has made and I am just scratching the surface and will use the media to help me build my business for the rest of my life. More importantly you can do the exact same thing that thousands of experts and I have done in our careers. If you Google® my name, which is not an uncommon name, you will find me on page one number one. If you Google® "Perpetual Wealth Systems" you will find that I dominate the first 5 pages of Google® with almost nobody else being allowed into those pages. This publicity has brought me many clients and much income. If you had done this same exercise just a few short years ago, you would not have been able to find me or my brand online unless it was many pages deep. These high rankings bring me a steady supply of leads of people who want the knowledge I have and may choose to do business with me in the future. Just for one quick example, I did an interview for a financial podcast and from that interview I received several leads and one immediate client that was worth over $25,000 of gross income to my business! This interview didn't cost me a dime and was only 30 minutes in length. You can do the exact same thing and achieve even stronger results.

The marketing chapter is critical to any business but when combined with media strategies you can explode any business (assuming that business has good products and services) in a very short period of time. I love marketing but I love the media even more! When I market, I usually have to invest money into the marketing campaign. This is, of course, a great investment and if done properly and depending on what you are selling, you could make loads of money. You can sometimes make 10 and 20 to 1 income ratios for marketing dollars spent. However, you will require the seed capital to get that profit machine up and running. Using the media to grow your business can even be more powerful.

If you were to take out a half page add in your local, large newspaper how much might that cost your business? This will depend on the circulation and the publication, but several thousand dollars would be the starting point, going up to six figures for the right publication. If you spent $10,000 on that ad but it was a clunker of an ad that just didn't pull much if any business or leads, your $10,000 would be gone forever. If this ad was successful and brought you a 4 to 1 return and you created $40,000 in sales, in most industries this would be considered a wildly successful ad campaign and would probably be repeated until it did not pull good numbers anymore. Your advertisement would be easily identifiable as an ad by the general public and be treated the way ads always are—with skepticism.

What if you could be written up in a story about how to save $2,000 next winter on your utility bills that was given the half page right next to your paid advertisement? The cost of this half page article is zero to you and brings with it so much more than just a paid advertisement. The fact you are being written up in the paper automatically makes you more credible (whether you actually deserve the credibility or not) than your competition who took out the advertisement. I remember this line from one of my first marketing and media mentors and I have never forgotten it and have verified for myself its validity: "People will believe much more of what others say about you than what you say about yourself."

When you or your company appear in a story of some kind in the media this gives you a certain cache and credibility with many people in the general public. The media is given a certain trust by the general public; no matter if that's right or wrong, the fact is that it's true. As my friend and guest author Steve says, you can cash in on that trust by making yourself "mediagenic" so the press seeks you out for your opinion. Once you are written up or interviewed in the media you can then leverage that story into other media appearances. If you are written up in a magazine, you could send that article to other magazines in similar genres and suggest a different slant on the story you are sending for their review.

Once you are interviewed by a radio station, you can post that interview on your site so that other radio producers can give it a quick listen to hear that you are an entertaining guest. This will also lead to bigger radio shows and television appearances in the future. The more media that you do, the more opportunities come your way from the media. I call it the "media snowball" and you should take time to start the snowball rolling!

There is also a whole other topic we need to cover and that is turning your experience and expertise into an income stream for your business. This will be done by teaching what you know to others who would like to have your knowledge. This is one of the most underused revenue streams in any successful business. If you have achieved expert status in any endeavor then there are always people that would like to have you teaching them what you know so they can become an expert as well. This is called the information business and people and businesses of every imaginable kind are taking part in this almost secretive business.

I am joined in this chapter by my friend Steve who is an expert in both the worlds of receiving free media attention and selling information as a business. Steve has a company and that's his full-time business: educating business and thought leaders on these points. I have been a student of his for several years and am very excited he agreed to help me bring this powerful information to your business.

John, I am really excited to be a part of your book and contributing to this chapter. I don't think there is another financial book that has included these strategies as part of its content. I look forward to sharing my years of knowledge about obtaining media with your readers and students.

In all my years showing people how to become famous and grow their businesses it never ceases to amaze me what kind of businesses can use my information to gain media attention. I have a client who has a septic tank business who we were able to help become famous in his hometown and make more profits for his business. The outsider might say, "How in the heck does a guy who inspects and installs septic tanks get the news media to do stories on him?"

The answer is that term you used earlier in the chapter. He made himself "Mediagenic" by letting the media know how he could help the community and give the news a great story at the same time. He decided to tell the media the importance of regular inspection and maintenance of people's septic tanks and septic fields. He created 7 facts about your septic tank that you don't know and could cost you thousands of dollars.

In his particular community many people have septic tanks so he was able to create a high degree of interest in these 7 facts. He put together a very simple "pitch" and began sending that pitch out to different media outlets and before long he was featured on the local television channel and other publications. He has since become the go to guy for the media when it comes to these kinds of stories and his business has flourished. Surely, if a man who deals in septic tanks can get written up in the media and interviewed on television you can as well!

What will be critical to make this happen for you is first you need to identify a problem or a trend going on in your industry. Then offer some good information on how to solve that problem or take advantage of the trend. We all take for granted how much each of us knows about a particular topic. Almost all of us are experts at something but most of us either don't believe we are experts or don't know how to take advantage of our expert status.

Let the media know about these problems or trends and suggest they do a show or article on this situation with you as the expert. Many people may be experts in your industry as well but almost none of them will actually deploy a plan to notify the media. The media have an insatiable appetite for stories and this has never been truer than in this "information age" of the 21st century. I heard a statistic several years ago that I'm sure is outdated by now. That statistic was that the media in all its formats needs 10,000 guests per day to satisfy its needs. Now with the even bigger explosion of online outlets that figure I am sure has increased dramatically. You can help fill that need.

Develop what is known in the industry as a "one sheet" that quickly tells the media the problem or trend, and then tell them why you are the expert that can help with this problem or trend and then suggest several show or article ideas. If you would like an example of a one sheet just go to www.wealthwithoutstocks.com and download John's one sheet from his Press page. Use that as a template for your own one sheet. Then get the one sheet out to the media via email and fax (whichever they choose) and then be consistent in your efforts. Be patient and be persistent and don't take any rejection personally because it's never personal. Also, just because they don't do the story today doesn't mean they might not do it next month etc.

When possible make your pitches tie into something relevant in the news over the last days or weeks. You may also try tying into the particular time of the year. Set up a calendar and try to tie in as much as possible every month when you pitch. Depending on the type of media you are pitching, there will always be some type of lead time. Radio and television will normally be weeks while daily newspapers might only be a week or two. Monthly publications might be planning 4 to 6 months out so remember that when trying to tie into a specific time of year.

The sky is the limit but you might try contacting smaller local papers, stations, and other outlets when you're first getting started with your media campaign. This is especially true if you have a local business or a good local story. Once you have any kind of media coverage put it up on your website and add to it continually. This will not only give credibility to your business and brand but it will also give other media a place to see that you have been interviewed by other outlets.

John was sharing with us earlier in the chapter another huge benefit that is very important in this day and age and that is Google® rankings along with other search engines. He told us that in less than two years he went from many pages down in rankings to page one and number one for his name. John Jamieson is not that uncommon of a name and even though he has the domain of www.johnjamieson.com he still was not very high in search engines.

He also shared that his company and brand of "The Perpetual Wealth System" went from nowhere to dominating the first 4 or 5 pages on Google®. He has almost every spot on the first 5 pages of Google® and here is how it happened for his name and business.

1) He started doing radio shows and advertising in the Radio and TV interview report (RTIR) and receiving calls from radio shows and some podcasts from all over the country. My company started and still runs RTIR and we helped John design his advertisements. He did every interview from 3 minutes to 1 hour in length. When he was done with the show the interview would be posted on the stations website and he made sure he was sent the MP3 of the broadcast. He would add them on his site as well. No matter how big the station was, all these links created synergy for his name and brand and sky-rocketed him in the search rankings very quickly. He also made sure

to send out thank you notes to the host and producers of the show to start to build a long-term relationship. One never knows where that host or producer will go in their career so make a great first impression and stay in touch

2) John also started submitting articles to nicely sized personal finance websites every few weeks. One site was AOL's personal finance website called Daily Finance, www.dailyfinance.com, where he was a consistent contributor for almost a year. This created dozens of articles on that site covering many of his core topics. Many of those articles ended up as full chapters in this book. Because that site has so many eyeballs coming to it along with links, and likes from places like Facebook® and Twitter® the site has very high credentials in the search engine rankings. This catapulted him in the search rankings. He also posts in similar sites whenever he can. John says he can also attribute much direct business from those interviews and articles. Start a blog and start writing even if you don't think anyone is reading your blog. Submit articles to bigger sites as well and watch the snowball effect this will have in your online presence. One last point about posting on the internet to keep in mind. John shared with me that he no longer submits new articles to Daily Finance but the articles he wrote are all still out there generating views, reads, eyeballs, and leads back to his website. This is what he likes to call "Perpetual Media."

The fact is that many consumers are using a search engine to research people and businesses even before they reach out to inquire about doing business with the company. Looking strong on search engines gives credibility to media and prospects alike so start to write on your topic and keep writing and doing interviews. With this writing strategy you can take a startup or newer business and give it instant credibility combined with an online presence. Also, start to post short training videos in your articles when possible and also by themselves on YouTube®.

I have another client who started out as a local veterinarian and started using these strategies and now has been on some of the biggest talk shows in the country. These are shows like "Regis and Kelly" (now "Live with Kelly and Michael"), and "The Today Show," just to name a few. He has graduated to a favorite guest of these shows and has been on many of them several times.

You must remember an important point about persistence when pitching the media. Once you have been featured in some kind of media and done well for that media outlet, many will invite you back several times. You might talk about slightly different things but you can have several placements on the same show or other media outlet. I know John has been on the same radio show 4 times! There also will be times that you pitch the same place a dozen times with no luck and then BANG! You're invited to be featured. When you think you're wasting your time and thinking about giving up, keep this in mind. Your next door is ready to open just keep pushing on them with all your power. Be patient and persistent.

The veterinarian's business has exploded and he has added other revenue streams to his existing practice that he couldn't have even dreamed of in the early days. He has deals with different pet providers for product endorsements along with other ventures. This all started from a seemingly ordinary veterinary practice and has turned into a national brand and big business. Media can make your brand and business get to another level and with almost no cost to you, unlike traditional advertising and marketing.

When you write your one sheet and other ads, remember that the headline is critical to getting your foot in the door. You will also need a good "hook" to get the readers interest. Some of John's hooks are:

a) Why investing in a 401k is a sucker's bet and what to do instead
b) How to create wealth without stocks or mutual funds
c) Why buying your car might be a better place to put your money than a 401k

When you're writing your own headline, think of the National Enquirer® and their headlines as a rough guide. Headlines should really grab the reader and get them to want and need more information after the headline.

Another way to get attention is to be contrary to traditional thinking.

Do you have a valid point or case to challenge long held beliefs? This book is a great example of a hook and being contrarian to most traditional thoughts when it comes to the stock market and mutual funds. How could you take a different position in your own business that flies in the face of the conventional norm?

1) 401ks are for suckers
2) Never lose a dime in the next stock market crash
3) Use equity you don't even have yet

Some other great hooks, titles, or going against the norm that have been wildly successful;

1) Chicken Soup for the Soul®
2) What the rich teach their kids about money that we don't
3) Wealth Without Risk
4) Start Late, Finish Rich™
5) The 4-Hour Workweek

Take the time to write some good headlines and hooks and start pitching the media! Here is a game plan that will help you get started

A) Develop your one sheet.
B) Create a one page press release using the examples here and provided for you online.
C) Do some research and find out who is the correct person to pitch at local newspapers, magazines, radio shows, and television stations. These will usually be the producer or assistant producer for bigger shows and publications. Also find out how they preferred to be contacted.
D) Design a calendar for pitches and a battle plan of action.
E) Start to pitch all your local sources.
F) Plan on pitching them every 4 to 8 weeks or whenever you have a great tie into existing stories they're already running.
G) Stay open-minded about changing a headline or a hook if it isn't pulling any response.

H) Be prepared in advance that most people will not even reply to your pitch due to the massive numbers of pitches they receive.

I) When you do get coverage of any kind start your media page and leverage that initial success.

J) Use the same source as Chicken Soup for the Soul® and the Rich Dad® authors by investing in advertisements in RTIR, the main source many radio producers use to book guests. This is also the publication John used to get his media blitz launched.

K) Be patient and be persistent. Most people quit if they don't get immediate gratification. Be the champion that moves forward and makes things happen for their business.

Get more education on this topic and surround yourself with like-minded people. I, of course, sell products and services that might be a perfect fit for you and your training. There is no way to not make this sound self-serving but facts are facts. My company helped launch many brands but two of the most famous are Chicken Soup for the Soul® and Rich Dad Poor Dad®. We can help you attract media just like we helped Jack Canfield, Mark Victor Hansen, and Robert Kiyosaki. We even helped a relative new comer who was a college dropout named John Jamieson launch his brand and now his second book! If there's hope for him, there's hope for everyone!

Become a highly paid expert and consultant

Most people don't think anyone would pay them for their expertise. Now I am not talking about charging for services that you actually perform in your business. It's a given that if you're running a business and you are operating with the public there will be fees and profit margins generated on products or services. I am really talking about training others to be experts in your field. There is a multibillion dollar world of consulting, coaching, and training in almost every conceivable area of expertise.

We often refer to it as the expert industry and it can be an entirely new income stream for your business and it might even become your main business. Here are some examples of how you might train others and get paid for your knowledge.

One way that most people think of is to write a book but understand there is not much money in the book unless you sell tens of thousands of copies or more. This is entirely possible but should be a bonus and not the main goal of your book. There should be several other goals before worrying about making money with your book sales. The book should help you build a database of potential prospects that might do business on a higher level with you either now or in the future. The wealth for me in this book and for John is not in book sales even if he sells a million copies of the book. Both John and I know that a certain percentage of readers will do business with our companies on some level which will mean way more income and wealth than whatever we might make selling books. We will also be able to help change lives for generations to come if we get even a small percentage of readers as clients. This gets us excited and keeps us both on purpose every day. Another goal could be to offer higher priced items after they like your book. It is impossible to put everything you know into a book without making it thousands of pages and who wants to read that many pages?

This is why you might have other products such as:

1) Home study course with audios and or videos with a manual or two
2) Group coaching on an ongoing basis to really work with people at a deeper level which should produce better and faster results
3) Online trainings that could be offered for sale for a one shot training or an ongoing series of trainings. This allows you to teach more and therefore ask more for the investment in the program. This also allows you to do your trainings for very little cost and have attendees from all over the world. Make sure you record all these trainings and repurpose them into other products and promotional items
4) Live seminars and multi-day retreats
5) Joint ventures with other similar or even totally different businesses that have great databases for what you offer and maybe vice versa.

6) Smaller group coaching or maybe even one on one coaching with you or your right hand people. The more of your time and greater access the client gets the more the investment from the client

This list looks daunting and there are also more ways but don't get intimidated. Start small and test the water. Maybe offer a group coaching teleconference call to train your heart out on one topic. Better yet, ask people that would be your target group of prospects what they would need more information on to be better at their jobs or business. If you get a similar theme going after you asked 10 people that might be the subject to focus your initial trainings, books, or pamphlets.

John was telling me this list looked almost undoable and an incredible amount of work but he was able to have most of these done within 1 to 2 years. From his book he spent some time and recorded a home study course on private banking. He then offered a live event and recorded the event both with audios and videos. Now he has several of the items above and can use them or sell them whenever he feels the time is right.

Once you have these products they can be sold and generate revenue for years to come and could become a huge income generator for your business. Start with one and graduate from there to another product. The easiest way to create a great high end product is to have a seminar and record the event. You make money on the seminar and you get a product you can resell for many years. It might require some updating from time to time but most of its core message could be relevant for decades!

I would encourage you to start to present and work on your presentation skills. I know that thought might scare some of the readers but overcome those fears. Start small and even give your own presentations first with nobody listening. Make enough PowerPoint slides to give a 15 minute presentation and then deliver it as if people were watching you live. You can also record these into a telephone and record the audio. Do whatever is needed to become confident at presenting. You don't have to be the best speaker in the world but you will need to present with confidence. The best way to be confident is to know your material up one side and down the other side.

Technology has changed every industry and the expert industry is no different. The internet gives you the ability to generate leads and deliver paid content all over the globe or in your own backyard. There are many tools you will add to your arsenal as you grow but for starters you need the ability to give and record trainings. There are several players in this niche and the most widely used is Go to Meeting® and Go to Webinar®. Simply Google® them and look up current price points. The bill will be dependent on how many people can join you on your webinars. You can get an entry level account for around $30.00 per month. This gives you the ability to train and record your trainings all over the world. I know John uses his webinar service every week to train and go over numbers with potential clients all over the country from his own office, from his house, or from his patio.

You will also want an email database service. There are a wide range of choices but start your search at IContact® or Constant Contact®. This will allow you a place to store and email addresses and mail information out to your list. These services are very inexpensive when you're starting out. This is very low cost and a high impact way to keep in touch with customers and potential customers. Building your email list will also make your business more valuable because of your ability to instantly get a message and offer to a list of people who have opted into your site. If you were looking to invest in an existing business would you rather buy one with 100,000 opt in subscribers or the business with 100? John also has included great chapters on marketing and internet marketing as part of this book. Make sure you spend time reading and rereading that section.

John was sharing with me that he and two partners made over $50,000 in sales from their very first webinar by utilizing a list of just over 8,000 subscribers. Within the next 6 months they sold over $250,000 of products and services to that same list. If it costs you a few dollars a month to employ a good email hosting and blasting service it is money well spent.

Levels of Access

You have the ability to build your expert business based on your lifestyle and goals. Do you want to work with small groups personally? Then you might offer a 6 week course of once a week using live webinars with you providing killer content that can help people obtain their goals. This might be priced at $1,500 for example and maybe limited to 20 attendees so you can have time to work with them personally on these calls and answer all their questions. These people might have come into your email and lead funnel from a book, article, pamphlet, or any other of two dozen ways. Maybe this will be the first purchase for them of any of your products. You will also have people who bought a less expensive program from you which could have been CDs and manuals, online content, or even a book. They liked your information so much they want more access to you personally and now are willing to pay more money for that access and service.

Many people will also offer a more expensive course with maybe only 5 people at $9,995 or a one on one with you alone for $30,000 or more. The next level is to have someone fly to your city or somewhere else you both agree to for a 3 or 4 day mentorship and be with you personally for 8 hours per day. These can cost from $30,000 to $50,000 depending on the niche the expert is in and how well known the expert is in the field.

Start off small and own the fact that you are an expert. You don't have to be the top #1 expert to sell your services. You certainly need to be a legitimate expert but many of you have sets of skills you have never even thought of hiring out or turning into their own separate business. We help people identify those talents and bring them to market to produce revenue.

One point that will be critical to your success is to own your expertise and be proud of the knowledge it probably took you years to learn. Don't be concerned about what others may think about your new venture. Negative forces will always try to drag you down because you are making them feel uncomfortable by stretching your comfort zone. Ask yourself this simple question: Could spending time with me and obtaining my training on my area of expertise greatly benefit the student? Could they make more money in their business, get in much better shape, have better relationships, be more confident in their own lives? Could your knowledge bring joy, peace, and happiness to your students? If the answer is yes than you owe it to them and yourself to get the knowledge in their hands as soon as possible. If people make some kind of an investment with you they are showing they are serious about improving one or several areas of their lives. Don't be afraid to charge for your expertise and know you are worth every penny and more.

In closing, I would just like to say that the seemingly secretive world of gaining media attention need not be secretive to you or something of which to be afraid. Use the strategies in this book to get your expert machine up and running. My company has given some really nice free downloads that will help you get started on your path to gaining free media exposure and building your expert status. Just visit www.wealthwithoutstocks.com for your free downloads.

You will also have the ability to work with us at a higher level by contacting us through that site.

"In dog years, you would only be 7 years old.
Chase some squirrels and see if it
makes you feel younger."

Chapter 12

Create Your Own Private Pension

HOW TO TURN YOUR IRA AND 401k OR ANY OTHER MONEY INTO A LIFETIME PAYCHECK MACHINE

This is a great chapter for those of you who have some money you would like to set and forget. This is not for everyone, but no matter what your circumstances now and how active of an investor you are, there will always be money you should set aside and let grow without your intervention. This is the place to grow both IRA and non-qualified monies on a set it and forget it basis.

As you can tell from the second chapter and my first book, I love properly designed whole life insurance for all the reasons already discussed. There is no other account that offers all those many benefits in one spot. However, a life insurance policy does have one drawback.

You can't use your current IRA and other qualified accounts to fund it without incurring a penalty and heavy tax burden. How much tax and penalty will depend on how much you withdraw, your tax bracket, and from what kind of qualified plan you withdraw your money to fund the policy.

However, as a general rule, you will pay any tax due from a traditional qualified plan (remember the money put inside your 401k or traditional IRA has not been taxed yet and neither have any profits you have realized) plus a 10% penalty if you take the money out before you are 59 and ½ years old. This is one of the major reasons we teach people other things to do with their money that don't have all the taxes and penalties. It should be noted that if your money is in a Roth style account, your money has already been taxed so you will just be liable for the penalty for accessing the money before the above mentioned age, which at this time is 10%.

When it comes to use and control of your money, the qualified plan is not a good fit at all and unfortunately most people don't realize this until they go to access the funds. Many people get discouraged because they have just read this book and love what they read and are ready to fund their policy and start to use volume and velocity in their favor. Then they realize that most of their net worth is inside of these qualified plans; especially if they have been working for a good number of years.

That is the weak link of the program as I have had many people share with me after they find out these disappointing facts. Most clients make the decision to stop funding their 401(k)s and other qualified plans and use that money to start funding a life insurance policy, but that still usually leaves significant monies in that account. If they start withdrawing the money prematurely, they get killed in taxes and penalties.

So what to do?

If you want to be an active investor and invest in nontraditional assets mentioned in this book, make sure you read the chapter on self-directed IRAs. These can be tremendous accounts to grow wealth at an accelerated rate. You can also rollover IRA money income and penalty free. Remember however, that these investments will require some of your time and much of your knowledge to be successful. How about if you just want to take some funds whether they are qualified funds (IRA, old 401 or 403) or non-qualified funds, and just make sure they are protected from loss and have an opportunity for nice growth? You also want to accomplish this with no time invested on your side or specialized knowledge.

Well, there is another very powerful product that offers many benefits that might be perfect for your qualified funds. This product CAN be used with qualified funds with zero taxes or penalty from the government for rolling over your funds. Once the funds are rolled over you will experience all of these benefits:

1) A signing bonus of up to 5 to 10% of your first year contribution into the account. This is paid on the rolled over monies and on any new funds placed into the account during the first 12 months after setting up the account (bonus amounts vary by state so contact us to see about yours).

2) Principal put into the account is always guaranteed. So once the account is set up and the stock market tanks 20%, your capital is guaranteed not to lose money from that serious downturn.

3) Potential for strong cash growth and the power of tax-deferred compounding.

4) Your account will follow the market indexes (markets you select that could be stock, bond, and even commodities indexes) up but never participate when they're down.

5) The ability to purchase a lifetime income rider that will guarantee your retirement income accumulation will go up every year even when the markets are down (amount of guaranteed increase is dependent on company and product selected but is us usually between 4% and 7% compounded growth). Some products offer guarantees of a smaller amount but then will also credit you more if the indexes go up giving you a chance at substantial income growth with no downside market risk

6) Many of these riders also offer other benefits such as increased income if you ever need home health care or long-term care (certain factors must be met to qualify).

7) Some companies and products also offer the ability to purchase a rider that will guarantee you leave more money behind when you die for your family or favorite charity.

8) When you purchase a lifetime income rider, many times you can designate the rider as a joint income rider so you will be guaranteed by the company that the retirement income will be paid for life no

matter how long either you or your spouse survive. Try that with mutual funds!

9) If you or your spouse live to be a ripe old age and the cash is used up, you still get your guaranteed income stream for both of your lives. If you both die younger and there is money left in the account, your estate gets the money.

10) Many products offer the ability to access a certain portion of the account value every year without penalty giving you a certain amount of liquidity in emergency situations. Of course the more capital you take out before you activate your income stream, the less guaranteed income you can take out for life.

This kind of product takes a humdrum, risky 401k and IRA and turns it into a guaranteed pay check machine for life regardless of how the markets perform. This takes out any downside risk of losing valuable capital before or during retirement. So, in effect, you have set up your own private pension that is even better than a company sponsored pension from the old days.

The traditional pension had many drawbacks such as:

1) It took many years until you could participate in the pension (be vested) and if you left the company you usually received nothing from the pension fund.

2) You very rarely could actually get access to the cash inside the pension fund. In other words, you could get the income but if you had an emergency and wanted the actual cash you had put into the fund, it was usually not accessible. If it was accessible you had to jump through the hoops chosen by your employer and the pension fund servicer.

3) When you and your spouse passed away, if there was any of the money left inside the fund your family did not receive it but rather you donated it to the fund for other pensioners.

When I hear people long for the old days of guaranteed income every month, such as with a traditional pension, they usually only remember the good and not the bad points of those programs. Your private pension has all of the good points with none of the above bad points. Yes John, but as with the rest of the book this just sounds too good to be true! Yes it does but it is completely true and is done every day across this country by people who are not totally dependent on the stock market.

There are also a couple downsides of this program you need to be aware of to determine if this is the right program for some of or all of your retirement account money. My dad told me many times, "Son, it ain't all beer and skittles." This program is not a place to put monies that you will want access to for the next 5 to 10 years (or prior to 59½) due to early withdrawal penalties.

When you fund one of these accounts and receive all the benefits above from the insurance company, that makes all the guarantees, they need certain assurances from you as well. So for them to make enough money on your money to give you all these benefits, they need to be reasonably sure they will actually get to use the cash. Depending on the product you choose there is almost always a penalty (usually between 6 and 12% of your initial purchase amount) for an early surrender of your contract. For example, if you put in or roll over $150,000 into this account and then decide you need all $150,000 out next year, then you can expect to give back any signing bonus you might have received, plus a penalty (exact percentage varies on company, product, and state). To avoid this is very simple and there is no need to experience these penalties. The first way is to know what the penalties are in advance and be reasonably certain you will not need access to this money during the heavy penalty years. The penalty is usually on a sliding scale with its highest penalty in the first few years and the penalty declines over 10 years (depending on the actual carrier, product you choose to purchase, and the state in which you live).

Another way to avoid needing these funds is to make sure you have other sources of liquid savings that you can tap into first before ever needing to tap your private pension. That liquidity or plain old cash can be placed in several different areas. This is one of the many reasons to set up the whole life policy we discussed earlier. One of those many benefits is liquidity which means easy access to your cash. These life policies can be a winning strategy for all kinds of income levels and are not just for the wealthy and high income earners. I have clients who fund these polices with just several hundred dollars per month. I have other clients who are funding these polices with large sums of money and then I have everything in between. So if you can fund $5,000 or $10,000 into a policy every year, start with those amounts. It would also be prudent not to withdrawal all of your cash value just because you have that option. Leave a rainy day fund in there for easy fast access to cash. This all ties back to the 11 pillars of wealth (7 gears of riches and 4 wealth drains)

You can also have savings, checking, and money market funds as a place for emergency liquid cash. By using this system you will have plenty of other places to draw cash from if needed. This way you can let the money inside the pension grow and compound so when you are ready to start drawing income from that private pension you will draw out the maximum possible. Even if you do need to tap that pension for extra funds, many good products will allow you to withdraw cash from the account before you start your normal income draw. This can be done without penalty. In the example above in which you put $150,000 into your private pension, you could draw out $15,000 that year without penalty but remember, that is less money that will grow and your eventual income draw will be reduced. If you withdraw more than the 10%, any amount above the 10% will be subject to penalties, if you are during the penalty phase of the contract. However it is nice to know that if you need emergency cash you can access some of it without penalty.

The product we use to accomplish all these great benefits is called a Fixed Indexed Annuity. This chapter is not designed to be a full training on all annuities and how they work. For some comparison, let's talk about the basic structure and operation of each kind of annuity. "Before we do that, John, lets first understand what an annuity is," I can hear you saying. So let's do that first.

An annuity is a financial structure administered by insurance carriers that is designed to take lump sums of money and structure a payout of that money over time. The structure of the payments and length of the payments is up to the purchaser and the provider at purchase. There are two basic types of annuities: immediate and deferred.

If you purchase an immediate annuity, the annuity payouts (annuitization) begin shortly after you fund the annuity. With a deferred annuity, you are deferring those payments for the future; in essence you are accumulating money first with the annuity payouts to be opted at a later date. For example, you plan to retire in 10 years and want to "annuitize" or begin the payouts at that time; this is deferring the payments.

There are 3 basic sub-types of annuities that you can purchase:

1) Fixed Annuity
2) Variable Annuity
3) Fixed Indexed Annuity

A fixed annuity is just as it sounds. You receive a fixed return during the time before you start taking income from the annuity with principal guarantees. It might look like this, for an example:

You purchase a fixed annuity that pays you 2.5% guaranteed for 10 years. Then you start to withdraw an income from the original amount that purchased the annuity and any growth over that 10 year period. Using our example above of the $100,000 let's see what it might look like over that 10 year period.

You purchase a $100,000 fixed annuity paying 2.5% that will start to pay you an income stream after a 10 year growth period. At the end of 10 years there is a little over $128,000 inside that annuity minus fees (more about fees to come). You now decide to "annuitize" the $128,000 over the next 20 years to provide a monthly income. So you would collect $500 to $1,000 every month for the next 20 years to help with retirement income. The amount you get paid will depend greatly on the terms of the annuity and the insurance carrier you choose.

You might also have chosen a lifetime income clause or rider when you purchased the annuity. This option will come with a fee, but instead of collecting monies for 20 years the insurance company guarantees that you will collect the income for the rest of your life even if you live to be over 100.

This income rider can usually be added on as a "joint income" rider, which means you and your spouse will receive income for both of your lifetimes. This rider can usually be purchased on any of the three types of annuities.

Now let's talk about a variable annuity, but not for long as I do not like them at all for retirement purposes. This is an annuity contract whose performance "varies" based on the ups and downs of the market (usually stock market). This type of contract shifts the burden of performance away from the carrier to the purchaser of the annuity contract. Your money will be invested in "sub accounts" and will perform based on market performance. This is very much like a mutual fund inside of the annuity contract. So during up times your money grows. During down times your money goes down in sympathy with the underlying sub-accounts. One of the reasons we like annuities and life policies is for the guarantees. Many of these guarantees are not present in the variable annuity. You can have a guarantee of lifetime income but that income will be based off of market performance.

Many people think I am anti-stock market and that is simply not true. I am "anti" all of your retirement money being in the stock market. The stock market can be a great place to have some huge successes but you must be ready for the hard downs as well. If you want to pursue those homeruns with some of your money I say do it but why do it inside of a variable annuity contract?

Well, there are two selling points that agents will often bring up in favor of the variable annuity. First of all an annuity by its structure offers tax-deferred growth even if the money that purchased it was not from a qualified account. So it has the same tax status as a traditional IRA or 401K as far as tax deferral of growth. Please check with a qualified tax attorney or C.P.A. for your tax questions. If you put $100,000 into that variable annuity and it grows by 30% over a 5 year period, that $30,000 was not taxable during that time but rather is taxable when you start drawing out income. So if you have big gains inside of the annuity, they will be tax deferred. That will be one sales pitch to have you buy a variable annuity. The tax deferral on annuities is not just for the variable annuity. These apply to fixed products and fixed indexed products as well. However, you must also remember that an annuity is taxed very much like a traditional IRA and has similar penalties from Uncle Sam if you access the money before you're 59 and ½ years of age. If you access funds before that time you will be subject to IRS penalties for early withdrawal from the account.

The second selling point is the ability to eventually get lifetime income when you elect to draw out the money as income. Your actual cash will go up and down during the annuity growth period just as a mutual fund but when you do take out income draws you can set it up where they are guaranteed for your lifetime and your spouse's lifetime. The actual amount you can take is anybody's guess because remember your growth or principal is usually not guaranteed with this kind of product.

Along with the lack of guarantees and certainty, there is another problem that goes along with a variable annuity more than a fixed or fixed indexed annuity. The fees in these types of annuities are generally quite high. Why could they be higher than the other two kinds of annuities? The subaccounts are invested and managed very actively and that creates more fees to be charged. Now let's make peace with fees and talk about them openly.

Everything you do in life, you can rest assured that someone somewhere is making money on that activity in almost every walk of life. In other words, people don't work at a profession for free. They might donate their time and money to worthy causes but when they work they get paid. The financial and insurance industry is no different. I have never had any problem with people making money on what I do but I always want to know what kind of value do I get in exchange for my fees? Remember it's not about what you make but what you keep.

As an example, assume you invest $100,000 somewhere and your investment doubled over five years to $200,000. Assume that as part of that investment package the person who set up that investment gets 10% of the profits. So your net would be a $90,000 profit on your $100,000, which is a very high, solid return. Without fail when you tell your brother or neighbor about your great deal they will focus on the high fee you paid rather than the value you received for the fee.

Your brother and neighbor invested the same $100,000 into a low fee program and lost 10% over 5 years or $10,000. They only have to pay a 2% fee and they are pleased as punch and think you are a sucker for paying that high fee. I think you are wise investor who looks at both sides of the coin and not just the side that says "fees." In reality, who paid the much higher "fee" on their transactions?

Back to your variable annuity example as it pertains to fees. I have seen variable annuity fees as high as 6% and see them routinely at 3 to 4%. This is based on the amount in the annuity. Is that too high? I would submit that you don't have enough information to make that determination. What do you get for your fees? If my money went backwards by 10% and they charged me 4 to 6% for "management," then I would think I got hosed. In fact if my money went backwards by 10% and they only charged me 2% I am not sure what my value was for that transaction? If my money went forward, my eventual retirement income went forward and does so every year then I would say a reasonable fee is in order for those guarantees. I think I received plenty of value for my fee.

Also if my income was guaranteed for both me and my spouse's life and it was guaranteed not to go down or maybe even up with the cost of inflation, then a reasonable fee is well spent. The point of this entire exercise is to start to think like a businessperson. The consumer focuses only on the expense and rarely the value. They also have a fixation on what other people must be making instead of focusing on how to make more them and their family. The successful businessperson wants to know how much my fees are, but focuses much more on what those fees buy for them and their family.

As a general rule, 1 to 2.5% is considered by most (and by me) to be a reasonable fee if there are plenty of valuable things put into the agreement. To pay more than that and sometimes double or triple that amount for not much value seems disproportionate. If you currently have an annuity but would like it analyzed to see what type of annuity it is and what type of fees you are actually paying, contact our office today for a free analysis of your existing annuity.

If you have a solid product with reasonable fees we will tell you that with no obligation on your part. If you have a lousy program and would rather have a more solid product with more stability and benefits there is good news. There is 1035 exchange provision that allows you to do a tax-deferred exchange from one annuity product or life insurance policy to another like kind account. It may be possible to exchange your current annuity to one that offers more value and maybe fewer fees as well. You can tax-free exchange one annuity for another but that does not mean there might not be costs. Remember those early termination or withdrawal fees? They might apply from your current carrier. We will be able to tell you what the penalties are if you exchange from one carrier to another. There usually will be no fees from Uncle Sam if we do a 1035 annuity exchange but let's find out what the fees are from your carrier. Please keep in mind that we have had many clients who in fact had a penalty for early termination of the contract but were able offset that expense by the signing bonus received from their new annuity. Contact us to let us know you would like to have this free analysis done at info@theperpetualwealthsystem.com and we will send you over some simple documents to get the ball rolling.

The last type of annuity is called a Fixed Indexed Annuity and that is the program we use most often at our company. We believe it offers tremendous upside potential with no risk of market loss. I believe it's the best of both worlds from the fixed and the variable programs. When you open up a properly designed fixed indexed annuity (FIA) you will receive many benefits and usually for reasonable fees. To begin with your purchase price of the annuity and future contributions are principal guaranteed no matter what transpires in the markets you will be tracking. What is tracking you say? Your cash will track different indexes (what indexes depends on the ones that are offered by the annuity carrier and within a certain product you are considering) such as the S&P 500 and other available indexes.

During years when your tracked index is up in price your money will grow in sympathy. During the years the indexes are down your money does not go down but rather stays the same. So your cash did not grow that year but you also did not participate in any market loss. When the market falls off by 30% and takes 6 years to recover to its prior level your money did not go backwards but broke even in the down years but will still participate in the up years.

Some years your compound interest curve will slow (if there is no growth than there is no compounding that year) but will pick right up from its previous amount when the markets go up. That offers a huge benefit for safety and yet offers strong potential growth. Your money will always grow faster when it has no down years and only moves forward. Using this type of structure you get to play the market in this form but have none of the downside market risks of actually playing the market.

This program becomes even more attractive when a lifetime income rider is purchased when you take out the annuity contract. These income riders have fees and will vary, as does everything, based on carrier and the product that you purchase. A common income rider fee could be .50% to 1.25% of your account balance. What is a lifetime income rider? Let's talk about a common structure for these with some real life examples.

You decide you like the idea of setting up stability and lifetime future income for you and your spouse and your purchase a $200,000 annuity from a reputable insurance carrier. You like the benefits of a fixed indexed annuity combined with a lifetime income rider. Let's assume you do receive a signing bonus on this particular program of 10%. That bonus is not on all products and is not available at that amount in all states, but in this example it is offered in your state at 10%.

So your cash starts out at $220,000 and then tracks an index or indexes depending on the product. There are several ways to track an index of which we are not going to discuss here but the most common is annual point to point and the anniversary date is when the account is open, not the calendar year. Your cash will now perform based on the discussion above in tracking its index or indexes but will be protected from downside losses.

Your income rider is not actual cash that is growing but rather a mathematical calculation that will eventually be used to determine your lifetime annual income. In our example, that figure also gets a 10% bonus and starts out at $220,000. Now that $220,000 will grow differently than your actual cash. The most common income riders give you a set rate at which the original $220,000 will compound EVERY YEAR even in the down index years. In our example let's say it is 6% and you intend to start drawing income from this account in 10 years when you are 60 years old. After 10 years, your original $200,000 has grown to just under $364,000 on your income rider. The insurance company has agreed to pay you 5.5% for the rest of yours and your spouse's life but this percentage will depend on your ages. (This assumes we took out a joint income rider and not a single life rider) You will get annual income for two lifetimes in this example of just under $22,000, which is usually paid monthly. So with only $200,000 up front and given some time to compound with no risk of market loss, that $200,000 is guaranteed to pay you and our spouse $22,000 a year ($1,833.33 per month) for life. Again check with your tax professional as to the amount that might be taxable.

Is that enough to retire on? I would say not but it's a good start when combined with your social security. The income rider guarantees this amount to be paid regardless of how old you both become and even if the cash is eventually spent through distribution. That's why it's called a lifetime income rider and you pay a rider fee mentioned above for that stability and guarantee. In this structure your income rider will almost always outperform your actual cash because there will be years your cash stays even for the year because of a down market. Your income rider is guaranteed to go up every year by the 6% mentioned above regardless of market performance.

If you could give that $200,000 15 years to compound your income rider would have $490,000 inside of it and be eligible for 6% every year which equals almost $29,500 per year ($2,454 monthly). If you could fund either more up front and/or also fund the pension with more money over those 10 to 15 years you are really setting yourself up for a retirement time filled with options because you know the income will be there every month.

Be aware that this is just one example of a scenario. Another possible option is an income rider with lower guarantees on the growth but it will also give you the index growth in up years. So your guarantee might only be 4% but you will also get the index growth. Will this be better than the

6% guaranteed? Nobody knows but if you want the chance at a larger income rider over time it might be a better fit for you.

I just want to talk about one more downside of most fixed indexed annuities and that is the capped cash growth that many offer. This means that in up years of your index, your rate of return will be limited or capped. In a typical example, your index or indexes (you might follow several indexes and not just one) goes up 6% but your cash might be capped at 3.75%. Next year the indexes go up at 10% your cash goes up at 3.75%. The third year the indexes drop by 12%, your cash slides over with no losses and maintains its previous two year gains. Meanwhile, during this time your income rider was still compounding at 6%. Always remember your cash growth and income rider will act differently. In this scenario your cash is protected but is also limited as to how much it grows. When you are buying an annuity you are not concerned as much about cash growth as you are with lifetime income. You will have other parts of your plan that are focused on growth but this is more of an income play and stability of income for life.

There are also products through which your cash growth is uncapped. That example might look like: 6% index growth your first year, your cash would go up by 4.5%. The next year the index goes up by 10% and your cash would go up 8.5%. The next year the indexes drop by 12%, your cash will slide over and keep its original value plus the two years of gains. The difference in what you're credited and how the indexes actually perform is called the spread. The insurance carrier always maintains a spread, which is part of the cost of the product. In my opinion, that is a very well spent fee and gives tremendous value. In many products you only pay that spread during up years and not in the down years. In that scenario you make money, pay the spread. If you don't make money, no spread paid.

To watch a free video on this entire concept please visit www.perpetual-pensions.com and simply register and view a 25 minute presentation that will further enforce what you have already learned in this chapter. Always feel free to contact us for a no obligation, personalized analysis or wealth strategy session.

One last bonus (and I think it is a biggie) of this kind of product is that within your lifetime income rider, they can also be set up to provide home health care or long-term care coverage for the annuity owner. This is on a state-by-state basis and some states will not allow this kind of set up but if yours does, it could be a great extra feature that helps you sleep well at night.

If you ever can't perform several of your basic daily tasks without assistance and if you qualify under the rider's conditions (again, they all vary by carrier and product) you would get to draw double the amount of income for up to 5 years to help cover your extra home health care or long-term care needs. If this is offered in the product you are looking at its cost is normally already built inside of the lifetime annual income rider fee. So if that rider fee is 1%, many times that includes that extra benefit. Again, it seems like a well-constructed lifetime income rider offers many benefits for a reasonable fee.

I know you have figured out by now that my company does offer these programs and we have access to many of the top programs offered throughout the entire country. If you would like a free analysis or simply to ask some questions, please reach out to us and we would be glad to help. Before you do however, watch the video at www.perpetualpensions.com which explains a real life product that we have access to and most other financial advisors don't have the same access.

A properly designed, fixed indexed annuity that is set up to be used as your own private pension is one of the most powerful retirement vehicles that you can bring to bear in your wealth creation and preservation efforts. As with any financial program they are not for everyone and benefits and fees vary greatly. Take advantage of the free educational materials we offer and the ability to speak with us about your own personal situation.

"The word 'invoice' is too soft and friendly.
We need a new word that means 'pay up or die'."

Chapter 13

Mobile Home Park Investing

When I originally heard the term mobile home parks and investing I almost immediately discounted the notion because of wrongly held preconceived notions. This would be similar to you discounting owning income properties in Metro Detroit because you might not have all the facts before reading this book. Mobile home park investing can be a great way to produce very low maintenance cash flow. How can mobile home parks be low maintenance? The reason is because most of the time, you're going to own the land the mobile homes are parked on and not the actual mobile homes or "trailers" that sit on the land.

You could also own the mobile home itself but it's not necessary to make this a very profitable arena. My guest writers for this chapter have owned the actual mobile homes as well as the parks. You can own them both if you wish. I also have another friend from out west who bought and sold mobile homes to get started in the real estate business and then moved up to parks, single families, and apartment buildings.

Your responsibility as the owner of this land is to maintain the grounds in a nice, neat, orderly fashion. It's not your job in most instances to make repairs on existing mobile homes in the park. This very fact alone will cut down on any maintenance costs and headaches dramatically. Anytime you can turn the management of all the mechanics of a home or mobile home to the tenant or mobile home owner you have set yourself up for much fewer headaches and less work. One of the most important parts of any income property regardless of the actual property is the management.

I decided to bring two of my friends and business associates in on this chapter because much of their business is devoted to working in the investing of mobile home parks. They are based in the Columbia, South Carolina area, where they do real estate investing and brokerage. You will have the opportunity to work with their team if you choose to invest in properties (of all sorts, not just mobile home parks) in their popular growing area. Their names are Christy and Noah and they are experts in this type of investing.

I won't bore you with too many details about them or their operation because we have that available for you online at our website—you will just have to put in this code, **WWS15**, to download their complete information. They are recognized national experts on this topic and have spoken to thousands of investors of all skill levels across North America.

I have given them some topics I would like discussed so they will provide some great information in this chapter. This is part of our commitment to you our reader and potential customer or client to bring you the top experts in their fields. As with many chapters in this book, we cannot cover an exhaustive list of details due to space restraints, but we have given you the ability to obtain more free information online. With that being said, let's bring in Christy for a chat and hear her story.

Hi John, I want to thank you for asking us to participate in this fantastic project of Wealth Without Stocks or Mutual Funds. We're tickled pink to be involved and look forward to helping as many people as possible acquire cash flowing hard assets outside of the stock market!

Oftentimes I have people asking me how I got started investing in mobile homes. I was raised on a farm all my life. As I grew older, I paid attention to how hard my father worked to maintain the farm. He spent countless hours every day maintaining that farm for his family. From sun up to sun down he took care of over 200 cattle, bailed hay all day, and tended to our dairy farm as well. He worked and saved, worked and saved. I saw how hard my father worked and knew that there must be a better way. My family and friends are what's most important to me. I love my father and am very grateful for him providing for us. However, I didn't want my husband and me always at work or worrying about money. I wanted us to enjoy watching our children grow and experience life to its fullest.

When I graduated college, I began investing in real estate. If you had told me 10 years ago that I would own mobile home parks and be sharing this investment strategy with others, I would have told you that you were crazy! Like many mobile home investors, investing in single-family homes was my starting point. I started educating myself on how to create cash flow through rental properties. The concept of cash flow made a lot of sense to me. Renter pays the rent, which pays my expenses, what's left over I get to keep. I saw myself increasing my cash flow one house at a time, the problem was, that it was taking a long time. I was going into debt, buying a $150,000 house and making $300 a month (so long as it was rented). I began investing in Florida during 2006 when the market was peaking in prices; houses were getting bought up left and right. If I wanted to get into the real estate game I'd have to pay top dollar. I flipped a few houses along the way, making some quick cash, but my goal was (and always has been) passive income. With increasing housing prices and the bubble about to burst this concept seemed less and less attainable.

I didn't give up on real estate; I kept searching for the right investment and the right concept. That's when I discovered mobile home investing. One day I came home with a book called *Deals on Wheels*. This book was written by a man who would later become my mentor, Lonnie. I brought the book to my business partner to get her opinion on it and she was also excited at the prospects. We contacted Lonnie and he invited us to a mastermind meeting in a small town in Alabama. This training was at the perfect time in our lives but also in terms of market conditions and opportunities.

We realized that not only were mobile homes cheaper to invest in but the cash-on-cash return was amazing! I kept asking myself, why haven't I ever heard of this type of investment before? Does this mean there is very little competition? The real estate market in most of the country was red hot from 2006-2009. This was the perfect alternative to fighting it out with all the other investors and home owners who were driving up real estate values at that time. A small single family house in Florida was selling for $200,000 so how could we keep investing at these prices and get passive income? Those numbers didn't make sense or fit into my overall passive cash flow goal. I discovered that I could purchase a mobile home for under $15,000 and the cash flow would be much higher which means a much greater cash-on-cash return. It seemed too good to be true.

Shortly after our mastermind meeting in Alabama, tragedy struck close to my heart. One day while shopping at the mall with my business partner, Erica, she received a phone call from her father. Her mother was in the hospital. In less than 48 hours from that phone call Erica had lost her mother. She went in for a common surgery but there were complications and with a blink of an eye her whole world was turned upside down. As I mentioned earlier, friends and family are what matter most in my life and I felt as though being there for Erica and her father was the most important thing I could do at the time.

We ended up taking our business to South Carolina where Erica's family had lived. Even though we had just caught the mobile home "bug" from what we had learned at our recent mastermind meeting with our mentor Lonnie, we were still focused on the single-family housing market. Over time our mobile home sizzle turned to fizzle. Who knows why we waited so long, perhaps I really needed to see mobile homes making money to be a true believer. I had always invested in single-family houses probably because I had always lived in and near single family houses. Honestly, I had never even been in a mobile home. That was about to change and in a big way! I didn't know it at the time but I soon found out that South Carolina was considered one of the mobile home capitals of the United States!

In 2008 and 2009 many banks were in a financial crisis. Banks were changing the entire game when it came to their lending criteria making it much more difficult to borrow money. Many banks were in serious financial trouble and some were even going out of business! That meant that we could no longer go to a bank to finance our real estate investments. We had to get creative with our financing.

There are a lot of different ways to fund a real estate deal without going to the bank and many of which are extremely common with mobile home investors. I would recommend paying close attention to all the creative financing John discusses in other real estate chapters of *Wealth Without Stocks or Mutual Funds®*. Many of these strategies can be applied to the world of mobile homes very easily.

I began to pay close attention and looking in the local papers and trade publications for potential motivated sellers, particularly ones that offered seller-financing deals. When a seller offered their own financing that meant I didn't have to go to the bank for a loan. While reading one of those trade publications I met an elderly gentleman from Gaston, SC that was offering owner financing on land. He would offer owner financing for people to be able to buy his homes and move them on to his park. We talked for a bit and he told me of his story of how he built his wealth. Just like me, he had started out investing in single-family houses and went on to fall in love with mobile home investing.

What I realized by talking with this gentlemen, is that my assumption of the mobile home marketplace was true. There was very little competition! It wasn't that people weren't living in mobile homes, or that people weren't becoming wealthy by owning them, but it was just that the concept of mobile home investing was being overlooked. It was this lack of competition that gave me a much greater opportunity for becoming successful. Where else, besides a mobile home, can a new family, a transitioning couple, or a person on a fixed income get a home for $500/month? Nowhere! Doesn't it seem counter intuitive that the least expensive way to live in a home can, in fact, be an extremely profitable business?

Although we didn't do any business together, our brief conversation reignited both my partner's and my spirit to invest in mobile homes. This time we were determined that we would not let our fire fizzle!

We immediately began marketing for mobile home deals. Along with marketing for mobile home deals, we were also marketing for mobile home tenants. Our goal was to immediately have a tenant lined up for any of our new mobile home ventures. We started with the local trader paper; it was stacked full of potential leads for both parks and homes. What we found was that a lot of the older investors used the local paper as a means to sell versus the internet. Next we decided to market with bandit signs on the side of the road . . . you know that signs you pass every day and think does anyone really call these? Yes, they do! We also went into the mom and pop mobile home supply store and put the word out. These guys know every park owner in the county and everything going on with them and their current situation. They referred us to mobile home movers who have tons of leads on homes. Next we decided to go online and search keywords on craigslist such as "trailers" or "mobile homes." That brought us to other reference websites such as www.loopnet.com and www.mobilehomeparkstore.com. We found there were deals everywhere! John offers a free download of 100 ways to find real estate deals in an earlier chapter. Make sure you download that resource and then remember all (or most) of those sources on that list are valid sources for mobile home park deals as well.

Our phone was ringing off the hook! What I came to realize was that affordable housing was in high demand! Buying and selling mobile homes was servicing a niche that was and is very much under serviced. There was and continues to be a gap between the number of people that needed affordable housing and the number of these people that had good enough credit to get a loan or even qualify for an apartment. Solving this problem has resulted in a lot of cash flow for us and can for you as well!

Through our investing experiences we have come to find that there are several ways to profit from mobile homes investing. Each mobile home and Mobile Home Park that we have made money on has had its own story. Each deal has been different. There is no cookie-cutter deal.

It's important that as an investor you are aware of the different ways to profit. After a few single mobile home units, perhaps then it would be a good time to start looking at buying your own mobile home park. The important thing is to get educated and we hope this book will be your first step!

Each way to profit leads to what we call, an "exit strategy." An exit strategy is what your plan is to do with the property once you take control. It's important to always have your exit strategy in mind when getting into a deal. Let's start by looking at the 5 basic opportunities on how to make money with mobile homes. They are as follows:

Opportunity# 1—Owning the Mobile Homes but Not the Mobile Home Park

Opportunity #2—Owning the Park AND the Mobile Homes

Opportunity #3—Owning the Park and Not the Mobile Homes

Opportunity #4—Owning the Park and Seller Financing or Offering a Lease Option to Buy the Homes

Opportunity #5—Selling Out the Mobile Home Park for a Higher and Better Use

#1: Making Money by owning the Mobile Homes but Not the Mobile Home Park

You can make money by moving used mobile homes into existing parks. You own the mobile home and someone else owns the mobile home park. You pay lot rent to the park owner for keeping your mobile home in their mobile home park. You then rent out or seller-finance the mobile home for profit.

It's important to know that some mobile home parks do not let investors rent out mobile homes in their park. They would prefer that only owner occupants live in the park. In this case you would simply seller-finance the mobile home to a new owner, instead of renting to a tenant. The buyer would give you a down payment and you would receive monthly cash flow in the form of a note payment. The new owner of the mobile home would be responsible for the lot rent.

Example: You have found a small mobile home park with a vacant lot in the park or a vacant mobile home for sale. After speaking with the owner of the mobile home park, you have agreed to pay $200 lot rent per month to keep your mobile home in his park. Now that you have a lot in a nice park picked out, you then go and find a good used mobile home. After you pay to have the mobile home moved and settled into the new lot your acquisition costs and fees to move the mobile home come out to be $5,000. You decide to rent the mobile home for $550 per month. Your rent of $550 minus $200 lot rent would result in a positive cash flow of $350 per month ($4,200 annually) on your $5,000 investment! This is an 84% cash-on-cash return and you were able to do it with a very low investment, which automatically means very low risk!

Advantages: Less Risk, Great Cash Flow, if anything breaks within the park, like a water line, road, or if the septic gets clogged, it is the owner of the mobile home park's responsibility to repair.

Disadvantages: If the mobile home park charges a high lot rent, it could eat into your cash flow.

#2: Owning the Park and the Mobile Homes

When you own both the mobile home park and the mobile homes in the park, it creates a scenario for the highest amount of cash flow. When you control the park you control how much lot rent gets charged and increases. You will want to charge a rent to yourself even if you own the mobile homes. One day you might want to sell the mobile home park so it should have its own income stream and leases in place. This keeps the operation separate and each aspect of the investment must stand on its own merit.

Example: You own a small mobile home park free and clear and all the mobile homes in the park. Let's say there are 30 mobile homes in your park. If you rent each mobile home at $550 a month and all 30 mobile homes are rented, your cash flow from both operations would be $16,500 per month. We usually take 20% of rents and set that money aside for miscellaneous repairs, vacancies, insurance, and taxes. 20% of $16,500 is $3,300. So our cash flow of $16,500 minus $3,300 in expenses would result in a positive monthly cash flow of $13,200.

Advantages: Highest Cash Flow Possible.

Disadvantages: You are responsible for any repairs needed to the mobile homes. You would want to seriously consider using professional management at this stage.

Yes you could manage the park yourself but there is more than enough cash flow to pay someone else to deal with the week to week management so you can find more deals or sit on a beach in the tropics.

#3: Owning the Park and Not the Mobile Homes

With this strategy you own the mobile home park and rent the lot spaces to people looking to move their mobile home into your park.

Example: If you own a small mobile home park, you can rent your lots out to mobile home owners. If you had 30 lots fully rented and charged $200 per lot. That would be a monthly cash flow of $6,000.

Advantages: Low risk, less management

Disadvantages: Less cash flow

#4: Owning the Park and Seller Financing Homes in Your Park

With this strategy you own the mobile home park and the homes in the park. However, instead of renting the homes, you sell them. You can sell the homes outright or hold the paper and offer seller financing for the mobile home. This creates a steady amount of cash flow. You make money two ways with this strategy. Money is made on the lot rentals and secondly on the mortgage payments. It's similar to renting but if something needs to be repaired you're not responsible because you are not the owner of the mobile home.

Example: You own a mobile home park consisting of 30 lots. If all the lots are rented your cash flow from renting the lots is $6,000. If you sold all the mobile homes by offering financing on the mobile homes you would increase your cash flow. The cash flow in this example would vary because so many different variables make go each individual seller financing deal.

Advantages: Less risk and cash flow two ways.

Disadvantages: By selling the units instead of renting them you will generally experience less cash flow but also should have much less management.

#5 Rezoning the Park Either Now or Later for Higher and Better Use Adding Value

When you own the mobile home park this gives you maximum flexibility to possibly rezone this park to commercial status. Is this park close to other commercial properties? Do you see development moving closer to the park? What else might be able to be done with this property? Will you have the ability to build something else much more valuable on the land? Could you just sell out to a developer for big cash later? Could you possibly subdivide the land into residential lots giving the overall property much greater value? Could you possibly build an apartment complex on this land now or in the future? All of these would be the icing on the cake and something you might not know or be able to predict when you first buy the park. You are buying it for cash flow so make sure those numbers make sense. Then pay attention every year to what is going on around your property.

The most desirable exit strategy is going to depend on you, your goals, your situation, and how involved you want to be in your investments. It could also depend on the timeframe you want your initial investment returned and the circumstances of the buyers or tenant. No matter the chosen strategy, there is money to be made. Before you begin acquiring mobile homes always have in mind what types of exit strategies you will use to profit on your deal!

I think it's important to take a moment and reflect on not just what you want to make, but what you need to make. Before you start daydreaming about exotic vacations, your dream car, or your dream house, let's focus on what you need right now coming in to be financially independent.

Financial independence to me is having the ability to be self-sufficient financially. It's about having my assets generating income that is greater than my expenses. If you're setting out to be a multi-millionaire you must first get your monthly cash flow needs met. Once you have those cash flow needs met you can then come and go as you please without having to report to a job. You now have the ability to spend more time with family and friends and to work on your business. If these are also some of your goals than mobile home and mobile home park investing might be a perfect fit.

Take the time to list your currently monthly expenses. I meet so many people who know down to the penny what they have coming in every month. Yet, when I ask them what their current monthly expenses are they come up scratching their head with a ballpark figure. Find out exactly what you have going out with expenses. Then calculate how many mobile homes rentals producing you $300/each you need in order to cover your monthly expenses. If you need $6,000/month that could mean that with just 20 mobile homes, or 1 small mobile home park, you would obtain your goal of financial independence.

We are very excited to be a part of the Wealth Without Stocks® program and we would like to help you invest in deals similar to what we described above. We have the capability to help you with mobile home park deals in our own backyard along with other types of properties from single family homes to apartment buildings. We have given John and his team our contact information along with information about the areas we specialize so the readers of this book can reach out to us for our help.

Simply visit the website at www.wealthwithoutstock.com and find the team members tab or the mobile home park chapter synopis. Then put in this code, **WWS15**, and our information will be downloaded to you right now. We look forward to meeting you and helping you build your own passive income plan.

MORTGAGE DEPT.

"Do you still offer those mortgages with hardly
any money down, super low rates and
no payments unless you threaten me?"

Chapter 14

Mortgage and Debt Payoff in Record Time

This chapter is dedicated to creating wealth by paying off debts faster and reallocating the cash flow used to pay those debts elsewhere to create wealth. Many people in this country are finally starting to see some of their former home equity return after many years of serious equity declines. In the past, home equity loans enabled homeowners of all ages to treat their home as an automated teller machine or (ATM). Many of these people abused the ease of accessing their equity for use in paying for mostly personal expenses. Equity loans or lines of credit bought cars, boats, and paid off credit cards that were filled from buying too many depreciating assets. It seemed as if any time someone spent beyond their means they would just tap their home equity for a bailout and to finance a lifestyle they could really not afford. Why not, this is what the country is still doing as a whole.

Many people got away with this for years until either they lost their jobs, the value of their homes dropped dramatically, or both. Those situations left homeowners over financed and many lost their homes because they couldn't afford them anymore or because they decided to walk away from the home usually due to negative equity positions. These circumstances gave using home equity a bad name and also caused many banks to shy away from issuing these types of loans. Many of you might remember the days of 2007 and 2008 when lenders automatically froze access to lines of credit in an effort to get a grip on the rising tide of foreclosures.

Now that most real estate markets have stabilized, borrowers have the ability to use their equity in wealth creation efforts. The only reason you should ever tap into your home's equity is to further your wealth creation efforts. These loans are not to be used for boats, cars, vacations, and other big ticket junk that massively depreciate in value the moment you own the asset (and the debt that goes with that depreciating asset). I am not opposed to any of these luxury items and toys but you should be able to pay out of your own liquid funds and not rack up long-term debt. When possible, you should also use your properly designed life insurance policy to finance your own cars and other items. As we said before, if you borrow money from your own private bank (your life insurance policy) you should pay every dime back plus extra interest every time period! When you do this you are simply writing a check from your checking account and paying down your loan balance inside of your policy. This also creates more cash value that you can use again later as you see fit. You see, when you're the bank you are not making payments as much as you are simply transferring money from a taxable non-interest account over to a non-taxable account that is earning much better growth and dividends than your bank account. You still have access to the cash. This simple strategy seems difficult for many people to understand because we all think of making payments to outside lenders and giving up access to our cash with your payments. Time to rethink that old school mentality.

Think of home equity like any other tool. Your knowledge and use of that tool can build you a fantastic structure or that same tool can wreak havoc and destroy futures. This chapter is dedicated to showing you how to use these simple tools to grow your wealth and income.

I am going to share with you two creative and relatively safe ways to use both your home's current equity and your home's future equity to create more wealth for you and your family. Let's talk about your current equity position and let's assume you can qualify for a home equity line of credit (HELOC). The key to this strategy is to make sure you have an actual HELOC and not just a home equity loan. A HELOC will be a revolving line of credit where money can be borrowed multiple times and as you pay it back the amount available for a loan increases. You can access money multiple times per month and also make multiple payments per month if you choose. These lines of credit will always have adjustable interest rates and that is just fine because of how you will use these accounts. A home equity loan will almost always have a fixed rate and you will not be able to access funds multiple times once they are paid back to the lender. You will have a fixed payment that never goes up or down so if you make extra buy downs on your principal balance, your payment will stay the same but your loan term will pay off sooner. You want the revolving HELOC and not the fixed home equity loan.

There are several reasons you want the revolving line of credit but the main one is the ease of accessing funds multiple times and also making payments that effect your payment and not your loan term. Interest is calculated differently within each one of these loans. The fixed loan is also called an amortizing loan, much like most of your first mortgages on your properties. You are charged an interest rate at the loan closing and a payoff term. These two factors combined with your amount borrowed give you your scheduled payment for the agreed upon term. The interest on the entire loan amount is calculated and then amortized over a period of time from 3 to 30 years depending on what the loan is given to buy.

With a revolving line of credit, you are charged a monthly finance charge, which is based on your average daily balance of the loan over the previous 30 day period. You may have credit cards that will usually assess interest in the same way. This is why your interest rate might stay the same all year but the finance charge changes every month depending on what you owe on average for the month. With this type of loan you are being charged simple interest that is calculated based on your average daily balance.

Simple yet Powerful Strategy

Most of you reading this book have a checking account where much of your monthly income is deposited and sits in the account until you use the money to pay bills or to just live your life. We don't even give a second thought to this because this is how we have been conditioned for decades to use bank accounts. These days you earn 0 to almost 0% interest by keeping your money in that checking account and you will actually lose money if you get charged any kind of statement fee, convenience fee, ATM fees, or God forbid you bounce a check. Your checking account is a losing proposition but you have to deposit your income somewhere, correct?

Many sophisticated people elect to use their HELOC as a kind of checking account. They will "deposit" their monthly income into their line of credit instead of their checking account. In truth you can't actually "deposit" funds into a line of credit. You can only make payments and take loan draws out of that account. If you owed a balance of $10,000 on your line of credit and had a salary of $4,000 per month you could make a payment of $4,000 on your line of credit reducing the balance to $6,000. This would be great, except you see the obvious problem with this scenario. You will need most, if not all, of that $4,000 to pay your bills and to live on that month. You will have to take a draw against the line of credit in 2 or 3 weeks and take out $3,500 to pay your bills. So how does this benefit you and your family?

Do you remember the average daily balance we talked about when it comes to finance charges on your account? By making a payment of $4,000 on your $10,000 loan balance you have affected the average daily balance of that account by making it less than $10,000. Even if this was only true for two weeks and you had to re-borrow the money out again to pay bills you still affected that months finance charge. If the interest rate on that money is 5% you are being charged the 5% on a much smaller amount of money for a period of time. This means you will pay less interest and start to automatically pay down this loan faster. In this example, you also had $500.00 that month you did not use and you left it parked (in the form of a loan pay down) inside that line of credit. Next month you now owe $9,500 so not only will your interest be charged on $500.00 less, but you will repeat the process again next month.

You automatically and without any extra effort are paying that line of credit down at a much faster pace than normal. Let's project 6 months out and say we now owe only $5,000 down on the line of credit but we have an emergency and need some money. If this is a revolving line of credit, you can quickly borrow $5,000 to use in that emergency. You have just changed the place where that money sits from an account that does you no financial good and costs you money (your checking account) to an account that allows you to use your income to actually cancel out interest charges. Every day you can leave the balance alone on that line of credit cancels out interest. Every dime of your income is being used as efficiently as possible and not wasted inside a checking account.

Phase Two

Now that we understand how interest is charged and how we can alter our finance charges let's put that information to good use right away. Let's say for the sake of example that one of our goals is to pay off our house loan years early to be able to retire without worrying about making a mortgage payment. There are always arguments against this by people who say that your equity is dead and you are better off investing the extra you would pay on the principal balance in the stock market. It won't surprise you to know that this argument is most often made by people who invest your funds for you into the stock market! If someone really believes that, then arguing the contrary will be a waste of everyone's time. Did you know that you could have your house paid off and still put the equity to use as you choose? You can but for now let's talk about first getting that 30 year mortgage paid off much more quickly and almost painlessly.

The line of credit discussed before will naturally be getting paid down. Why not rotate the money out of that line of credit and do a principal buy down on our first mortgage? If you borrowed even $5,000 from your line of credit and applied that $5,000 to the first mortgage's principal you would automatically take years off your mortgage. You only need to find a free mortgage calculator online that runs an amortization schedule to find out how much in your own real life case. That $5,000 mortgage buy down has taken thousands of dollars in future interest out of that 30 year amortizing loan. Now even though your first mortgage payment stays the same, you are now paying more of that regular payment toward the principal balance than it was last month before the buy down.

You have shifted that debt ($5,000 of it for now) from amortizing interest over to your line of credit that is now calculating that money with average daily balance. We continue the program by using that line of credit as our main checking account or place to park our income until we need to use the income to pay bills and live life. Let's say in 7 months our equity line has gone from a $10,000 balance to a $5,000 balance and all our bills are paid for the month. Let's be like a shampoo bottle and rinse and repeat! Borrow out another $5,000 from the line of credit and send another $5,000 to the first mortgage holder. We have taken thousands more of interest out of that mortgage and as before, our payment stays the same but now even more of that payment is being applied to the mortgage balance because less is going toward interest and more toward the principal balance.

I have had clients take a mortgage with 28 years left on it and be on pace to pay it off in 5 to 10 years, saving sometimes six figures of interest. While this process is happening you could work with a lender who would periodically increase your line of credit. Your equity position is growing, so getting a large line of credit will enable you to access much of your "tied up equity." You might also decide to borrow money from your equity line to make investments that will provide future income. You will then use the system described above to pay down that equity line payment painlessly and relatively quickly. With this strategy you are in total control of if your home stays free and clear or if you would like to use some of the equity judiciously to create more wealth outside of the house. If not, let it sit there and sleep well at night that you have relieved that debt and payment out of your life. If a great opportunity appears, you can use your line of credit to seize that opportunity.

Many people (including myself) have elected to incorporate a piece of technology to help them quickly and easily determine how much money they should shift and at exactly what time from their line of credit to the first mortgage or other debts. There is a very powerful software program that is available if you are so inclined to bring every tool to bear in your wealth creation efforts. Please visit www.wealthwithoutstocks.com, and click on the Fast Mortgage Payoff tab to learn more and invest in the software, if you choose. If not, you're certainly free to wing it yourself, but that is not recommended and certainly not optimal. The first step will be to run a free evaluation to show you how quickly you could pay off your home and all other debts using this strategy.

Also, it is not required that you have an equity line of credit for the software to help you pay down your debts in record time. You will understand this more once you take the time and watch the 3 free quick videos at our site.

If I decided to use this equity line to help me create more wealth, where could I put this money that would provide lifelong income for me that I can set my watch by month after month? Where could I put it that has no stock market risk at all?

Read and pay close attention to the chapter on creating your own private pension, which will give you some great ideas of how to effectively and safely use your home equity to produce income.

Another Powerful Equity Strategy

Wouldn't it be great if you could use nonexistent equity in your home to create wealth? The equity line of credit described above assumes you have enough equity in the property to qualify for that type of loan. The equity has to already exist to use that type of strategy. There is, however, a program that has recently become available through which you could actually "equity share" any future equity in your home (or second home) with a hedge fund who wants to own real estate in many parts of the country.

This hedge fund would pay you a certain percentage of your properties value as a buy in for a percentage of your future appreciation. This is not a buy in of any current equity but only a buy in on any future appreciation. There would be no interest charged on this money or any loan payback schedule. The appreciation is based on a housing index measurement taken when the deal is struck and when the deal is exited. If the index in that particular area is higher at the time of sale, then you would split a portion of that gain with the equity share partner. Let's give this strategy some real life numbers:

Current value of your home: $500,000

You have a current mortgage balance of $200,000 with an equity line of credit for $50,000, bringing total debt to the property to a maximum of $250,000. You strike a deal with the equity partner to buy into your properties future appreciation. You agree to let them buy into the property for 50% of any future appreciation. The hedge fund agrees and pays you a $70,000 onetime payment today for the chance (but certainly not the guarantee) of a future profit on the sale of the home. The index used to track this deal stands at 100.00 when you enter into this transaction. Fast-forward 10 years and your mortgage of $200,000 has been paid off in full and your equity line has been raised to $250,000 but you have a zero balance on the line of credit when you sell. Your home is fully paid off and free and clear. Let's say you sold that home for $1,000,000 and the index has gone from 100 to 160. How much money does the equity partner receive?

According to the index, your value has increased 60% over 10 years, giving the property a value of $800,000 in your deal with the hedge fund. Even though your property sells for $1,000,000 the hedge fund's profit is based on the index. Maybe you made really nice improvements that popped your home's value above what most homes are selling for in your area. If this is the case, you get the benefit of that extra equity for your efforts.

You sell for $1,000,000

Sales price (artificial based on current index and your equity agreement) $800,000

Buy in value determined by appraisal at the time of $500,000

Profit to be split 50/50 based on a $300,000 appreciation from $500,000 to $800,000

Equity partner receives $150,000 which includes the $70,000 original investment for a more than doubling of their money over a 10 year period.

You receive at closing the entire $1,000,000 minus your payout to the equity partner of $150,000 and your costs of sale in the amount of $50,000 for this example. You net $800,000 out of the house.

Would you have netted more on the house sale if you had never accepted the $70,000 buy in 10 years ago? Yes, you would have netted $80,000 more (remember you did receive the $70,000 up front) when you sold the property. If this is the case, why enter into a deal like the one described?

What could make this attractive for you is what you did with the $70,000 you received 10 years ago. If you put that money into a solid, fixed, indexed annuity with principal protection and guarantees you might have close to $200,000 in your retirement income rider from that original $70,000. Make sure you read the chapter on this strategy (the private pension chapter) so you will understand how that might happen as we are not going to talk about it here and chew our cabbage twice. Now let's say that original $70,000 seed money is spitting out $10,000 per year for the rest of your life in retirement income. That is a nice income stream that is guaranteed for your entire life on just a $70,000 one-time upfront payment made 10 years earlier.

If you are a little more aggressive, you could take that same $70,000 and pay cash for a little income home somewhere in the country and let the rent accrue inside of your life insurance policy for 10 years. This would give you 10 years worth of net rental income plus the tax-free growth of the insurance policy available to you in the form of cash value in your life policy. You would also have the original $70,000 equity in the income property that might have grown during that same 10 year period. If you experienced even 5% appreciation that home would be worth $115,000 plus another $50,000 in pocketed income from the rent. However, remember that there is no guarantee of the rental property value gaining or even staying the same. You could also lose equity, but you would also have all the cash flow to offset or at least reduce any potential loss. Assuming you do achieve that modest appreciation rate, these numbers would hold very close to true to life. This would be a nice return on that original $70,000 and would produce lifelong income for as long as you owned the home. Once you sold the home you could take the proceeds and put that money into an immediate fixed indexed annuity to continue a nice hands-off income stream for the rest of your life.

Maybe you might want to take that $70,000 and put it down on a $400,000 mobile home park that would provide great net income and possibly a huge back end profit 10 years from now. You have loads of options with that original $70,000 buy in from the hedge fund. My hope is that you have more options after reading this book than you did before you read it cover to cover. What not to do is to blow that $70,000 on something silly such as luxury items. Home equity should either sit dormant or be used for wealth creation and income purposes and not for more garbage you don't really need.

What if our property we did this equity share deal with did not appreciate or even went down in value over that 10 year period? The hedge fund is in danger of losing all or a portion of the original $70,000 investment. Whether or not they are entitled to any of their $70,000 dollars back will be determined at the beginning of the agreement, based on how much they agree to give you up front. If you decide you don't agree to pay anything back on their investment if the value goes down, they will give you less money up front. If you agree to make sure they get all or a portion of their $70,000 back even if the value goes down then they will give you more money up front.

This is a great wealth and income building plan for the right person. It gives you the ability to utilize possible future equity to produce for sure income and wealth. There are obviously more details but this section is not meant to be a product brochure, but rather an educational opportunity to let you know that these programs exist.

Unfortunately this program is not available in all areas. Those areas will change and more are being added all the time, so if you interested to know more, reach out to our office. We are one of just a handful of companies authorized to offer this program. If you live in an area where it is offered we can help get this set up for you if you qualify.

Simply go to www.wealthwithoutstocks.com and go to the Equity Share tab, send us an email, and we will determine if you are located in an area and are in a price range of a home that will qualify for this program.

Chapter 15

Double Digit Returns
Paying Other People's Taxes

My first exposure to this entire strategy was by accident. I read a small book about tax liens and tax deeds and the basics of how they actually worked. It sounded nice, but I had no funds and needed to make quick money. However, after reading the book, I did a little research and it just so happened that there was a huge Michigan property tax sale taking place close to my mom's home. She was interested in this strategy and told me if I would do the research she would fund the investment and we would split 50/50 on any profits. I quickly agreed and went to work.

I found about 5 vacant parcels of land that were going up for auction and found out where they were located and their specifications such as size, current zoning, and if they were land locked or had any frontage. The starting bid on the parcel we ended up buying was a whopping $100.00 and this was for a full sized platted lot in a growing area, but was currently landlocked with no streets in front or rear of the property. We bid on the property and were the winning bidder at $750.00. This was the very first investment deal I had ever been a part of and I was at first excited. Then the self-doubt crept into my mind and worried what kind of lot was it if you could purchase it at such a low price? Surely this had to be a scam and I had just wasted $750.00 of my mom's hard earned money.

I went on to start buying and flipping single family homes and had almost forgotten about this little lot my mom and I had purchased. My mom paid the annual taxes on it, which were less than $30.00 because she believed that there would be more value if we just waited a little while. You should always listen to your mom because she is almost always right and mine certainly was in this case.

One afternoon, I happened to be visiting my mom and her phone rang. She was tied up elsewhere and asked me to answer the phone. A man quickly asked me if I was Mr. Jamieson. I said I was Mr. Jamieson but probably not the Mr. Jamieson he was looking for but could I help him anyway. (I was getting ready for a sales pitch.) He asked if I was the owner of a piece of land in Marysville, Michigan. My mom had once lived in that city but had moved quite a few years before this call. So I immediately said no my mom had sold her property there years ago and that he had some old records. Thankfully he did not take no for an answer and he said she was still the owner of record for a lot in Marysville and the light bulb went off in my head and I said oh yes she was in fact the owner of that property.

To make a long story short, a road had been cut into the next street over and this man bought the lot behind ours and built a house. He wanted to know if we would like to sell our lot to him. Over the next week we negotiated and eventually closed on that lot for a sale price of $20,000 cash. This was a full 8 years after we bought the property and it was like found money. We had purchased the lot for $750.00, had paid another $240.00 in property taxes over the years, and sold out for $20,000. How would you like to 20 fold your investment over 8 years? This is just one example of how people profit from tax liens and tax deeds every year all over the country. We wish we would have bought the other 4 lots that were in the same general area at the tax auction. What a great place to park a few thousand dollars they would have been.

Tax Liens or Tax Deeds are a different kind of animal than most real estate investing and here are some reasons why:

1) Very little marketing of these properties by the taxing authorities

2) These are all cash sales

3) Most of the properties will be vacant land (but certainly not all)

4) The state and local governments become your nonprofit taking partners

Property taxes are collected and used nationwide for local municipalities to fund a large portion of their operating budgets and city services, which include public schools. The municipalities rely on those taxes for most of their income. When property taxes go unpaid then every municipality has the right to collect those unpaid taxes by offering the land for sale at what is called a tax sale.

The structure of these tax sales varies dramatically depending not only on what state you are investing in but also which county in that state the subject property is located. Some states use a tax lien structure to sell these properties and some use a tax deed. This is also subject to change as I have personally experienced. My home state of Michigan was at one time considered the most attractive tax lien state in the country. The old rules stated that if you bought one of these properties at sale you would receive a tax lien certificate but not the actual title to the property at the sale. The owner of the property would be allowed 18 months to pay off those delinquent taxes. If they paid the tax lien buyer off in the first 12 months, the investor would receive 18% over and above what they paid for the property. If the redemption occurred between the 12th and the 18th month, the tax lien holder would receive 50% above and beyond their purchase price for the property! If the redemption was not done within those 18 months, then the tax lien holder could convert their lien to an actual deed and own the property. Michigan has since gone to giving winning bidders the deed at the time of sale and away from the tax lien certificate.

With those kinds of high returns it is tempting to buy any junk lot or property you can get your hands on, but don't make that mistake. You only get those returns if the owner comes in and pays the back taxes during their allotted time. If they don't pay, then you get the deed and own the property. The basic question becomes: would you like to own the property? Does it have real value either now or a high probability of having a much higher value in the future? If the answer is no, find another property.

Tax lien certificates are used by many states and all pay different interest rates on these certificates as well as have different time frames for redemptions. For a list of tax lien states, please go to our site at www.wealthwithoutstocks.com, and go to the Double Digit Returns in Property Taxes page for a non-guaranteed list of tax states and some details about interest rates and timeframes. You must then reach out to the county tax assessor in the state in which you are interested in purchasing for more details and bidding information.

Tax deeds are also used by many states and the same rules apply. After you receive the list from www.wealthwithoutstocks.com, on the Double Digit Returns in Property Taxes page, you must do your own due diligence to find out more details. Remember achieving more wealth without stocks or mutual funds will almost always require a little more effort on your part but the rewards are well worth the effort. Do your research on not only the rules of the sales but of course the property you will be trying to acquire. Some things to pay attention to during your research:

1) How large is the parcel? Even if there is a building on the property you always want to know the actual measurements because you might elect to try and upgrade the use of the land and its dimensions will be one factor in determining if that's possible. You also might be able to split the property up into multiple parcels, creating more value.

2) What is the current zoning? Any chance of upgrading the zoning to higher and better use? Commercial property is much more valuable per foot or per acre than agricultural or residential.

3) Does the property have access to city water, sewer, and or natural gas?

4) Will the property require a well and septic system and is the land suitable for those two systems?

5) Who already owns land around this parcel that might be interested in acquiring your parcel from you once you have clear title to the land?

6) Spend some time at the city and county and ask them to help you with these and other points.

7) Does this property have way more value now than you're going to pay?

8) Could you easily see how the value might 10, 20, or 30 fold over 5 to 10 years as my property did, as described above in my real life example?

Some other possible strategies with the land

Most of the properties you will acquire at tax sales will require a longer term strategy, but if you have the chance to 10 and 20 fold your investments it may be very much worth the wait! If you would like some other options that offer a quicker payout, then consider trading your land.

You may have the opportunity in your real estate travels to deal with someone who really wants to sell their property at a good price but you are not quite there yet in terms of agreeing upon a deal. How about offering your free and clear property as a bonus that would go along with your offer on their property? Maybe you only paid $500.00 for the property but you believe it is worth at least $3,000 to $5,000—why not offer this as an incentive? If you are acquiring a great property that you intend to flip for a nice chunk of cash, and that land you purchased for $500.00 puts you over the top, I think that would be a great use of $500.00.

I once knew an investor from Northern California who would buy properties from all over the country for usually hundreds of dollars each and then go trade them for down payments and inducements on improved properties. He was buying these properties at big discounts or great terms and created his own private land bank to help him build his holdings.

Another possible benefit of owning these properties would be for beefing up your financial statement, should you ever need more traditional financing. If you were trying to obtain long-term bank financing or even longer term private funds you could very easily and without much question assign a value of $2,000 to $3,000 per parcel that you might have only paid $300.00 for at the tax auctions. If you invested $30,000 in solid tax properties, they could easily look like $100,000 to $300,000 of net assets. You will NOT be able to get a loan from a bank with just these as the collateral because banks hate to foreclose on vacant land most of the time.

However, they could look like a nice asset on your balance sheet and also provide even more credentials to you in the lender's eyes in regards to your real estate experience.

That Self-Directed IRA Strategy again

You may use a self-directed IRA to invest in these properties if you choose. This might be perfect for some of your money if you have a long-term outlook. I know my mom wishes she would have bought $10,000 worth of similar properties to the one she did buy and just held them for some years. If they would have paid off as handsomely as the first one, her $10,000 would have turned into $200,000. She could have used her IRA and all that profit would have been tax-deferred or tax-free.

It's possible in certain instances that title companies will frown upon insuring the title when you resell these properties. Many view this as a forced taking of land and don't want the possible downside risks by insuring the title. It would be very rare (so rare I don't personally know of an actual case) that the former owner of the land would come back and claim rights to this property years after the sale. Most property forfeiture laws have been on the books for well over a century and are very clear. However, I have run into some title companies that would not insure the title when these properties are resold. Check with your local title companies and talk to their title examiners and not just the sales agents or front office staff. Ask them if they have any problems issuing a title insurance policy after a tax foreclosure.

If all else fails, file a quiet title lawsuit to take away any doubts of the title insurance agent. This is not complicated or expensive but will require some time from a real estate attorney and filing some papers.

Why are most of these properties vacant land and not improved properties?

The property tax foreclosure process can take years in some instances and if an owner of a property is getting into financial trouble or for whatever reason decides not to make payments on a property, the mortgage fore-closure process is far quicker. This means that some lender would have foreclosed and paid the property taxes long before the tax auction. Also in many states the lenders require you to put one year's property taxes in an escrow account up front when you buy the property. This will allow the lender tax reserves should you ever get behind on the taxes they will be paid out of those funds.

Having the property taxes paid is critical to the mortgage lender. Prop-erty taxes take a superior position to all other liens. This means that it is possible (but rare) for a property to be foreclosed on for back taxes and wiping out the bank's mortgage lien in the process. If the bank was owed $200,000 and had a secured mortgage on the property but let the property be foreclosed for back taxes that $200,000 would be wiped from the title. If you were the lucky bidder and paid $15,000 for the back tax liens you would own this property without the $200,000 lien and could sell or oth-erwise dispose of the property without paying off the mortgage. This is the reason banks are sticklers to make sure property taxes are paid and if you become delinquent they will usually pay the property taxes on your behalf and then add that amount to an escrow account and also require you to put another years taxes in advance. They will do this by raising your monthly payment. The payment you had of $1,000 just increased to $1,800 to pay the lender back for the back taxes and to future fund taxes on your behalf. Once the escrow account is funded only then will your payment go back to the $1,000 that it was before the tax default.

When I was an REO agent (real estate agent for the banks who were foreclosing on properties) we did have several occasions in which the prop-erty tax delinquency slipped through the lender's cracks and their mort-gages were wiped off the title of the properties. The mortgagee still owed the money but the lender lost their collateral for their note. We ran down to the city on behalf of the lender more than once to pay off property tax liens before they went to sale. You will occasionally see improved buildings on the land, but the bulk of tax sale properties will be vacant land.

If I am the winning bidder at a tax lien sale, will I have to play bill collector and hound the current owner?

Not at all, the owner simply pays the taxes through the county or city and they handle all money and paperwork to get you paid. If they never come in and pay, you simply inform the county tax collector and ask that your tax lien be converted to a tax deed. They will issue you the deed based on the rules of sale. Presto! You are the new owner of a free and clear property. Property tax sales can be a very lucrative investment but will require some expertise, time, and patience. Start by visiting your target county's website and see if they have dates for the next auction. Most municipalities only do these sales once a year but in larger markets they might hold several per year. Many of the property lists will be online or information will be provided regarding how to obtain the list of upcoming sales. Have some fun and get your feet wet in your hometown. Make plans to attend the next sale even if you don't intend to buy anything. This is a great way to get comfortable with the process and evaluate the kinds of deals that are bought out of that arena.

"You will want to get a hobby after you retire.
Hunting and gathering might be good."

Chapter 16

Network Marketing in the 21st Century

What runs through your mind when you hear the terms "network marketing, direct sales, and multilevel marketing," or MLM for short? Many people have a very negative outlook on these kinds of structures and refer to them as a "scheme," a "pyramid scheme," or even a "Ponzi Scheme."

They have visions of buying all kinds of products up front and then pestering their friends and family members to buy overpriced products of dubious quality. There is a reason many people believe these statements are true. The fact is that for many years these thoughts and statements were true of many companies and opportunities. The business model would usually look something like this:

1) You sign up to be a distributor of a product (let's say vitamins and health products for this example).
2) You buy a starter kit and an initial product package because after all you have to be a product of the product.
3) You commit to buy a minimum amount of product every month so you can be qualified to earn down line commissions.
4) You buy more products up front so you can have it on hand to sell to customers because you have been told the product will go flying off of your shelf.
5) You call on friends and family members only to receive the cold shoulder or grudging appointments to show them your new venture.
6) Your mom and sister might sign up to buy some products and to

become distributors but few others become members of your down line or even customers.

7) You receive more products every month for several months and then become frustrated and quit the business and usually stop receiving the products.

8) Your down line (mom and sister) quickly follow suit and your venture went from up and running to closed within weeks or a few months.

This unfortunately was all too common with many network marketing companies. Thankfully, many companies have changed much of that business model and modern technology has transformed the basic structure of many operations. The industry itself did very little to rein in overzealous distributors who promised untold riches with very little work for new recruits. Since that time, companies have changed their ways and government regulation has helped a more realistic picture to be painted for new prospects.

Network marketing, which is also commonly known as "The Direct Sales Industry," is nothing more than a different distribution channel for goods and services. Instead of spending loads of money upfront to market, distribute, and sell products through traditional retail outlets, Network Marketing companies choose a different route. They sell their products through a network of distributors (also known as associates and/or agents depending on the product) who sell directly to their own client base. These associates are also encouraged to recruit other associates in what is called a down line or team. These recruited associates will produce sales volume and that sales volume will be credited to other associates in the entire down line. If you recruit associates and they also recruit other associates you will receive commissions on all revenue generated from that entire group.

The amount you receive will be determined by the host company and will depend on what pay structure is utilized. There are all kinds of different pay structures and this book is not designed to be the bible of Network Marketing. Generally you would receive some percentage of sales from all associates in your group to a certain level number or "generations." You might receive less percentage from deeper generations. If your company pays to 7 generations, that means the 8th level would not generate any direct commissions to your business. However, many companies do offer bonus pools where that 8th level and beyond might generate revenue to a pool and if you qualify personally you may participate in that pool.

The old style of Network Marketing would require you to buy products up front and pass them out and sometimes even ship them yourself. The 21st century way would be to have the company automatically ship directly to your customers every 30 days (or on whatever cycle the customer requests) without your involvement as the distributor. The internet has also dramatically changed the way products are distributed and even delivered. This will, of course, depend on what kind of company you are using but sometimes the product or service can be distributed via the internet with no delivery costs. This would be true of information products or digital documents. You could just take your customer on to your website and get them signed up as a customer and/or a new associate right at your site. The host company tracks all sign ups and commission and pays them to you at a specified interval, such as monthly.

There are several things that make this kind of venture appealing to many people. Here are a few:

1) Potential for residual or passive income. Every time your customer buys a product you will be paid a commission on the new purchase. If you have direct customers that are buying products for years to come, that means years of passive income for your business. You sell the product one time and get paid for years. The best kind of income to generate is passive because it does not require much of your involvement to be paid after the initial sale is made. Think of this as your own royalty base of income. Most of us can't be professional song-writers but we could start our own direct sales business that would pay us "royalties" on all future sales. You also get paid on any sales your team produces during a particular cycle. This is leverage at its finest!

2) Very low startup costs for distributors. Unlike a traditional "brick and mortar" business for which you need office space, utilities, and

product to get rolling, you can invest usually less than $200.00 for a starter kit and to be signed up as a distributor and be qualified to earn money. This can be run from your home so start up and ongoing costs are very low.

3) The ability to tap into an existing company structure and brand without having to develop your own. Building a name and a brand can take many years and loads of money so if you can tap into an existing brand for a small amount of money, this may be a fit for you and your family. This would also be the case with buying a national franchise but without having to pay hundreds of thousands of dollars in a franchise fee.

4) The huge expenses of launching a new business are handled by the host company. Everything from research and development, product design, construction, office space, computer systems etc. are already done and ready for the agent to tap into for their own use.

5) Leave the income stream and business behind for future generations. Make sure the company you choose allows you to will your business and its income to future generations. Your family might choose to continue to build the business and make it even bigger or they might just receive the income for as long as your organization qualifies for commissions.

There is almost no limit to what can be marketed and sold through network marketing channels. From legal services to phone services and on to nutritionals are all available. If you're considering one of these ventures, I would recommend first and foremost you have a passion for the product and product line. If you don't have this passion, your chance of succeeding is very low. Without the passion you are just selling money. You are selling the business opportunity and the chance at riches but don't actually believe in the product or service. At best, this will produce very short-term, limited results.

I want to tell you a real life story about friends of mine who are deeply involved with a very solid network marketing company. However, they did not join the company to make money. They started out as a customer taking a nutritional supplement to help improve their health. Their names are Merv and Shirley from Kansas and they are both in their seventies. They reported that prior to taking this supplement they both were on multiple medications for several maladies such as high blood pressure, heart issues, and cholesterol, among others. They also reported just not feeling well and questioning if they could even live another year or two.

Then a good friend introduced them to this product line and shared with them the good things this supplement had done for their own health. Merv and Shirley decided to give it a shot for 6 months and the results they report are nothing short of amazing. They both report being able to be off all medications! (Merv still keeps a pill with him if his high blood pressure should spike but does not need to take it regularly any longer.)

They report feeling healthy and vibrant and are once again excited about life and their future. This product did so much for them that they naturally started telling other people and many of those people wanted to also try the product and even some other products from the same company. Their friend who was already in the business invited them to join as business associates and they were excited to do so because their story was so dramatic and they really wanted to help as many people as they could.

Within about 2 years of beginning their new venture, they have an impressive list of both direct customers and other associates in their down line. This produces a very handsome monthly cash flow for them even though they did not join this venture for the money. They were quite comfortable financially and did not need the extra income but Merv does report to me that they enjoy spending the extra funds! In their retirement years they have built a very successful business that is nationwide. They enjoy taking road trips together to visit with their customers and team members because many of those people have become good friends. They enjoy those trips even more now because they did so well with this business that the host company gives them an automobile allowance every month and they went out and got a beautiful Mercedes Benz cross over vehicle.

Merv and Shirley didn't need the extra income but I know millions of senior citizens do need more income. This could be a viable way to generate that extra $1,000 or $2,000 per month that might mean the difference between abundance and many options vs. scarcity and few options.

How many millions of families would have their lives greatly altered if they could just bring in an extra $1,000 to $2,000 every month and do it residually? If you could achieve that income goal what's wrong with shooting for $5,000 to $20,000 per month and beyond? Nothing is wrong with it you just need the right products or services, right company, and this be the right time in your life to make a serious change.

The most important reason Merv and Shirley have achieved this level of success is their initial passion because of what the products had done for their lives. Now they have made it their mission to simply tell their story and ask others to try it in their own lives.

If you're reading this book you are no doubt very interested in getting ahead in life and creating a high income and net worth. You also might already have those things but are looking for another way to either add to or replace your current income. Maybe you are making great money but at the expense of your health, family, and quality of life due to the hours required to make that income. Maybe you're not out to make a full-time income but would very much appreciate an extra $1,000 or $2,000 dollars every month. It's very possible to make huge income or a more modest income and create wealth while doing it in a reasonable amount of hours that you set yourself. There is nothing like having the freedom that kind of income can produce. However, be warned that if you are just chasing a buck, save your time and money. It's all about passion.

I have another dear friend and colleague named Tracie who wanted to reinvent herself both physically and financially. Tracie already made great income but her time was not her own. She was required to do much traveling to maintain the level of income that she wanted in her life. She felt that she missed out on too many things by being on the road speaking and training. She also felt that her health and fitness had suffered from a life-style of being on the road. She had a desire to create a new physicality and a new and different source of income. As we already said, passive income is an amazing thing that hits your bank account long after the effort to create that income is over. Make no mistake, Merv, Shirley, and Tracie work at their businesses but they know before they start every month that they will receive a paycheck from work they did months and years ago. I also refer this as "options income" because as the name implies, it gives you many more options with your time than the traditional linear income such as hourly, salary, or one-time commission income.

Tracie found a rock solid nutritional, cleansing, anti-aging and weight loss company where people were achieving truly life changing results in their physicality and much faster than traditional weight loss or nutritional programs were able to achieve. Tracie informed me she tells people she is in the energy and performance business. She started out as a customer before she dove into being an associate for the company. She was very impressed with her physical results and knew she could put her whole heart behind this set of products.

Tracie was shown this company by a very successful couple named Herb and Patty. They were able to start their Network Marketing business with this same top nutritional cleansing and weight loss company in 2006. From 2006 to 2012 (6 relatively lousy years in the overall economy), Herb and Patty had made 6 million dollars of income from their business. Much of this income was now passive and they were still building! The even more interesting part of the story is the couple was out of the Network Marketing industry for 17 years! They were compelled to return and start their own mission of health and wealth!

Once Tracie had that passion and had made her decision, she went to work sharing her story and results and educating people on health and wellness. She has had a dramatic improvement in her physicality and health while at the same time replacing a strong six figure income. Tracie shares with me this is the best thing she ever did for her life and wishes she had been more open to this kind of business years before.

Before Tracie really investigated this industry and her company, she had some limiting beliefs about Network Marketing companies much like the ones I shared earlier in this chapter. To her credit she was open-minded enough to take another look and the results have been great and are only getting better for her as she moves down her path. She also shared with me she is living with much more passion for life than ever before!

It's time to rethink the way you look at money, income, wealth creation, and long-held financial beliefs that are limiting your potential. The direct selling industry has been around for many decades now and is redefining the franchise concept and showing people another way to participate with an existing business model that works without having to spend hundreds of thousands of dollars for the franchise name and to launch the actual business. Don't let old truths stop you from exploring a potentially life changing venture.

Don't be just a sales representative or associate for the company, but focus on education and great information first. This is what Merv, Shirley, and Tracie do and their customers look on them not just as "salespeople" but as consultants and educators. This is one of the biggest reasons they have been successful and continue to grow their income and their passion for life. They also spend time leading their sales teams with training and product updates. Mostly they lead by example and blaze a path that others can follow if they have or can develop the same passion.

You may have noticed that I am a big believer in educating people with a lot of great information before they enter into any business or financial trans-action with my company. The truth is, an educated client is by far your best asset for your business and brand. The initial sale does take longer than if you gave the client just enough information to do business with you as opposed to fully educating the client. However, when the client truly gets what you do, they are much more likely to do business with your company on a larger scale and for a much longer period of time. They are also much more likely to refer others to check out your brand and educational materials.

The same is true for the networking business. Don't sign a customer or associate up until you're confident they have a total picture of the product and service you represent. If they're going to be an associate on your team, find out their goals and what they are prepared to do to achieve those goals. Once you understand what they're trying to achieve you can decide if you are prepared to help them down their path. The good solid Network Marketing companies will already have certain sales materials you can just tap into right away as a business associate. This will make your job of training easier but your new team member will always have questions, so set some time up right after they sign up on your team to give them some one on one phone time and get them rolling. This will also help you with retention of good long-term business associates. You should understand that many good associates will be heavily recruited by other companies. These could be companies in the same line of products (health and wellness, telecom, financial services etc.); however, they could be totally different companies with completely different product lines and markets.

This is why it is critical to take a little more time researching the company you are considering and really determine whether they are the best fit for your interests and talents. Once you really believe you are a great fit with the company, don't become a commission or product jumper. I have witnessed many people tell me how great their current product or service is, that their new company is the best and going to make them richer quicker. Then 6 months later the next new shiny object is dangled in their face and they bolt for that company. They lose all credibility with their established teams and never really make any money. They spend all their time selling the "new thing" instead of taking time to really understand what they perceive to be the "old thing."

Yes, it's possible to have multiple wealth streams and I am a big believer and teacher of the concept, but you must have laser focus on one opportunity at a time and implement others only when you have your first one solidly on the ground and making money. Then I recommend considering implementing another product line but it should complement what you already have in place. Make sure you know in advance what the rules are with your proposed first main company about offering any other products or services.

Tracie does this brilliantly by building her brand inside of her main company and using their products both personally and selling them professionally. She is in the health and wellness industry so she has started "Tracie's New Wealth and Wellness Company" which allows her to promote her own brand and maintain control of what she chooses to bring into her business. She loves her current company and believes she will be using only their products for the rest of her life. However, because of her extensive business background she understands that if for whatever reason that company changed its products, pay scales, or overall vision and she did not agree with those changes, she has the ability to bring in another set of products without having to rebrand for the new company. Tracie reports to me that she is thrilled with her current Network Marketing company because of the amazing results she sees in her life as well as others who use the product line.

The one thing in life that is guaranteed is that things change in every area of life, and networking companies are no different. By developing your own brand separate from the host company you are giving yourself maximum flexibility to build other revenue streams inside of your business and being able to turn on a dime if you need to in the future. With this kind of set up you have a brand that is expandable with any future opportunities that may arise. This brand and business of yours can be built and eventually sold if you choose. With Tracie's brand she could also bring in other products and services that complement her core business and bring added value to her client base.

Lastly, when you do enter a company, be a good student of strategies and techniques the larger income earners are using and replicate what they do as much as possible. Use technology to your advantage by doing webinars (record every one so you can build a library of training and education for future distributors and potential customers), having conference calls, three way calls, training videos on YouTube®, and social media strategies. Don't try and reinvent the wheel when starting your new venture. Follow what the successful people are doing and make sure you tune into several trainings per week.

Networking can be a very rewarding business if you in fact treat it like a business. Find something you have passion about and let the world know your story. Developing your story will be critical to your success. Network away!

Merv, Shirley, and Tracie have graciously offered their success tips and more about their stories at our website. Just go to www.wealthwithout-stocks.com, Networking in the 21st Century, for the free downloads.

Chapter 17

Wealth Without Stocks or Mutual Funds Game Plan

We are coming to the end of our initial journey together in this book. I truly hope you have received a thousand more times value than your small investment in these pages. There is an old saying that "knowledge is power!" In truth, knowledge is just potential power and requires consistent action for true power. How many people do you know that seemingly "know it all" and yet have very little true success in any area of their lives? Please take steps right now to make sure your name doesn't appear on anyone else's know it all list.

Instead, seek to be on people's go to list because not only do you have knowledge but you have taken steps to use that knowledge in your own life and achieved a measure of success. What some deem "successful" will vary greatly between people but the only person's opinion of your success that matters is your own. Once you obtain new information that you believe to have great value for your life it's imperative that you take some first step toward implementation right away and not just tomorrow. I have heard that once you set a goal no matter how big, you should not leave the spot of that decision without taking even one small step towards its accomplishment. That step could even be as small as scheduling an outbound call tomorrow that will take you toward your goal. It could also be going to our site and downloading some of the free tools and resources that have been offered through the book.

It is important that you immediately begin to write things down such as goals and lists. You must start to use a time planner of some kind or success is almost impossible. I personally use an old-fashioned time planner from Franklin Covey™ to keep track of goals and to do lists on a daily, weekly, and monthly basis. I also use my smart phone for actual appointments and keeping a schedule. I love the reminder feature and having my schedule with me at a moment's glance. This system has worked well for me and when I am true to following it I get much accomplished in a very short period of time. The reverse is also true that when I slack off and don't write everything down my productivity and subsequent income goes lower as well. I like to sit down at night in my easy chair and spend just 15 minutes looking at that day and planning out the next and giving a quick look to my week and month ahead. If for some strange reason you don't have a written system in your possession in the next 3 days, you are setting yourself up for failure before you really even start.

Now let's talk about the main groups of people who are reading this book:

1) People with many funds to protect and investments of $100,000 to over $500,000 and probable household income of over $100,000 from their profession
2) People with smaller funds to invest from $30,000 to $100,000 and probable household income from $50,000 to $100,000
3) People with nothing to $30,000 to invest who need to immediately increase their income so they will start accruing a surplus that they can save and invest more funds

This book is loaded with cutting edge wealth creation and income generating information. If you have high income and solid or high net worth you should obviously start in a different direction with this information than the other two groups. The truth is if you have high income and net worth, everything in this book is available to you in terms of money. However, you will not be able to digest and utilize all this information all at once. If you were to try and do this, you would be far too fractured and get very little done. Most of you with money have already figured out this simple truth: focus is the key to accomplishing all things in life.

I obviously don't know your individual situation and won't unless you take the time to reach out to my office to get our customized help. So for now let me give you the broadest of suggestions when it comes to a battle plan for each group. Even the general plans will vary group to group based on other factors such as age, goals, and time available being the most critical.

Group #1

People in this group are already doing well people but feel like they should be doing much better financially and have a desire to do improve through their wealth creation and preservation efforts.

If you are a high income earner, I would immediately start by creating an income tax plan to make sure you are paying as little as legally possible from your income to various taxing authorities. Remember it's not about what you make but what you keep. Get that wealth drain of taxes under control first and you will automatically give yourself a pay raise without having to ask anybody for their permission. If you feel you have overpaid your previous 3 years' taxes based on new information from Patrick, than consider getting an analysis done to see if it might be advisable to amend your last few years' tax returns. You might literally have thousands or tens of thousands of dollars owed to your family. Reach out to our office for Patrick's help if you wish. We offer a great educational program and when you invest in it you also get access to Patrick's personal Tax Attorney whose office can help you start implementing a simple tax plan that will save you a fortune and enable you to take those savings and put them into your wealth plan. Patrick has been kind enough to include some great exclusive bonuses to the readers of *Wealth Without Stocks or Mutual Funds®*

If you're a successful business owner and have maximized deductions, but still are paying over $150,000 of income taxes, you also owe it to yourself to get a free analysis of our income efficiency strategy which can help you greatly reduce that income tax figure. Contact one of our professionals today.

I would also recommend looking into whether you qualify for a home equity line of credit that will work in the way we describe in this book. Next, start harnessing that high income to make sure every dollar that comes into your life either gains you interest or cancels out other interest you are set to pay. This will automatically start to grow your wealth and you will get even further ahead faster. Consider using the technology of a software system that not only tracks balances of all your debts and accounts but also figures out complicated algorithms on the internals of all those accounts and will direct you to the quickest way to be debt free. Go to www.wealthwithoutstocks.com, Fast Mortgage Payoff, for a quick video on how it works and why you should be bringing this weapon to bear in your wealth creation efforts. You can also use this strategy to grow wealth outside of your house faster while still paying off your home in record time.

I have clients who use this amazing software and the software will actually tell them down to the penny when to take money out of their line of credit or bank account and do a principal buy down on their mortgage. You can do exactly what the software says or you might vary the direction. If it tells you to take $7,000 from your line of credit or savings account and pay down your first mortgage, you might decide to pay down only $4,000 on the mortgage and send the other $3,000 to an investment account. The software will tell you exactly how that will alter your plan to be debt free in real time. This kind of knowledge allows you to make great financial decisions almost effortlessly.

Consider setting up your own family and business bank by setting up your own properly designed life insurance policy. Treat these policies like retirement accounts and fund them with as much as you can for the greatest benefit. Go back and reread those two chapters and then reach out to our office directly so we can get you set up with the optimal type of policy from the best carrier for your own situation. We spend much of our days designing these policies and they're not your typical life insurance policy your standard agent will have access to or know how to create. Once set up, start to volumize and velocitize some of the cash value by doing productive things with the policy loan. You might refinance some of your existing debt from outside lenders to your own loan inside of your life policy. Some of you will also use these funds to acquire cash producing real estate or other assets. The choice is yours but you have to get it set up first and we can take all the work and worry away from you for this step.

Will you still put money into your 401k or IRA and then put the money into the stock market? Would you consider not funding the 401k or IRA in favor of a properly designed policy for all the benefits discussed in that chapter? If you would like greater control and access to your funds the answer will be a big yes!

These initial steps will get your money flowing in the right direction and build you an incredibly solid base from which to invest. Speaking of investments, let's take a look at what you already might have and see if we can reallocate funds to protect you from possible long-term care or home health care needs. Many life insurance policies might give you a level of protection in the event you need long-term care in the future. Contact our office for a free no obligation consultation and ask us to prepare an illustration based on your own needs.

If you have existing IRAs and qualified accounts and are looking to diversify your stock holdings or get out of the market altogether, consider two options. These options can work together or totally separately depending on the type of investor you are and your goals.

1) Open up a self-directed IRA and consider investing in real estate using one or all of the strategies discussed in this book. Some of the investment options are turnkey and ready to be put in the place with a couple phone calls on your part. While others will require you to take some time and get some lead generating systems set up in your own backyard. If you're too busy for this, consider bringing in a joint venture partner and pay them to find the deals and bring them to you for a portion of the profits. Consider getting involved with a real estate mentorship program to walk you through your first couple deals. We

have seasoned real estate investors who are at your disposal via our real estate coaching and mentoring programs. Our office will have more details. I am very proud of the real estate chapters in the book but no book on the planet can take the place of personal mentorship.

2) Take the time to go back and study the chapter on using fixed indexed annuities to grow and protect money. These products can be used by your IRA money via a tax-free roll over from your current account to the annuity. Exactly what product is best for you will depend on many factors. Please contact our office and we will give you a simple questionnaire to help you determine which product might be the best fit for you and your plan. Remember this is not a place to put money that you want to actively invest in real estate or another business venture. This is set it and forget it money that is put in place to protect the funds against downside market risk and to grow your retirement income every year guaranteed. You could even roll over a portion of your current IRA to a self-directed account for your more active real estate investments and at the same time roll over a portion of your funds into the fixed indexed annuity. This is true diversification to different asset classes other than stocks, mutual funds, or bonds.

Lastly, take a look at our marketing strategies to help you make more money in an existing business or launch a new business venture successfully. Consider becoming part of our referral agent network and simply give out this book and direct people to our training modules about money and wealth creation, that are already done for you. We track all your referrals so you are assured you get proper credit for your referrals and create income for your family when we are able to help them set up certain financial products. You will need a life/health insurance license to do this, but they are not difficult to obtain and you will like the education you get when preparing to take the licensing test.

You might also consider seeing if you're a candidate for the advanced equity strategy described in the chapter about paying off mortgages and other debts in record time. If you're in an area that qualifies, that program can be a great way to obtain funds without having to make payments or have interest accrue at all. Remember, the hedge fund is buying into your future equity position and not any current equity you have in the property.

Group #2

This group should immediately start to increase their income by taking home more money with proper tax strategies. Consider starting a small business as described in the income tax chapter. You may also decide to work with my company as a referral agent as described above. I think this is a higher priority for you because your income needs to grow to give you more options. Think of what your life would look like if you started taking home $500.00 more per month from your current job (with proper tax strategies) while at the same time starting another revenue stream by working with my company as a referral agent. This income stream could eventually eclipse your normal job or current business if you ever decide to make sharing these strategies your full time endeavor.

Take steps to start your own life insurance policy and use those funds as your own bank or finance company. Even if you can only put in $300.00 to $400.00 a month into the program, your policy will grow and in seemingly no time you will be ready to take out your first policy loan. Don't worry if you can't put in much right now, just start from wherever you are and move forward. The key word in that last sentence is start. Many people start funding these policies to take the place of contributing to a 401k or IRA. They're putting the funds into a tax-favored account but don't have all the rules and entanglements of the 401k and IRA. They are also not locking up access to the money, so they'll be able to put those funds to use in other business and investment areas of their life.

I would also pay close attention to the chapter Fast Turn No Equity Homes and become better versed on the strategies described in the book. There are all kinds of deals in your own backyard once you know what to look for and develop a business plan. You might want to consider further instruction on real estate from our office. You may also want to give networking some serious consideration for you or your spouse. Find a company and product line that you can really get behind and consider becoming a distributor. Make sure you get the tips and insights from Tracie, Merv, and Shirley, whose stories were told in that chapter.

Also start to maximize your income by using a properly designed home equity line of credit as a way to cancel out interest and put money to work for your future. Use this account to strategically pay down debt and let your cash flow pay down the account and then rinse and repeat. If you elect to use the software program in this endeavor it will tell you how many years and months away you are from being debt free. Every time you put money into the program or take money out of the program, you will updated in real time on your screen what that deposit or withdrawal means to your overall plan. This software will be your financial GPS, crystal ball and a valued tool for the rest of your life.

Lastly for this group, I want to talk about the non-sexy topic of plain old budgeting. I challenge you to do a month end from all your accounts for the last quarter. Find every expense and drop of income to see where you stand. I am partial to increasing net income via tax strategies and business strategies as well. However, look at your expense and challenge yourself to find no less than $500.00 and preferably $1,000 per month from your expenses that could be reduced. I have compiled dozens of things to do that will help you chop expenses and included them on my site. Spend some time on the site and download those suggestions. Remember if you can save $500.00 per month and contribute that to your life policy, that will be $6,000 every year plus the tax-free compounding. You are setting yourself up for a much larger and fruitful retirement.

Group #3

This group is near and dear to my heart because this is where I was when I started out in business at 21 years old. I literally had no money, no job, and no credit. I was fresh out of dropping out of college after my sophomore year. I didn't drop out due to grades and I didn't flunk out at all. My grades were respectable but I hated every second of those two years in college. I knew I had to create something on my own and began my own journey. I was told I was crazy, would never amount to anything, couldn't be an entrepreneur, etc. etc. and I was determined to prove people wrong. Many of the strategies in this book can be used by people in this same group. However, if I had to start again and had this book to help me, here is what I would do to get my income up as soon as possible:

1) Become an affiliate agent with Perpetual Wealth Systems and obtain proper licensing with our help. Once this is done, begin to hand out this book to anyone you know who is interested in getting ahead. Tell them to keep it for two weeks and read the chapters on private banking, insurance policies, and fixed indexed annuities. Set an appointment with them to meet to discuss their thoughts. Ask for the book back or the cover price so they can keep the book. Use your affiliate checklist that we provide to kick your marketing into overdrive. We have systems set up that you can tap into online where we will do all the training. We will work directly with your referrals and compensate you accordingly. Without sufficient income, life is much more difficult and has far fewer options. You would just have to pass out the book, and send people to our weekly online webinars for further training. Once you're an affiliate agent you will be given your own link that you can use in your marketing efforts to direct people through your link to all of our online trainings and webinars. Our system will tag that person as coming from your customized link and any business they choose to transact with our company would trigger referral commissions for you upon closing of the client. Pass out a book, pass out a link, do some friendly follow up, and then let us do everything else with that client. Then collect a check. We have made making extra income while helping people incredibly easy! You just have to tap into what is already built to reap great rewards.

2) Study the chapter again on fast turning low equity homes and begin to put together some marketing material and look for online and newspaper ads that sound promising and begin to call these leads. Start to build a buyers list of people who would love a long-term rent

to own solution so when the first deal presents itself you have several people interested. Collect your first check and repeat the process.

3) Pay close attention to the online marketing section of the book and focus on bringing in leads for your insurance referral business (we have the entire system built for you to drive traffic to and make sure you are credited with any eventual sales) and your real estate business.

4) Start to put money away into savings and when your income gets more stable start your own insurance policy. You will want the policy for all the benefits already described but also because it will give you more credibility when you're practicing the program you're offering to others.

Just because you don't have much financially now doesn't mean you have to be in the same position in 6 to 12 months. Once your income is stable and you have some money in the bank, you can go into wealth creation mode and utilize more strategies from this book. You also have the benefit of being able to have all the additional strategies in your toolbox so when you start to create more income you will know how to grow wealth with that money faster and safer than traditional methods.

I don't care what group you're in, there are strategies in this book that will help you get to your next level. The key is to develop a battle plan of your first one or two strategies to implement. If we can help you in your journey please reach out to our office.

Coaching for all groups

No matter which group most resembles you, I want you to consider entering a coaching program to help you move farther faster. If you had a qualified coach to help you implement many of these strategies, it would make your journey quicker and give you a feeling of much more confidence. You're going to pay for the coaching one way or the other. Pay a coach a known and predetermined amount of money which should be considered an investment in your business. This will save you years of time and give you a much higher chance at success. You will still have to put in the time and effort, but with a coach you are not searching for answers in the dark.

Reach out to our office and visit us online to see how we might be able to help you in your wealth creation efforts.

I want to thank you for allowing me to be your wealth without stocks or mutual funds coach and I truly hope our relationship will move forward for both of our benefits. I challenge you to begin to implement some of these strategies right away. Review the sections that are most appropriate for your current situation. When possible, reach out to us for further assistance. We have a mission to help people from all walks of life grow and protect wealth and increase their incomes. It's your decision as to whether or not you will be one of those people. Please email us any success stories you have to tell us on what you were able to do with the information in this book. These stories give hope to those who will come after you and lets them know success is attainable for them using these systems.

In closing, I would like to ask you not to believe all the negative forces that will surround you in your wealth creation efforts. You will be making people around you uncomfortable because of your actions and beliefs. That's their problem and not yours. When you stretch yourself, the 97%'ers get nervous and start to ask themselves some internal questions. Most will not like the answers to those questions and rather than change themselves, they will find it easier to rain on your parade. Always pack an umbrella and understand you are in total control. There are always outside factors that you can't control but you certainly can control how you feel about those factors and how you adjust your approach. There is no such thing as failure, there are only learning experiences. Take the feedback even if it was a negative outcome, and alter your approach. Study what successful people do in any field and study champions. When you begin to adopt their mindsets, the future will hold more opportunities and wonderful possibilities than you ever dreamed possible. Now go take your first step to achieving your goals and dreams!

Wishing you all the Best,

John Jamieson and the staff of Perpetual Wealth Systems

About the Author

John Jamieson

John is a life-long student of money, business, and real estate who began investing in properties at the age of 21 years old. When John started his career he had just dropped out of college and had no money, no job, and no credit yet established. Despite these seemingly insurmountable obstacles he purchased millions of dollars worth of real estate in a short period of time. Although John left college after only two years he has been a veracious seeker of knowledge from successful people from all over the world.

He has a massive private collection of books and training programs as well as having attended numerous training programs in person all over the country. John is constantly looking for better and smarter ways to transact business as well as help others create more income and wealth in their own lives. His first book, *The Perpetual Wealth System,* is a number one bestseller and continues to help many people all over the country grow and protect their wealth.

In his 25-year business career John has bought and sold tens of millions of dollars of real estate as an investor and an agent. He has set up millions of dollars of financial products for clients from all over the United States. John has managed real estate for clients and been a corporate trainer for Century 21 teaching sales and marketing strategies. He has launched several businesses from nothing more than an idea and made them into successful ventures.

John has been fortunate to have spoken to thousands of people from all over the country and been asked to speak by some of the biggest names in business. He has been on training stages at the request of Robert Allen, Donald Trump, Robert Kiyosaki, and several other well-known wealth trainers. He now speaks to various groups including real estate professionals, insurance professionals, physicians, and small business owners all over the country on the topics of increasing income, investing, wealth creation, sales, and asset preservation.

He is a highly sought after business coach and mentor who loves showing people alternative ways to increase their income and wealth without needing the stock market or mutual funds. Along with books he is the author of several complete educational programs on money, business, and real estate.

He has written numerous articles on income and wealth for dozens of print and online news media such as AOL, Re/Max®, and the Florida Realtors Magazine.

One of his favorite topics is how anyone regardless of formal education or degrees can lead an abundant financial life. There is more opportunity now than at any point in history for people to get ahead and a college degree is not mandatory to make that a reality. There is world-class education available to anyone who wants to get ahead and much of it will not be found on a college campus.

John has put together power teams located in many cities throughout the United States to help people achieve their financial goals regardless of where those people are starting from in their quest for abundance. It does not matter if you're just starting out like he was 25 years ago or if you're already financially successful; John can help get you to your next level.

He is a lifelong resident of Metro Detroit where he lives with his wife and sons.

Would you like to become a
Wealth Without Stocks Team Member?

We are looking for go getters who are looking for an opportunity to help others while at the same time creating a new powerful stream of income for their families. You must already possess or be willing to obtain certain licensing. Most of this licensing will be through your home state and can generally be obtained by taking an approximate 40 hours on-line training course and then passing your state exam.

You must also be honest, trustworthy, easy to work with, and coachable. You must strongly desire to put the needs of your customer first; above and beyond your compensation.

Once properly licensed you can help us get this powerful much needed message to the public and qualify to collect income based on your efforts. This can be a part time venture to start but could blossom to significant full time income if you are serious about being successful. We provide training once licensed and a complete turnkey marketing system that you can plug into immediately to launch your business.

We will do 95% of the training and selling for you to your prospects. You just have to give your prospect this book and ask them to read the chapters most appropriate for their situation. You also would invite them to attend an on-line training we will hold each week, from the comfort of their own home. Our wealth strategy team would take over from there and answer all your customers questions and build any financial structure that would benefit your customer.

When these financial structures get set up and funded by your client you will be paid a commission! The amount will vary but could be very substantial. If this sounds like a business you would like to pursue, please send us an email with resume or personal fact sheet to info@wealthwithoutstocks.com and make the subject line "new agent" and we will send you more details and resources you can use to begin your journey to join us in this very rewarding business.

We reserve the right to choose who we will and won't work with and not everyone will qualify.

More education from John and Perpetual Wealth Systems

Perpetual Financing Home Study course complete with 13 CDs, 5 DVDs, and full manual.

This educational package will show you how to be your own bank using a properly designed life insurance policy. The information contained in this program will change yours and your family's life for generations to come. It comes with a 30-day money back guarantee and is available for 50% off its normal price to *Wealth Without Stocks or Mutual Funds'* readers. Go to www.perpetualwealthsystems.com and click on the Buy Now tab to look at this and other products. Use Promo Code **WWS50** to apply the discount at checkout.

Foreclosure and Real Estate investment course complete with 6 CDs and manual.

Step by step instruction on how to be an active and successful real estate investor. Find out how to dominate the foreclosure market in your own backyard. Readers receive a 50% discount on their order. Use Promo Code **WWS50** to apply the discount at checkout.

Perpetual Wealth System recordings (audio and video) of a Live 3-Day Boot Camp hosted by John.

This program is loaded with world class information on topics such as:

1) Setting up your private pension
2) How to never lose money in the stock market again
3) Advanced income and real estate strategies
4) Private lending and banking strategies
5) Advanced Insurance strategies
    And more!

These are the actual recordings from a live 3-day event that was offered to students for $1,495. By using the already discounted price plus the 50% off reader bonus you will pay a fraction of that amount for the same great information. Use Promo Code **WWS50** to apply the discount at checkout.

Sites to keep in contact with us:

www.johnjamieson.com (will act as a portal to all other sites)

www.wealthwithoutstocks.com

www.perpetualwealthsystems.com

www.doctorsbuildwealth.com

www.realestateagentsbuildwealth.com

www.perpetualpensions.com